Thriving in Android Development Using Kotlin

Use the newest features of the Android framework to develop production-grade apps

Gema Socorro Rodríguez

Thriving in Android Development Using Kotlin

Group Product Manager: Rohit Rajkumar

Publishing Product Manager: Vaideeshwari Roshan

Book Project Manager: Sonam Pandey

Senior Editor: Hayden Edwards

Technical Editor: Simran Ali

Copy Editor: Safis Editing

Indexer: Manju Arasan

Production Designer: Prashant Ghare

DevRel Marketing Coordinators: Anamika Singh and Nivedita Pandey

First published: July 2024

Production reference: 2180924

Published by Packt Publishing Ltd.

Grosvenor House

11 St Paul's Square

Birmingham

B3 1RB, UK.

ISBN 978-1-83763-129-2

www.packtpub.com

To Amaia and Aitor, for giving me the incredible privilege of being your mom and inviting me to be part of your extraordinary worlds, filled with magic and wonder.

To Roberto, for believing in me more than I ever could myself. Thank you for being my greatest support in every challenge I face, and for spending countless nights working alongside me while I wrote this book.

I love you all.

– Gema

Contributors

About the author

Gema Socorro Rodríguez is a Google Developer Expert for Android with over 15 years' experience. In 2009, after finishing her studies, which included building a mobile project, she started working on more mobile apps and fell in love with Android. Since then, she has worked on mobile apps as part of several teams. As her experience grew, she realized that she wanted to share with the community what she had learned; hence, she started giving talks and organizing workshops. She has also been an instructor at a mobile-specialized boot camp. She currently works as a senior Android engineer at Cabify, a popular ride-hailing company with a presence in Spain and the majority of Latin American countries.

I want to thank the wonderful Packt team for supporting and helping me write my first technical book.

I also want to thank my family, friends, and colleagues for listening to me talk about this book for months and their unwavering support.

Finally, I want to thank the Android community for being one of the most open and welcoming communities, contributing to the growth and development of countless Android developers.

About the reviewer

Hema Sai Charan Kothamasu (a.k.a. hemandroid) is a seasoned mobile app developer, armed with a B.Tech in electronics and computer engineering from Usha Rama College and a decade of expertise in Android and Flutter. Hema's professional journey includes spearheading projects by leveraging his proficiency in frameworks such as Android, Flutter, and iOS and his adeptness in design patterns and architecture. A stalwart in the developer community, Hema is also a technical speaker at GDG Hyd Community, where he captivates audiences with dynamic talks, and a co-organizer at Flutter Hyd Community, where he fosters growth and collaboration, mentoring aspiring developers. Hema's insightful blog offers a wealth of knowledge on mobile development.

Table of Contents

3

Backing Up Your WhatsPackt Messages   103

Part 2: Creating Packtagram, a Photo Media App

4

Building the Packtagram UI   141

5

Creating a Photo Editor Using CameraX   185

8

Adding Media Playback to Packtflix with ExoPlayer   311

9

Extending Video Playback in Your Packtflix App   351

Preface

As an Android developer, I consider myself honored to be part of a community that has the power to touch and improve the lives of users worldwide. Android development is not just about writing code; it's also about creating experiences that resonate, inspire, and connect people in meaningful ways. I have to recognize that my passion for Android development stems from the profound impact we, as developers, can have on individuals and communities.

The Android community is a vibrant and dynamic ecosystem, characterized by innovation, collaboration, and a relentless pursuit of excellence. From the early days of simple apps to the complex, feature-rich applications of today, Android developers have continuously pushed the boundaries of what is possible. This book is a tribute to that spirit of innovation. It aims to help you gather the skills and knowledge to build applications that offer real value to users.

Whether you are creating messaging apps, social networking platforms, or video streaming services, as we will do in this book, the core principles of Android development remain the same – a commitment to quality, a focus on user experience, and an eagerness to learn and adapt. As you embark on this journey, remember that you are part of a global community of developers who share your passion and dedication. Together, we can continue to innovate and create apps that make a difference in the world.

Who this book is for

If you are a mid-level Android engineer, this book is for you, as it will teach you how to solve issues that occur in real-world apps and can be used as a reference for your day-to-day work. This book can also help junior engineers, as it will start exposing them to complex problems and the best practices to solve them.

It will be beneficial to have a basic understanding of Android and Kotlin concepts such as Views, Activities, lifecycles, and Kotlin coroutines.

What this book covers

In *Chapter 1*, *Building the UI for Your Messaging App*, you will begin by building the WhatsPackt messaging app, focusing on making critical technical decisions and creating the necessary structure for development. This chapter will guide you through defining the app's structure and navigation, setting up and organizing modules, and selecting a dependency injection framework. You will also gain hands-on experience with Jetpack Navigation and Jetpack Compose to build the main screen, chats list, and messages list, resulting in a solid foundation for the app's user interface.

In *Chapter 2, Setting Up WhatsPackt's Messaging Abilities*, you will explore how to connect the WhatsPackt messaging app to a backend server using WebSockets, enabling real-time, one-to-one conversations. This chapter covers establishing WebSocket connections, handling messages within ViewModels, and implementing best practices to update the user interface and manage message storage. Additionally, you will learn to manage synchronization and error handling and implement push notifications to alert users of new messages. By the end of this chapter, you will have a comprehensive understanding of the essential technologies needed to create a robust messaging system.

In *Chapter 3, Backing Up Your WhatsPackt Messages*, you will focus on data handling and persistence in the WhatsPackt messaging app, ensuring messages are stored correctly and can be quickly retrieved, even in the event of device failures or accidental deletions. This chapter introduces Room, a persistence library that simplifies database management in Android, and guides you through its architecture and implementation. You will also learn to create effective caching mechanisms, set up and secure Cloud Storage for Firebase for backups, and use WorkManager to schedule asynchronous tasks, ensuring the safety and reliability of your chat data. By the end of this chapter, you'll have a robust data persistence strategy for your messaging app.

In *Chapter 4, Building the Packtagram UI*, you will begin creating Packtagram, an Instagram-like social networking app, starting with setting up a robust project structure and defining the file hierarchy and modules. This chapter covers the essential aspects of project organization and choosing the right architecture pattern for scalability. You will then develop user-friendly interfaces for the news feed and stories, ensuring seamless navigation and interaction. Additionally, you will learn to retrieve data from servers, using Retrofit and Moshi, and implement effective data caching strategies to improve performance and user experience by reducing network calls.

In *Chapter 5, Creating a Photo Editor Using CameraX*, you will enhance the Packtagram app by integrating CameraX, a powerful tool for seamless photo capturing and editing. This chapter will guide you through implementing CameraX to transform the photography experience, allowing users to tweak and personalize their shots with intuitive editing tools. Additionally, you will explore using machine learning to recognize photo themes and suggest relevant hashtags, adding an intelligent layer to the app's functionality.

In *Chapter 6, Adding Video and Editing Functionality to Packtagram*, you will elevate the Packtagram app functionality by integrating video capabilities, transforming it into a comprehensive multimedia platform. This chapter covers capturing high-quality videos using the CameraX library and enhancing them with FFmpeg to process tasks, such as adding captions and filters. You will also learn to efficiently upload videos to Cloud Storage for Firebase, ensuring the smooth handling of large files and an improved user experience. By the end of this chapter, you will have significantly enriched Packtagram, making it a versatile platform for both photo and video sharing.

In *Chapter 7, Starting a Video Streaming App and Adding Authentication*, you will begin creating Packtflix, a video streaming app, focusing on multimedia content delivery and user authentication. This chapter starts with setting up the project structure and modules from scratch. You'll implement robust user authentication using OAuth2 to ensure secure access to accounts and personal preferences. Following authentication, you'll use Jetpack Compose to build dynamic and responsive lists to showcase movies and create detailed screens for each movie or series, providing users with all the necessary information. By the end of this chapter, you'll have a solid foundation for your streaming app.

In *Chapter 8, Adding Media Playback to Packtflix with ExoPlayer*, you will enhance the Packtflix app by integrating robust video playback capabilities using ExoPlayer, a versatile library offering extensive customization and support for various media formats. This chapter begins with an overview of media options in Android, highlighting ExoPlayer's advantages. You will learn the basics of ExoPlayer, including its architecture and key components, and how to integrate it into your app. Following this, you will create a responsive video playback UI, manage playback controls, and adjust video quality. Additionally, you will add subtitles to ensure accessibility, enriching the user experience with high-quality video content.

In *Chapter 9, Extending Video Playback in Your Packtflix App*, you will expand the capabilities of the Packtflix app with extended video playback features, focusing on **Picture-in-Picture (PiP)** mode and media casting. This chapter will guide you through creating a miniature video player that overlays other apps, allowing users to continue watching while multitasking. Additionally, you will learn to use MediaRouter and the Cast SDK to transfer video playback to larger screens, such as TVs with Google Chromecast. By the end of this chapter, you'll have a solid understanding of PiP functionalities and media casting, significantly improving the user experience of your Android app.

To get the most out of this book

Software/hardware covered in the book	Operating system requirements
Android Studio Jellyfish | 2023.3.1	Windows, macOS, or Linux

You will need to have Android Studio installed on your computer, as it will be the primary development environment used throughout the chapters. Additionally, a basic understanding of Git is recommended, as you will need it to download and manage the code repositories provided in the book.

If you are using the digital version of this book, we advise you to type the code yourself or access the code from the book's GitHub repository (a link is available in the next section). Doing so will help you avoid any potential errors related to the copying and pasting of code.

Download the example code files

You can download the example code files for this book from GitHub at https://github.com/PacktPublishing/Thriving-in-Android-Development-using-Kotlin. If there's an update to the code, it will be updated in the GitHub repository.

We also have other code bundles from our rich catalog of books and videos available at https://github.com/PacktPublishing/. Check them out!

Conventions used

There are a number of text conventions used throughout this book.

Code in text: Indicates code words in text, database table names, folder names, filenames, file extensions, pathnames, dummy URLs, user input, and Twitter handles. Here is an example: "For example, in the build.gradle file of the :app module, include the following code in the dependencies section."

A block of code is set as follows:

```
class MessagesRepository @Inject constructor(
    private val dataSource: MessagesSocketDataSource
): IMessagesRepository {

    override suspend fun getMessages(): Flow<Message> {
        return dataSource.connect()
    }
```

When we wish to draw your attention to a particular part of a code block, the relevant lines or items are set in bold:

```
Scaffold(
    topBar = {
        TopAppBar(
            title = {
                Text(stringResource(R.string.chat_title,
                uiState.name.orEmpty()))
            }
        )
    },
```

Bold: Indicates a new term, an important word, or words that you see on screen. For instance, words in menus or dialog boxes appear in **bold**. Here is an example: "Android Studio will offer us a set of templates to start with. We will choose the **Empty Activity** option, as shown in the following screenshot:"

> **Tips or important notes**
> Appear like this.

Get in touch

Feedback from our readers is always welcome.

General feedback: If you have questions about any aspect of this book, email us at customercare@packtpub.com and mention the book title in the subject of your message.

Errata: Although we have taken every care to ensure the accuracy of our content, mistakes do happen. If you have found a mistake in this book, we would be grateful if you would report this to us. Please visit www.packtpub.com/support/errata and fill in the form.

Piracy: If you come across any illegal copies of our works in any form on the internet, we would be grateful if you would provide us with the location address or website name. Please contact us at copyright@packtpub.com with a link to the material.

If you are interested in becoming an author: If there is a topic that you have expertise in and you are interested in either writing or contributing to a book, please visit authors.packtpub.com.

Share Your Thoughts

Once you've read *Thriving in Android Development Using Kotlin*, we'd love to hear your thoughts! Scan the QR code below to go straight to the Amazon review page for this book and share your feedback.

https://packt.link/r/1-837-63129-8

Your review is important to us and the tech community and will help us make sure we're delivering excellent quality content.

Download a free PDF copy of this book

Thanks for purchasing this book!

Do you like to read on the go but are unable to carry your print books everywhere?

Is your eBook purchase not compatible with the device of your choice?

Don't worry, now with every Packt book you get a DRM-free PDF version of that book at no cost.

Read anywhere, any place, on any device. Search, copy, and paste code from your favorite technical books directly into your application.

The perks don't stop there, you can get exclusive access to discounts, newsletters, and great free content in your inbox daily

Follow these simple steps to get the benefits:

1. Scan the QR code or visit the link below

https://packt.link/free-ebook/9781837631292

2. Submit your proof of purchase

3. That's it! We'll send your free PDF and other benefits to your email directly

Part 1: Creating WhatsPackt, a Messaging App

In this part, you will learn to build and structure a messaging app called WhatsPackt, implement real-time communication using WebSockets, and ensure data persistence and backup with Room and Cloud Storage for Firebase. You will gain hands-on experience in creating user interfaces, handling message synchronization, and implementing push notifications, culminating in a robust and reliable messaging system.

This part includes the following chapters:

- *Chapter 1, Building the UI for Your Messaging App*
- *Chapter 2, Setting Up WhatsPackt's Messaging Abilities*
- *Chapter 3, Backing Up Your WhatsPackt Messages*

Building the UI for Your Messaging App

In this first chapter, we're going to start building a messaging app called WhatsPackt (referring to a popular messaging app that you probably already know about). At this point in the project, we must make some important technical decisions and create the structure needed to build it. This is what we will be focusing on, as well as working on the app's user interface.

By the end of this chapter, you will have hands-on experience creating a messaging app from scratch, organizing and defining the app modules, deciding which dependency injection framework you will use, using Jetpack Navigation to navigate between the app features, and using Jetpack Compose to build the main parts of the user interface.

This chapter is organized into the following topics:

- Defining the app structure and navigation
- Building the main screen
- Building the chats list
- Building the messages list

Technical requirements

Android Studio is the official standard **integrated development environment** (IDE) for developing Android apps. Although you can use other IDEs, editors, and Android tools if you prefer, all the examples in this book will be based on this IDE.

For that reason, we recommend that you set up your computer with the latest stable version of Android Studio installed. If you haven't already, you can download it here: `https://developer.android.com/studio`. By following the installation steps, you will be able to install the IDE and set up at least one emulator with one Android SDK installed.

Once installed, we can start creating the project. Android Studio will offer us a set of templates to start with. We will choose the **Empty Activity** option, as shown in the following screenshot:

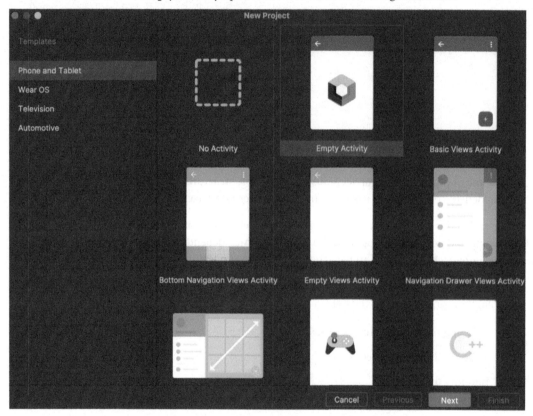

Figure 1.1: Android Studio new project template selection with the Empty Activity option selected

You will then be asked to select a project and package name:

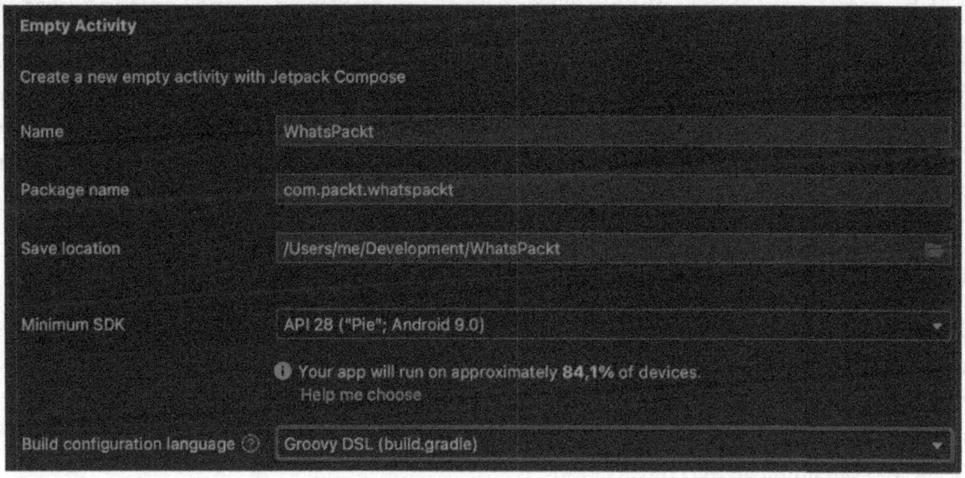

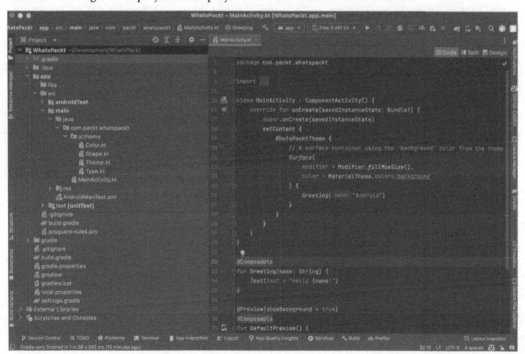

Figure 1.2: Android Studio – adding a new project name and package name

After that, you're all set! Android Studio will generate the main folders and files needed so that you can start working on our project. Your project structure should look as follows:

Figure 1.3: Android Studio – project template structure

Note that all the code for this chapter can be found in this book's GitHub repository: `https://github.com/PacktPublishing/Thriving-in-Android-Development-using-Kotlin/tree/main/Chapter-1/WhatsPackt`.

Now, we are ready to start coding our new messaging app. To do so, we will have to make some important technical decisions: we will have to decide how our project is going to be structured, how we will navigate between the different screens or features, and how we are going to set and provide the components needed (defining and organizing the dependencies between every component).

Defining the app structure and navigation

Before designing the app structure, we must have a basic idea of the features it should include. In our case, we want to have the following:

- A main screen to create new or access already existing conversations
- A list containing all the conversations
- A screen for a single conversation

As this is going to be a production-ready app, we must design its code base while considering that it should be easy to scale and maintain. In that regard, we should use modularization.

Modularization

Modularization is the practice of dividing the code of an application into loosely coupled and self-contained parts, each of which can be compiled and tested in isolation. This technique allows developers to break down large and complex applications into more manageable parts that are easier to maintain.

By modularizing Android applications, modules can be built in parallel, which can significantly improve build time. Additionally, independent modules can be tested separately, which makes it easier to identify and correct errors.

While the most common way to create modules in Android development is by utilizing the Android libraries system via Gradle dependencies, alternative build systems such as Bazel and Buck also facilitate modularization. Bazel provides a robust system for declaring modules and dependencies, and its parallelized building capabilities can lead to even faster build times. Similarly, Buck also supports modular development by providing fine-grained build rules and speeding up incremental builds.

By exploring various build systems, such as Gradle, Bazel, and Buck, developers can find the most suitable modular approach to structure their Android applications. Each build system offers unique features for managing dependencies and organizing code, enabling developers to implement various patterns to achieve a modular architecture.

Among the organizational patterns, the most common ones are modularization by layers and modularization by feature modules.

Modularization by layers

It is common to structure an app by grouping its components based on a set of layers depending on the architecture chosen by the developers. One popular architecture is clean architecture, which splits the code base between the data, domain (or business), and presentation layers.

With this approach, each module focuses on a specific layer of the architecture, such as the presentation layer, domain layer, or data layer. These modules are usually more independent of each other and may have different responsibilities and technologies, depending on the layer they belong to. Following this pattern, our app structure would look like this:

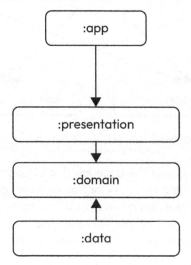

Figure 1.4: App modularization by layers

From this diagram, you can see why layer modularization is also referred to as vertical modularization.

Modularization by feature

When modularizing an app by feature (or using horizontal modularization), the application is divided into modules that focus on specific features or related tasks, such as authentication or navigation. These horizontal modules can share common components and resources. We can see this structure in the following figure:

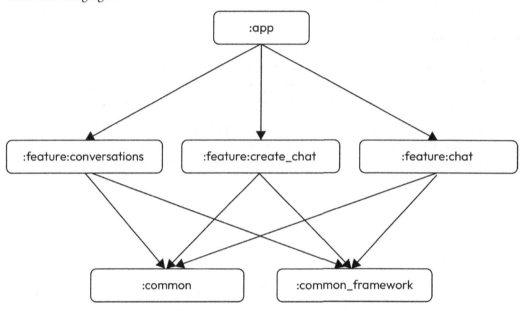

Figure 1.5: App modularization by feature

In our case, we are going to have a main app module that will depend on every one of the feature modules that our app needs (one for every one of the features we are going to implement). Then, every one of the feature modules will also depend on two other common modules (in this example, we have divided them into common and common_framework, using the first to include framework-independent code, and the second to use code that depends on the Android framework).

One of the main advantages of this pattern is that it can scale with the company if it evolves into a feature-based team (where every team is focused on a single or group of features). This will enable every team to be responsible for one feature module, or a set of feature modules, where they have ownership of the code in those modules. It also allows teams to be easily autonomous regarding their problem space and features.

WhatsPackt modularization

In our WhatsPackt example, we are going to combine both modularization approaches:

- We will use a modularization based on features for our features.

- We will use a modularization based on layers for the common modules. This will allow us to share common code between the feature modules.

The structure of our modules and its dependencies will be as follows:

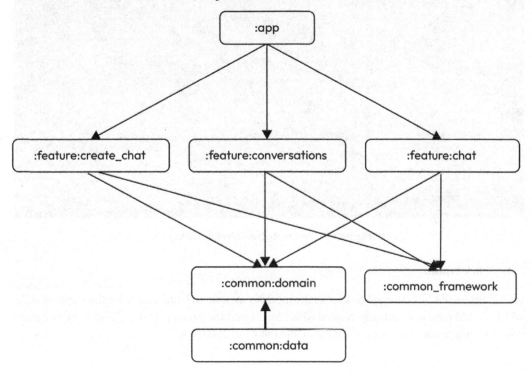

Figure 1.6: Our app modules structure and dependencies

Now, we are going to start creating this structure in Android Studio. To create a module, follow these steps:

1. Select **File | New... | New Module**.

2. In the **Create New Module** dialog, choose the **Android Library** template.

3. Fill in the **Module name**, **Package name**, and **Language** fields, as shown here:

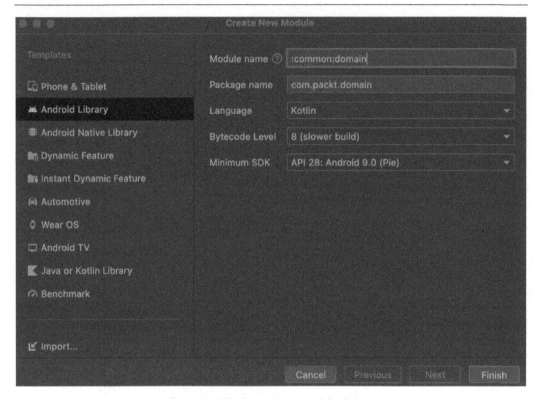

Figure 1.7: The Create New Module dialog

4.   Click **Finish**.

We will have to do this same process for all the modules we want to build, except for the `:app` module, which should have been already created when we created the project. This is going to be our main point of entry to the app. So, we must create the following modules:

- `:common:domain`
- `:common:data`
- `:common:framework`
- `:feature:create_chat`
- `:feature:conversations`
- `:feature:chat`

Once we've done this, we should have built the following project structure:

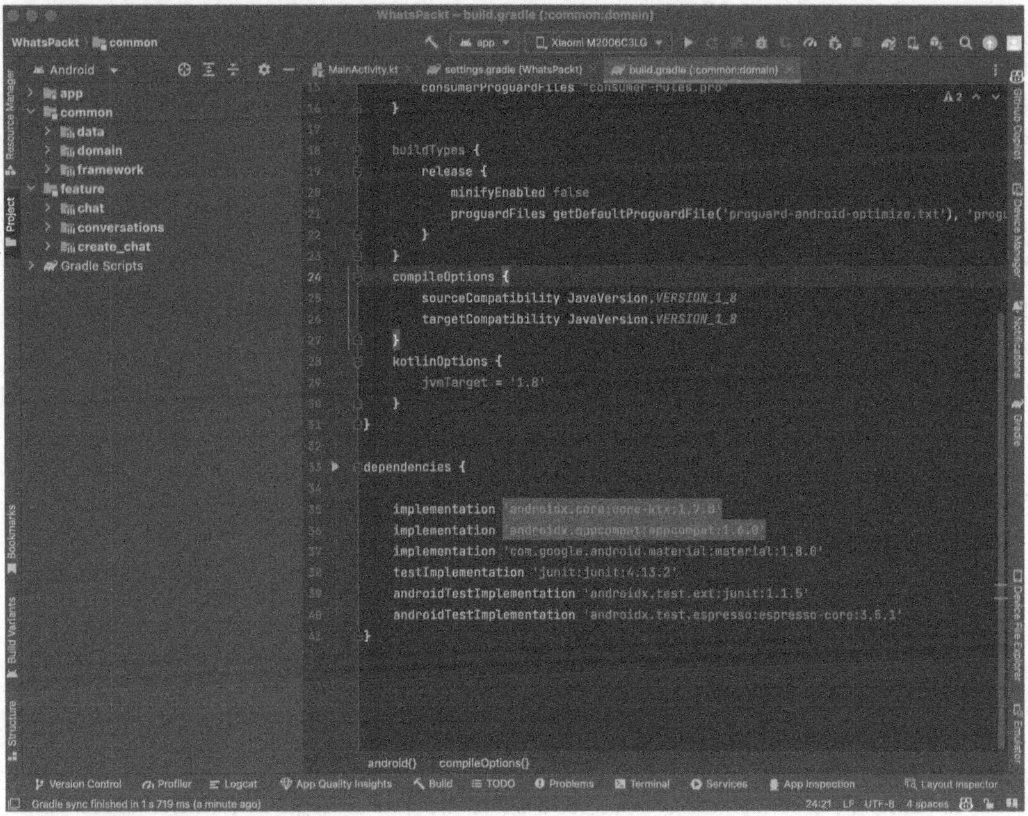

Figure 1.8: Project structure, including all modules

The next step is to set the dependencies between modules. We will do this in the `build.gradle` file of every module. For example, in the `build.gradle` file of the `:app` module, include the following code in the `dependencies` section:

```
dependencies {

    implementation project(':feature:chat')
    implementation project(':feature:conversations')
    implementation project(':feature:create_chat')
    // The rest of dependencies
}
```

Now that our app modules are ready, we can start working on the next step: dependency injection.

Dependency injection

Dependency injection is a design pattern and technique that's used in software engineering to decouple the objects in an application and reduce dependencies between them. In Android, dependency injection involves providing an instance of a class or a component to another class, rather than creating it explicitly within the class itself.

By implementing dependency injection in an Android app, you can make the app's code more modular, reusable, and testable. Dependency injection also helps improve the maintainability of the code base and reduce the complexity of the application architecture.

Some of the most popular dependency injection libraries that are used in Android development are as follows:

- **Dagger** (`https://dagger.dev/`): Dagger is a compile-time dependency injection library developed by Google that uses annotations and code generation to create a dependency graph that can be used to provide dependencies to the app's components. Its main advantage is that it builds this dependency graph at compile time, whereas other libraries (such as Koin) do it at runtime. For larger apps, this can imply a performance problem.

- **Hilt** (`https://dagger.dev/hilt/`): Hilt is a dependency injection library built on top of Dagger that provides a simplified way to perform dependency injection in Android apps. It reduces the boilerplate code required for Dagger and provides predefined bindings for Android-specific components, such as activities and fragments.

- **Koin** (`https://insert-koin.io/`): Koin is a lightweight dependency injection library for Kotlin that focuses on simplicity and ease of use. It uses a **domain-specific language** (**DSL**) to define the dependencies and provide them to the app's components, which makes it easier to do the setup and start using it.

Ultimately, the choice of dependency injection library depends on your specific requirements and preferences, and both Dagger and Koin are worth considering, depending on your needs. In this case, we are going to use Hilt as it is the current recommendation by Google.

To set up Hilt in our project, follow these steps:

1. Add the Hilt Gradle plugin to your project-level `build.gradle` file (replace `[version]` with the latest version available for you):

```
buildscript {
    repositories {
        google()
    }
    dependencies {
        classpath "com.google.dagger:hilt-android-
            gradle-plugin:[version]"
```

```
        }
    }
```

2. Apply the Hilt Gradle plugin and enable view binding in your app-level `build.gradle` file:

```
apply plugin: 'kotlin-kapt'
apply plugin: 'dagger.hilt.android.plugin'

android {
    ...
    buildFeatures {
        viewBinding true
    }
}

dependencies {
    implementation "com.google.dagger:hilt-
        android:[version]"
    kapt "com.google.dagger:hilt-android-
        compiler:[version]"
    ...
}
```

3. Finally, create an `Application` class in our `:app` module. The `Application` class serves as a base class for maintaining the global application state (this refers to data or settings that need to be maintained throughout the entire life cycle of the application). While it's not created by default, creating a custom `Application` class is crucial for initialization tasks, such as setting up dependency injection frameworks or initializing libraries. In this particular instance, to make Hilt work, you should annotate your `Application` class with the `@HiltAndroidApp` annotation:

```
@HiltAndroidApp
class WhatsPacktApplication : Application() {
    // ...
}
```

With that, we are all set – we will continue defining the modules and dependencies once we advance in this project.

Navigation

The next step is to decide what our approach to handling the navigation between screens and features in our application will be. It is important to note that we are going to use Jetpack Compose to build the user interface of our app, so the chosen approach must be compatible with it.

In this case, we're going to use Navigation Compose as it provides a simple and easy-to-use way to handle in-app navigation within an Android app. Here are some benefits of using Navigation Compose:

- **Declarative UI**: Navigation Compose follows the same declarative approach as Jetpack Compose, which makes it easier to understand and maintain the navigation flow in your application.

- **Type-safety**: With Navigation Compose, you can define your navigation graph and actions in a type-safe way. This helps prevent runtime crashes caused by incorrect navigation action names and arguments.

- **Animation and transition support**: Navigation Compose provides built-in support for animating screen transitions, making it easy to create smooth and visually appealing navigation experiences.

- **Deep linking**: Navigation Compose supports deep linking, allowing you to create URLs that can directly navigate to specific screens or actions within your app. This is useful for implementing features such as app shortcuts, notifications, or sharing content.

- **Integration with Jetpack Compose**: As part of the Jetpack Compose family, Navigation Compose works seamlessly with other Compose libraries and components, allowing you to build a consistent UI and navigation experience across your app.

- **Modularity and scalability**: Navigation Compose enables you to build modular navigation graphs, making it easier to scale your app and manage complex navigation flows.

In summary, Navigation Compose simplifies navigation management, improves the robustness of our app, and will help us to create a more consistent, accessible, and visually appealing user experience.

To start using Navigation Compose, we must do the following:

1. First, we need to include the dependencies that are required in our Gradle files:

    ```
    dependencies {
        implementation "androidx.navigation:navigation-
        compose:2.5.3"
    }
    ```

> **Note**
>
> The version used in the previous code is the latest stable one at the time of writing this book, but there will likely be a new version by the time you are reading this.

2. Next, in the `app` module, create a new package called `ui.navigation`. Then, create a file called `WhatsPacktNavigation`.

3. Now, create a `NavHost` composable and provide a `NavController` instance. The `NavHost` composable functions as a container for managing navigation between different composables in an app. It acts as the central hub where navigation routes are defined and composables are

switched in and out based on the navigation state. Each screen or view in your application corresponds to a composable that NavHost can display. Here, we will start by creating the WhatsPacktNavigation composable function. This will be responsible for holding NavHost:

```
import androidx.compose.runtime.Composable
import androidx.navigation.compose.NavHost
import
androidx.navigation.compose.rememberNavController

@Composable
fun WhatsPacktNavigation() {
    val navController = rememberNavController()

    NavHost(navController = navController,
    startDestination = "start_screen") {
        // Add composable destinations here
    }
}
```

4. Once we've created the first screen (which we'll call MainScreen), we will complete NavHost, as follows:

```
NavHost(navController = navController,
startDestination = "start_screen") {
    composable("start_screen") {
    MainScreen(navController) }
}
```

5. We can also include dynamic parameters in the route, like so:

```
NavHost(
    navController = navController,
    startDestination = "start_screen"
) {
    composable("start_screen") {
        MainScreen(navController) }
    composable("chat/{chatId}") { backStackEntry ->
        val chatId =
            backStackEntry.arguments?.getString(
                "chatId")
        ChatScreen(navController, chatId)
    }
}
```

Here, we have a second composable that defines another navigation destination associated with the `"chat/{chatId}"` route. The `{chatId}` part is a dynamic parameter that can be passed when navigating to this destination.

Using these two configurations – that is, navigation with and without parameters – should have us covered but since we are using feature-based modularization, we might encounter the problem of having to navigate from one module to another where there isn't a direct dependency between them. In those cases, we will use deep links.

Deep linking allows users to navigate to specific screens or actions within your app using URLs. When defining your composable destinations within `NavHost`, you need to add a `deepLink` parameter with the URI pattern you want to use for that destination. This pattern should include a scheme, a host, and an optional path. In our example, if we have `ChatScreen`, which takes a `chatId` argument, we can add a deep link URI like this:

```
NavHost(
    navController = navController,
    startDestination = "start_screen")
{
    composable("start_screen") { MainScreen(navController)
    }
    composable(
        route = "chat?id={id}",
        deepLinks = listOf(navDeepLink { uriPattern =
            "whatspackt://chat/{id}" })
    ) { backStackEntry ->
        ChatScreen(
            navController,
            backStackEntry.arguments?.getString("id"))
    }
}
```

One common practice to keep our `NavHost` leaner and delegate the definition of routes and URIs to every screen is to define the route with constants. Here is an example:

```
@Composable
fun ChatScreen(
    ...
) {
    object {
        val uri = "whatspackt://chat/{id}"
        val name = "chat?id={id}"
    }
}
```

By doing this, developers can easily manage, update, and maintain the routes in a centralized manner.

Then, in `NavHost`, we would define `uriPattern` using these constants:

```
composable(
    route = NavRoutes.Chat,
    arguments = listOf(
        navArgument(NavRoutes.ChatArgs.ChatId) {
            type = NavType.StringType
        }
    )
) { backStackEntry ->
    val chatId = backStackEntry.arguments?.getString(
        NavRoutes.ChatArgs.ChatId)
    ChatScreen(chatId = chatId, onBack = {
        navController.popBackStack() })
}
```

Instead of adding this information to every screen, a better option is to create a class where we are going to put all the route constants:

```
object NavRoutes {
    const val ConversationsList = "conversations_list"
    const val NewConversation = "create_conversation"
    const val Chat = "chat/{chatId}"

    object ChatArgs {
        const val ChatId = "chatId"
    }
}
```

Having the route's definition in the same place will facilitate reading and maintaining our code so that we can easily manage, update, and maintain the routes in a centralized manner, while also improving code readability and reducing the possibility of errors caused by hardcoded or duplicated strings throughout the code base.

We will place the file that contains this class in our `:common:framework` module as we will need to access those constants from every feature module. Another common practice is to create a dedicated `:common:navigation` module and add the definition of the route and even the `NavHost` definition there. In our case, we will define the routes using the latest approach – that is, route constants:

```
package com.packt.whatspackt.ui.navigation

import androidx.compose.runtime.Composable
import androidx.navigation.NavGraphBuilder
```

```
import androidx.navigation.NavHostController
import androidx.navigation.NavType
import androidx.navigation.compose.NavHost
import androidx.navigation.compose.composable
import com.packt.feature.chat.ui.ChatScreen
import androidx.navigation.navArgument
import com.packt.framework.navigation.NavRoutes

@Composable
fun MainNavigation(navController: NavHostController) {

    NavHost(
        navController,
        startDestination = NavRoutes.ConversationsList)
    {

        addConversationsList(navController)

        addNewConversation(navController)

        addChat(navController)

    }
}
```

In the preceding code, we completed our NavHost definition.

In our app, we will want to navigate to three different parts of the app (conversations list, create new chat, and the single chat screen). The navigation destinations can be added to NavHost by using extension functions on NavGraphBuilder. These extension functions are defined as follows:

```
private fun NavGraphBuilder.addConversationsList(
    navController: NavHostController
) {

    composable(NavRoutes.ConversationsList) {
        ConversationsListScreen(
            onNewConversationClick = {
                navController.navigate(
                    NavRoutes.NewConversation)
            },
            onConversationClick = { chatId ->
                navController.navigate(
                NavRoutes.Chat.replace("{chatId}", chatId))
```

```
            }
        )
    }
}

private fun NavGraphBuilder.addNewConversation(
navController: NavHostController) {

    composable(NavRoutes.NewConversation) {
        CreateConversationScreen(onCreateConversation = {
            navController.navigate(NavRoutes.Chat)
        })
    }
}

private fun NavGraphBuilder.addChat(navController:
NavHostController) {

    composable(
        route = NavRoutes.Chat,
        arguments = listOf(navArgument(
        NavRoutes.ChatArgs.ChatId) {
            type = NavType.StringType
        })
    ) { backStackEntry ->
        val chatId = backStackEntry.arguments?.getString(
            NavRoutes.ChatArgs.ChatId)
        ChatScreen(chatId = chatId, onBack = {
            navController.popBackStack() })
    }
}
```

Here, addConversationsList(navController) sets up ConversationsListScreen and defines click listeners for navigating to the NewConversation and Chat destinations.

Then, addNewConversation(navController) sets up CreateConversationScreen and defines a click listener for navigating to the Chat destination upon creating a new conversation.

Finally, addChat(navController) sets up ChatScreen and extracts the chatId argument from backStackEntry. It also defines a click listener for navigating back to the previous screen using navController.popBackStack().

Now, we are almost ready to hit the **Run** button for the first time. But first, to avoid compilation problems, we should create the screen's composables in their respective modules:

- `ConversationsListScreen` in `:feature:conversations`
- `CreateConversationScreen` in `:feature:create_chat`
- `ChatScreen` in `:feature:chat`

For example, we can create `ChatScreen` and leave it as follows:

```
package com.packt.feature.chat.ui

import androidx.compose.runtime.Composable

@Composable
fun ChatScreen(
    chatId: String?,
    onBack: () -> Unit
) {
}
```

We are missing one last change (for now). We need to include the `MainNavigation` composable as the content in `MainActivity`:

```
class MainActivity : ComponentActivity() {

    override fun onCreate(savedInstanceState: Bundle?) {
        super.onCreate(savedInstanceState)
        setContent {
            WhatsPacktTheme {
                val navHostController =
                    rememberNavController()
                MainNavigation(navController =
                    navHostController)
            }
        }
    }
}
```

As we can see, we've added `navHostController`, which we created using `rememberNavController()`. This is used to remember the navigation state across recompositions. Here, `navHostController` manages the navigation between different composables in the application. Then, the `MainNavigation` composable is called with `navHostController`.

So far, we have chosen and created the module structure for our app, chosen a dependency injection framework, added the dependencies we need, and structured the navigation that defines how our screens are going to be accessed. Now, it's time for us to start working on each of the screens we need to build this app.

Building the main screen

Now that we have the main structure of our app ready, it is time to start building the main screen.

Let's analyze what components our main screen will have:

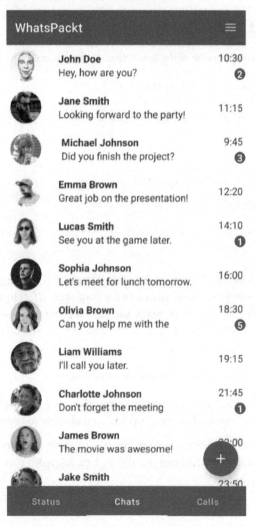

Figure 1.9: The ConversationsList screen

As you can see, we are going to include the following:

- A top bar

- A tab bar to navigate to the main sections (note that this book will only cover the development of the chat section; we will not cover the status and calls sections)

- A list containing the current conversations (which we will complete later in this chapter)

- A floating button to create a new chat

Let's start with the main screen.

Adding a scaffold to the main screen

Previously, we created an empty version of the first screen (ConversationsListScreen), as follows:

```
package com.packt.feature.conversations.ui

import androidx.compose.runtime.Composable

@Composable
fun ConversationsListScreen(
    onNewConversationClick: () -> Unit,
    onConversationClick: (chatId: String) -> Unit
) {
// We will add here the ConversactionsListScreen components
}
```

Now, it's time to start working on this screen. The first component we are going to add is a **scaffold**. This is a composable that provides a basic structure for your app's UI. It helps you create a consistent layout by providing slots for common UI elements, such as a top app bar, a bottom app bar, a navigation drawer, a floating action button, and content. By using Scaffold, you can easily organize your app's layout and maintain a consistent look and feel across different screens.

Here's a brief overview of the main components of Scaffold:

- topBar: A slot for placing a top app bar, typically used for displaying the app's title and navigation icons. You can use the TopAppBar composable to create a top app bar.

- bottomBar: A slot for placing a bottom app bar, typically used for actions, navigation tabs, or a bottom navigation bar. You can use the BottomAppBar or TabRow composable to create a bottom app bar.

- `drawerContent`: A slot for placing a navigation drawer, which is a panel that displays the app's navigation options. You can use the `Drawer` or `ModalDrawer` composable to create a navigation drawer.

- `floatingActionButton`: A slot for placing a floating action button, which is a circular button that hovers above the content and represents the primary action of the screen. You can use the `FloatingActionButton` composable to create a floating action button.

- `content`: A slot for placing the main content of the screen, which can be any composable that displays the app's data or UI elements.

In our case, we are going to use `topBar`, `bottomBar` with `TabRow` (to navigate between tabs), `floatingActionButton` (to create new chats), and the content, where we are going to place our main content – in our case, the list of conversations.

Let's create the `Scaffold` composable in our `ConversationsListScreen`. We will add the modifiers for all the components we want to include, but we'll leave them empty (for now):

```
@Composable
fun ConversationsListScreen(
    onNewConversationClick: () -> Unit,
    onConversationClick: (chatId: String) -> Unit
) {
    Scaffold(
        topBar = { /* TopAppBar code */ },
        bottomBar = { /* TabRow code */ },
        floatingActionButton =
            { /* FloatingActionButton code */ }
    ) {
        /* Content code */
    }
}
```

The `Scaffold` composable we have created includes `topBar`, `bottomBar`, `floatingAction Button`, and the content of the main area of the screen. We will continue implementing each of those components.

Now, depending on your Android Studio version, you may see the following error:

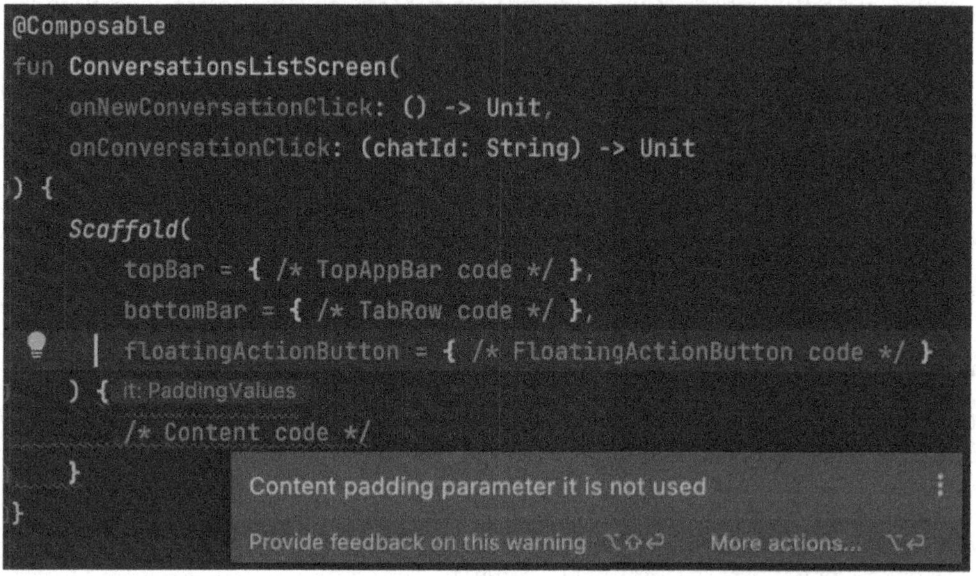

```
@Composable
fun ConversationsListScreen(
    onNewConversationClick: () -> Unit,
    onConversationClick: (chatId: String) -> Unit
) {
    Scaffold(
        topBar = { /* TopAppBar code */ },
        bottomBar = { /* TabRow code */ },
        floatingActionButton = { /* FloatingActionButton code */ }
    ) { it: PaddingValues
        /* Content code */
    }
}
```

Content padding parameter it is not used

Provide feedback on this warning ⌥⇧↵   More actions... ⌥↵

Figure 1.10: An error with the content padding parameter

This is happening because the `Scaffold` composable provides a padding parameter to the content Lambda. We will need to take this padding into account when we place the inside components since the scaffold could overlap them if we don't. For example, in our case, we must consider the padding because otherwise, our content will be kept behind `bottomBar`. We will use this parameter layer when we build the content.

Now, we will add a `TopAppBar` composable to the `Scaffold` composable.

Adding the TopAppBar composable to the main screen

The `TopAppBar` composable represents a toolbar located at the top of the screen and provides a consistent look and feel across different screens in your app. It typically displays the following elements:

- **Title**: The main text that's displayed in the app bar, usually representing the app's name or the current screen's title

- **Navigation icon**: An optional icon located at the beginning of the app bar, usually used to open a navigation drawer or navigate back into the app

- **Actions**: A set of optional icons or buttons located at the end of the app bar, representing common actions or settings related to the current screen

To add a `TopAppBar` composable, we must create the `conversations_list_title` string in the module's `strings.xml` file.

Then, we are going to create the `TopAppBar` composable while setting the title to `WhatsPackt` and adding `IconButton` with a menu icon. Here, `IconButton` has an `onClick` function where you can define the action to perform when the button is clicked:

```
topBar = {
    TopAppBar(
        title = {
            Text(stringResource(
            R.string.conversations_list_title))
        },
        actions = {
            IconButton(onClick = { /* Menu action */ }) {
                Icon(Icons.Rounded.Menu,
                contentDescription = "Menu")
            }
        }
    )
},
```

Next, we are going to create a `TabRow` composable.

Adding the TabRow composable to the bottom of the main screen

The `TabRow` composable is a horizontal row of tabs that allows users to navigate between different views or sections within an app. The `TabRow` composable mainly consists of the following elements:

- **Tabs**: A collection of individual `Tab` composables that represent different sections or views within the app. Each `Tab` composable can have a text label, an icon, or both to describe its content.

- **Selected tab indicator**: A visual indicator that highlights the currently selected tab, making it easy for users to understand which section they are viewing.

Before creating the `TabRow` composable, we'll have to provide a list and the tabs it is going to contain:

```
@Composable
fun ConversationsListScreen(
    onNewConversationClick: () -> Unit,
    onConversationClick: (chatId: String) -> Unit
) {
    val tabs = listOf("Status", "Chats", "Calls")
    Scaffold(
```

```
        topBar = {
...
```

Then, we can add TabRow:

```
bottomBar = {
    TabRow(selectedTabIndex = 1) {
        tabs.forEachIndexed { index, tab ->
            Tab(
                text = { Text(tab) },
                selected = index == 1,
                onClick = { /* Navigation action */ }
            )
        }
    }
},
```

For every row, we are adding a Tab composable, where we indicate the title (using a Text composable), the selected value when the tab is selected, and the onClick action (which we are not implementing).

After that, we can make our code more readable by creating a data class to store the title of the Tab composable:

```
data class ConversationsListTab(
    @StringRes val title: Int
)

fun generateTabs(): List<ConversationsListTab> {
    return listOf(
        ConversationsListTab(
            title = R.string.conversations_tab_status_title
        ),
        ConversationsListTab(
            title = R.string.conversations_tab_chats_title
        ),
        ConversationsListTab(
            title = R.string.conversations_tab_calls_title
        ),
    )
}
```

Then, we can change our `TabRow` code:

```
bottomBar = {
    TabRow(selectedTabIndex = 1) {
        tabs.forEachIndexed { index, _ ->
            Tab(
                text = { Text(stringResource(
                    tabs[index].title)) },
                selected = index == 1,
                onClick = {
                    // Navigate to every tab content
                }
            )
        }
    }
}
```

`TabRow` composables are usually combined with a pager, where the content will be shown. When clicking and navigating between tabs, the main content that's displayed should change.

Now, let's add the pager to our screen content.

Adding a pager

A pager is a UI component that allows users to swipe through multiple pages or screens horizontally or vertically. It is commonly used to display screens or views in a carousel-like fashion.

We are going to use `HorizontalPager`, which, as its name suggests, allows the user to horizontally swipe between screens or composables. One of its main advantages is that it will not create all pages at once; it will only create the current page and the immediate previous/next pages, which will be off-screen. Once a page is out of this three-page window, it will be removed.

To do so, we are going to have to tweak some of the previous code we had in our `Conversations ListScreen` composable:

```
@OptIn(ExperimentalFoundationApi::class)
@Composable
fun ConversationsListScreen(
    onNewConversationClick: () -> Unit,
    onConversationClick: (chatId: String) -> Unit
) {
    val tabs = generateTabs()
    val selectedIndex = remember { mutableStateOf(1) }
    val pagerState = rememberPagerState(initialPage = 1)
```

```
    ...
}
```

First, since `HorizontalPager` is part of the foundation API and is (at the time of writing) an experimental API (which means that it could change its public interface in the future), we need to add the `@OptIn(ExperimentalFoundationApi::class)` annotation.

Second, we have added a new field called `pagerState`. Its responsibility is to hold the state of the pager, including information about the number of pages, the current page, the scrolling position, and the scrolling behavior.

Next, we will add `HorizontalPager` to the content function, as follows:

```
content = { innerPadding ->
    HorizontalPager(
    modifier = Modifier.padding(innerPadding),
    pageCount = tabs.size,
    state = pagerState
) { index ->
    when (index) {
        0 -> {
            //Status
        }
        1 -> {
            ConversationList(
                conversations = emptyList(),
                onConversationClick = onConversationClick
            )
        }
        2-> {
            // Calls
        }
    }
}
    LaunchedEffect(selectedIndex.value) {
        pagerState.animateScrollToPage(selectedIndex.value)
    }
}
```

Here, we will be using a `LaunchedEffect` function. This function is used to manage side effects, such as launching tasks that have been completed asynchronously in the context of a composable hierarchy. Side effects are operations that can have an impact outside of the composable function itself, such as network requests, database operations, or, in the case of the previous example, scrolling to a specific page in a pager.

LaunchedEffect takes a key (or a set of keys) as its first parameter. When the key changes, the effect will be re-launched, canceling any ongoing work from the previous effect. The second parameter is a suspending Lambda function, which will be executed in the effect's coroutine scope.

The main advantage of using LaunchedEffect is that it integrates well with the Compose life cycle. When the composable that called LaunchedEffect leaves the composition, the effect will be automatically canceled, cleaning up any ongoing work.

Coming back to our code, in our case, we are changing the current page in pagerState and animating the scroll to the next selected page. This will be triggered every time selectedIndex. value is changed.

The next component will allow the user to create a new chat – we will create this button using a FloatingActionButton composable.

Adding the FloatingActionButton composable

The FloatingActionButton composable is a Material Design composable that represents a circular button floating above the UI. It's typically used to promote the primary action in an application (for example, adding a new item, composing a message, or starting a new process). Following the Material Design guidelines (you can check them here: https://m3.material.io/), we are going to use it to create a new chat from ConversationsListScreen:

```
floatingActionButton = {
    FloatingActionButton(
        onClick = { onNewConversationClick() }
    ) {
        Icon(
            imageVector = Icons.Default.Add,
            contentDescription = "Add"
        )
    }
}
```

Our FloatingActionButton composable is taking an onClick modifier. Here, we will include the code to navigate to the create chat screen. Inside this button, we have included an Icon composable, which we are using as an image of one of the Icons.Default predefined images.

At this point, our conversations list screen should look similar to this:

Figure 1.11: The conversations list screen with a top bar, tab bar, and floating action button

With that, we have created our Scaffold composable with all the elements we need to help the user navigate. Now, we are ready for the last step (and the most important one) to complete the screen: creating the list of existing conversations. To do that, we are going to start creating a conversation item.

Creating the conversations list

In this section, we are going to create all the pieces we need to show the conversations list. We will start with the UI data model, which will represent the information that the app is going to show in the list, the Conversation composable, which will draw every item of the list, and finally the list composable itself.

Modeling the conversation

First, we are going to model what is going to be the entity we will be using through our conversations list components: the `Conversation` model.

As part of the conversation model, we want to show the avatar of the other participant (we are just doing one-to-one conversations), their name, the first line of the last message, the time the message was received, and a number indicating how many unread messages there are.

Taking that information into account, we will start creating a data class to hold the data we'll need:

```
data class Conversation(
    val id: String,
    val name: String,
    val message: String,
    val timestamp: String,
    val unreadCount: Int,
    val avatar: String
)
```

As the avatar could be reusable across the app, we are going to create it first. We can include it in the `:common:framework` module so that it is visible and can be reused from the other feature modules.

Jetpack Compose doesn't include support to asynchronously load images from a URL out of the box, but there are plenty of third-party libraries that will help us accomplish this. The most popular options are Coil and Glide, which, in terms of performance, caching, and image loading, are quite similar. We are going to use Coil just for simplicity and because it is Kotlin-first (whereas Glide is programmed in Java).

As always, we need to include the dependency in our module's `build.gradle` file:

```
dependencies {
...
implementation "io.coil-kt:coil-compose:${latest_version}"
...
}
```

At this point, we're ready to create our `Avatar` composable:

```
@Composable
fun Avatar(
    modifier: Modifier = Modifier,
    imageUrl: String,
    size: Dp,
    contentDescription: String? = "User avatar"
) {
```

```
AsyncImage(
    model = imageUrl,
    contentDescription = contentDescription,
    modifier = modifier
        .size(size)
        .clip(CircleShape),
    contentScale = ContentScale.Crop
)
}
```

Here, we are creating an avatar using `AsyncImage`, which will load an image provided by a URL. This image will be modified to have a circular shape. Also, we should pass the size of the image when using this composable (we have chosen 50 density-independent pixels).

Now, we can create `ConversationItem`:

```
import androidx.compose.foundation.layout.*
import androidx.compose.material.MaterialTheme
import androidx.compose.material.Text
import androidx.compose.runtime.Composable
import androidx.compose.ui.Alignment
import androidx.compose.ui.Modifier
import androidx.compose.ui.text.font.FontWeight
import androidx.compose.ui.unit.dp
import com.packt.feature.conversations.ui.model.Conversation
import com.packt.framework.ui.Avatar

@Composable
fun ConversationItem(conversation: Conversation) {
    Row(
        modifier = Modifier
            .fillMaxWidth()
            .padding(8.dp),
        verticalAlignment = Alignment.CenterVertically
    ) {
        Avatar(
            imageUrl = conversation.avatar,
            size = 50.dp,
            contentDescription =
                "${conversation.name}'s avatar"
        )
        Spacer(modifier = Modifier.width(8.dp))
        Column {
            Text(
```

```
                text = conversation.name,
                fontWeight = FontWeight.Bold,
                modifier = Modifier.fillMaxWidth(0.7f)
            )
            Text(text = conversation.message)
        }
        Spacer(modifier = Modifier.width(8.dp))
        Column(horizontalAlignment = Alignment.End) {
            Text(text = conversation.timestamp)
            if (conversation.unreadCount > 0) {
                Text(
                    text =
                    conversation.unreadCount.toString(),
                    color = MaterialTheme.colors.primary,
                    modifier = Modifier.padding(top = 4.dp)
                )
            }
        }
    }
}
}
```

Let's take a closer look at what this composable does:

- The ConversationItem composable accepts the following parameters: name, message, timestamp, avatarUrl, and an optional unreadMessages with a default value of 0.

- A Row layout is used to arrange the contents horizontally. It has a fillMaxWidth() modifier to occupy the full width of the parent and a padding of 8 density-independent pixels.

- The Avatar composable is used to display the avatar. We already know how it works – the only thing to remark on is that we want it to have a size of 50 density-independent pixels.

- A Spacer composable with a width of 8 density pixels is added to provide some space between the avatar and the text content.

- A Column layout is used to arrange the name and message text vertically. The Column layout has a Modifier.weight() modifier, which ensures that it takes up all the available space between the avatar and the timestamp.

- Inside the Column layout, a Text composable is used to display the name with a bold font weight and a font size of 16 scale-independent pixels. Another Text composable is used to display the message with a maximum of one line and an ellipsis overflow.

- Another Column layout is added to the main Row layout to arrange the timestamp and unread messages badge vertically. The Column layout has a horizontalAlignment value of Alignment.End to align its children to the end of the available space.

- Inside this second `Column` layout, a `Text` composable is used to display the time with a font size of 12 scale-independent pixels and a gray color.

- A conditional statement checks if there are any unread messages (that is, `conversation.unreadMessages > 0`). If there are unread messages, the unread messages count shows a text with a circular background drawn using the `drawBehind` modifier.

Now that we have our `ConversationItem` composable, it is time to finish this screen. Let's create the `ConversationList` composable!

Creating the ConversationList composable

As the last step for this screen, we are going to create the list of conversations:

```
@Composable
fun ConversationList(conversations: List<Conversation>) {
    LazyColumn {
        items(conversations) { conversation ->
            ConversationItem(
                conversation = conversation
            )
        }
    }
}
```

The `ConversationList` composable takes a list of `Conversation` objects and uses `LazyColumn` to display them efficiently. The `items` function is used to loop through the conversations list and will render `ConversationItem` for each conversation.

Finally, we will include the list in the `HorizontalPager` logic, in our `ConversationsListScreen` composable:

```
HorizontalPager(
    modifier = Modifier.padding(innerPadding),
    pageCount = tabs.size,
    state = pagerState
) { index ->
    when (index) {
        0 -> {
            //Status
        }
        1 -> {
            ConversationList(
                conversations = emptyList(), // Leaving the
```

```
                                        list empty
                                        for now
            onConversationClick = onConversationClick
            )
        }
        2-> {
            // Calls
        }
    }
}
```

If we want to test it, we can fake the data of the conversations:

```
fun generateFakeConversations(): List<Conversation> {
    return listOf(
        Conversation(
            id = "1",
            name = "John Doe",
            message = "Hey, how are you?",
            timestamp = "10:30",
            avatar = "https://i.pravatar.cc/150?u=1",
            unreadCount = 2
        ),
        Conversation(
            id = "2",
            name = "Jane Smith",
            message = "Looking forward to the party!",
            timestamp = "11:15",
            avatar = "https://i.pravatar.cc/150?u=2"
        ),
//Add more conversations here
```

Note that here, I'm using a random avatar generator just to make it as similar as possible to how it would be when we connect this UI with real conversations.

The following screenshot shows what our app would look like with more conversations:

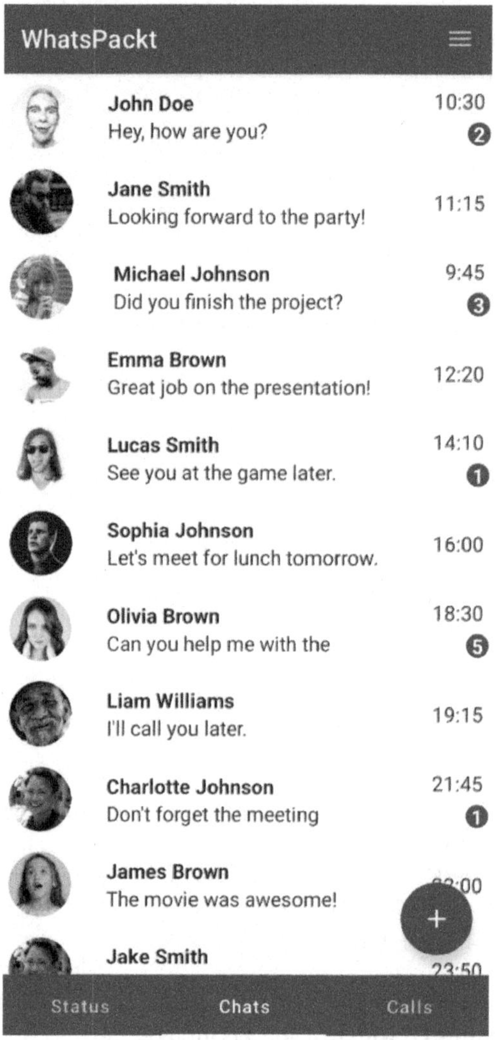

Figure 1.12: ConversationsList screen completed

Now, let's switch to the chat screen, also known as the messages list. Whereas the conversations list is a list showing all the conversations we have, the messages list will show the list of messages we have with one user (a single chat screen).

Building the messages list

In this section, we are going to create the UI models that are needed to create the chat screen and the messages two users could have exchanged. Then, we will create the `Message` composable, and finally, the rest of the screen, including the list of messages.

Modeling the Chat and Message models

Taking into account the information we have to show on the chat screen, we are going to need two data models: one for the static data related to the conversation (for example, the name of the user we are talking to, their avatar, and so on) and one data model per message. This will be the model for the `Chat` model:

```
data class Chat(
    val id: String,
    val name: String,
    val avatar: String
)
```

In this case, we will need the ID of the chat, the name of the person we are talking to, and their avatar address.

Regarding the `Message` model, we will create the following classes:

```
data class Message(
    val id: String,
    val senderName: String,
    val senderAvatar: String,
    val timestamp: String,
    val isMine: Boolean,
    val messageContent: MessageContent
)

sealed class MessageContent {
    data class TextMessage(val message: String) :
        MessageContent()
    data class ImageMessage(val imageUrl: String,
        val contentDescription: String) : MessageContent()
}
```

In this case, we need the sender's name, their avatar, the timestamp, whether the message is mine or not (which we will take into account so that we can arrange the message one to the left or the right), and the content of the message.

Since our application is going to have two types of content (messages and images), we need two different kinds of `MessageContent`. That's the reason it has been modeled as a sealed class. We have two data classes with the data needed for every type of message content.

Now, we need to convert these models into some composables.

Creating the MessageItem composable

The `MessageItem` composable is going to draw each of our chat messages.

To start, we will create a `Row` layout. We will set the arrangement of the row contents depending on the message's author:

```
@Composable
fun MessageItem(message: Message) {
    Row(
        modifier = Modifier.fillMaxWidth(),
        horizontalArrangement = if (message.isMine)
        Arrangement.End else Arrangement.Start
    ) {
    ...
    }
}
```

Then, inside this row, we are going to place the rest of the components of the message. We will start with the avatar; we will only show the avatar if the message is not from the user:

```
if (!message.isMine) {
    Avatar(
        imageUrl = message.senderAvatar,
        size = 40.dp,
        contentDescription = "${message.senderName}'s
                            avatar"
    )
    Spacer(modifier = Modifier.width(8.dp))
}
```

Then, we are going to add a `Column` layout so that we can arrange the rest of the message information:

```
Column {
    if (message.isMine) {
        Spacer(modifier = Modifier.height(8.dp))
    } else {
        Text(
            text = message.senderName,
```

```
                    fontWeight = FontWeight.Bold
            )
    }
    when (val content = message.messageContent) {
        is MessageContent.TextMessage -> {
            Surface(
                shape = RoundedCornerShape(8.dp),
                color = if (message.isMine)
                MaterialTheme.colors.primarySurface else
                MaterialTheme.colors.secondary
            ) {
                Text(
                    text = content.message,
                    modifier = Modifier.padding(8.dp),
                    color = if (message.isMine)
                    MaterialTheme.colors.onPrimary else
                    Color.White
                )
            }
        }
        is MessageContent.ImageMessage -> {
            AsyncImage(
                model = content.imageUrl,
                contentDescription =
                content.contentDescription,
                modifier = Modifier
                    .size(40.dp)
                    .clip(CircleShape),
                contentScale = ContentScale.Crop
            )
        }
    }
    Text(
        text = message.timestamp,
        fontSize = 12.sp
    )
}
```

The message will include the following information:

- **The name of the sender (if the author is not the current user)**: To know if the message is from the current user, the app will check if the author of the message is the current user using if (message.isMine. If this is positive, we will add a Space composable; if the message author is not the current user, we will show the Text composable and their name.

- **The content**: The app will show a bubble containing text if the content is text. The color of the bubble will depend on whether the sender of the message is the current user and the time the message was created. A timestamp with the date and time of creation will be shown at the bottom of the message.

Now that we have MessageItem, it's time to create the rest of the chat screen.

Adding the TopAppBar and BottomRow composables

As we did for the conversations list, we are going to add the Scaffold structure and its TopAppBar and BottomRow composables to this screen:

```
@Composable
fun ChatScreen(
    chatId: String?,
    onBack: () -> Unit
) {
    Scaffold(
        topBar = {
            TopAppBar(
                title = {
                    Text(stringResource(
                    R.string.chat_title, "Alice"))
                }
            )
        },
        bottomBar = {
            SendMessageBox()
        }
    ) { paddingValues->
        ListOfMessages(paddingValues = paddingValues)
    }

}
```

Note that we are hardcoding the title of the chat. This is just for preview purposes; we'll correct that in the next chapter.

In the case of the bottom bar, we are adding a new composable that will contain `Textfield` and the send button needed to send a message. This is what this composable will look like:

```
@Composable
fun SendMessageBox() {
    Box(
        modifier = Modifier
            .defaultMinSize()
            .padding(top = 0.dp, start = 16.dp,
                end = 16.dp,
            bottom = 16.dp)
            .fillMaxWidth()
    ) {

        var text by remember { mutableStateOf("") }

        OutlinedTextField(
            value = text,
            onValueChange = { newText -> text = newText },
            modifier = Modifier
                .fillMaxWidth(0.85f)
                .align(Alignment.CenterStart)
                .height(56.dp),
        )

        IconButton(
            modifier = Modifier
                .align(Alignment.CenterEnd)
                .height(56.dp),
            onClick = {
                // Send message here
                text = ""
            }
        ) {
            Icon(
                imageVector = Icons.Default.Send,
                tint = MaterialTheme.colors.primary,
                contentDescription = "Send message"
            )
        }
    }
}
```

Here, we are creating a Box composable to arrange the children composables accordingly (the text field at the left and the Send button at the right). Then, we're defining a property called text to store text field changes and using the remember delegate to remember its last value between recompositions.

As shown in the preceding code block, the main components of this composable are as follows:

- OutlinedTextField: To write the message. It will take its value from the text property and modify it every time the value of the text field changes.

- IconButton: To send the message. Its onClick parameter is not doing anything yet (apart from restarting the text property value). We will configure this in the next chapter.

With that, our chat screen is almost ready. The last thing we need to do is add the messages list.

Adding the messages list

Earlier, we were adding the messages list as a composable in the content parameter of the Scaffold composable. This composable will look as follows:

```
@Composable
fun ListOfMessages(paddingValues: PaddingValues) {
    Box(modifier = Modifier
        .fillMaxSize()
        .padding(paddingValues)) {
        Row(modifier = Modifier
            .fillMaxWidth()
            .padding(16.dp)
        ) {
            LazyColumn(
                modifier = Modifier
                    .fillMaxSize(),
                verticalArrangement =
                    Arrangement.spacedBy(8.dp),
            ) {
                items(getFakeMessages()) { message ->
                    MessageItem(message = message)
                }
            }
        }
    }
}
```

With that, we have added `LazyColumn`, which will show the list – every item in the list is a `MessageItem` composable.

Since we haven't connected it to any kind of data source yet, we are using a function to generate a list of fake messages just for preview purposes:

```
fun getFakeMessages(): List<Message> {
    return listOf(
        Message(
            id = "1",
            senderName = "Alice",
            senderAvatar =
                "https://i.pravatar.cc/300?img=1",
            isMine = false,
            timestamp = "10:00",
            messageContent = MessageContent.TextMessage(
                message = "Hi, how are you?"
            )
        ),
        Message(
            id = "2",
            senderName = "Lucy",
            senderAvatar =
                "https://i.pravatar.cc/300?img=2",
            isMine = true,
            timestamp = "10:01",
            messageContent = MessageContent.TextMessage(
                message = "I'm good, thank you! And you?"
            )
        ),

    )
}
```

You can add more messages if you want by adding them to the list that's been created inside the `getFakeMessages()` function.

Finally, we should have a screen that looks like this:

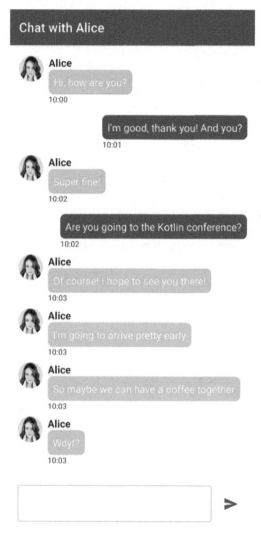

Figure 1.13: Chat screen UI finished

With that, we are done with the user interface for now. We will continue working on this app during the next two chapters!

Summary

In this first chapter, we started our first project, WhatsPackt, a messaging app.

We accomplished several initial tasks to build this app, such as organizing modules, preparing dependency injection and navigation, constructing the main screen, creating the conversations list, and building the messages list.

Throughout this process, we've learned about modularization and the various approaches to organizing it. We've also learned about popular libraries for managing dependency injection, how to initialize them, and how to set up Compose navigation. Additionally, we became familiar with using Jetpack Compose to create our user interface.

As we move forward, it's time to give some love and life to our chats. In the next chapter, we will explore how to retrieve and send messages and integrate them into our recently created user interfaces.

2

Setting Up WhatsPackt's Messaging Abilities

In the previous chapter, we created the structure and UI needed for our messaging app, WhatsPackt.

One of the core features of any messaging app is the ability to facilitate 1:1 conversations between two users, so in this chapter, we will delve into the process of connecting our messaging app to a backend server using WebSockets, handling messages within `ViewModel` instances, and managing synchronization, error handling, and push notifications.

We will begin by exploring **WebSockets**, a powerful technology that enables bidirectional communication between client and server, providing a solid foundation for real-time messaging in your app. You will learn how to establish a WebSocket connection, send messages, and handle incoming messages from the server.

Next, we will demonstrate how to receive messages in your **ViewModel**. We will discuss best practices for updating the UI, managing message storage, and handling user interactions, ensuring a smooth and responsive messaging experience for your users.

The chapter will also cover the essential aspects of synchronization and error handling. You will learn how to manage message delivery status, handle intermittent connectivity issues, and gracefully recover from errors, resulting in a resilient and reliable messaging system.

Finally, we will dig into the topic of push notifications, which are vital for alerting users of new messages even when the app is not in the foreground.

By the end of this chapter, you will have gained a comprehensive understanding of the key components and technologies involved in creating a modern messaging app that supports 1:1 conversations using WebSockets and push notifications.

So, in this chapter, we will cover the following topics:

- Using a WebSocket connection

- Receiving messages in our `ViewModel`

- Handling synchronization and errors

- Adding push notifications

- Replacing the WebSocket with Firestore

Technical requirements

As in the previous chapter, you will need to have installed Android Studio (or another editor of your preference).

We are also going to assume that you followed along with the previous chapter. If you haven't, you can download the previous chapter's complete code from here: `https://github.com/ PacktPublishing/Thriving-in-Android-Development-using-Kotlin/tree/ main/Chapter-1/WhatsPackt`.

The code completed in this chapter can also be found at this link: `https://github.com/ PacktPublishing/Thriving-in-Android-Development-using-Kotlin/tree/ main/Chapter-2/WhatsPackt`.

Using a WebSocket connection

As mentioned, WebSockets is a powerful technology that enables bidirectional communication between client and server. In this section, we are going to use a WebSocket connection to connect with our server to obtain and send messages. But before we do that, it is essential to understand the alternatives and the rationale behind choosing WebSockets for our messaging app.

Why WebSockets?

There are several options for enabling real-time communication between clients and servers, including the following:

- **Long polling**: This is when the client sends a request to the server, and the server holds the request until new data is available. Once the server responds with the new data, the client sends another request, and the process repeats.

- **Server-Sent Events (SSE)**: SSE is a unidirectional communication method where the server pushes updates to the client over a single HTTP connection.

- **Real-time cloud databases** (for example, Firebase Firestore): Real-time cloud databases provide an easy-to-use, scalable solution for real-time data synchronization. They automatically push updates to clients whenever data changes, making them suitable for messaging apps.

- **WebSockets**: WebSockets provide full-duplex, bidirectional communication between clients and servers over a single, long-lived connection. They are widely supported across platforms and are an ideal choice for real-time communication in messaging apps.

Considering these alternatives, we choose to use WebSockets for our messaging app because they offer the following advantages:

- **Bidirectional communication**: WebSockets enable simultaneous data transmission between clients and servers, allowing for faster message exchanges and a more responsive user experience

- **Low latency**: Unlike long polling, SSE, and some real-time cloud databases, WebSockets provide low-latency communication, which is crucial for a real-time messaging app

- **Efficient use of resources**: WebSockets maintain a single connection per client, reducing the overhead on both client and server compared to long polling

- **Flexibility and control**: Implementing custom WebSocket communication allows for more fine-grained control over the messaging infrastructure, avoiding potential limitations or constraints imposed by real-time cloud databases

For sure, WebSockets also have their disadvantages that we must take into account, such as the following:

- **Battery and data usage**: Maintaining a persistent connection can lead to increased battery drain and data usage, which may be a concern for mobile users.

- **Complexity**: Implementing WebSocket communication is typically more complex than using RESTful services. You have to handle various scenarios such as reconnection on network changes, which are common in mobile environments.

- **Scalability**: If your application scales to a large number of users, maintaining WebSocket connections for all of them can be resource-intensive on the server side.

Although there are some disadvantages, the advantages of using WebSockets — such as real-time bidirectional communication and lower overheads compared to traditional HTTP polling — significantly outweigh these issues, making them a powerful choice for interactive applications.

Let's start learning how we can integrate WebSockets.

Integrating WebSockets

There are several libraries available for integrating WebSockets in Android applications. Some popular options include the following:

- **OkHttp**: A popular HTTP client for Android and Java applications that also supports WebSocket communication

- **Scarlet**: A declarative WebSocket library for Kotlin and Java applications, built on top of OkHttp

- **Ktor**: A modern, Kotlin-based framework for building asynchronous servers and clients, including WebSocket support

For our app, we will use Ktor due to its ease of use, native support for Kotlin, and extensive documentation.

What is Ktor?

Ktor stands out for its coroutine-based architecture, which allows for non-blocking asynchronous operations, making it particularly suitable for I/O-intensive tasks such as network communication. It's lightweight and modular, allowing developers to pick and choose only the features they need, thereby avoiding the overhead of unnecessary functionality.

The framework is built on top of coroutines, a feature in Kotlin that makes your code cleaner and more readable, and simplifies asynchronous programming by allowing functions to be paused and resumed at later times. This provides a powerful way to handle concurrency with a more straightforward and expressive syntax compared to traditional callback mechanisms.

Ktor is versatile, supporting both server-side and client-side development. On the server side, it can be used to build robust and scalable web applications and services. On the client side, it provides a multiplatform HTTP client that can be used on Android, allowing for seamless interaction with web services.

Ktor's WebSocket client allows for easy setup and management of WebSocket connections, handling complexities such as connection lifecycle, error handling, and message processing. Its **domain-specific language** (**DSL**) provides a concise and expressive way to define the behavior of WebSocket interactions, making the code more readable and maintainable.

Integrating WebSockets with Ktor

To integrate Ktor in our Android app, follow these steps:

1. In our app's `build.gradle` file of the `:feature:chat` module, add the following Ktor dependencies for the WebSocket client. Make sure to replace `$ktor_version` with the latest version available (for the examples in this book, we are using version 2.2.4):

    ```
    dependencies {
        implementation "io.ktor:ktor-client-
    ```

```
            websockets:2.2.4"
    implementation "io.ktor:ktor-client-okhttp:2.2.4"
}
```

Each dependency serves a distinct purpose:

- `io.ktor:ktor-client-websockets`: This dependency provides the necessary functionality to manage WebSocket connections in our application. It includes high-level abstractions for opening, sending messages to, and receiving messages from WebSocket servers, facilitating real-time data exchange in a seamless manner. By using this library, we can easily implement WebSocket communication without handling the complex underlying protocols and handshakes manually.

- `io.ktor:ktor-client-okhttp`: While Ktor is a multiplatform framework, it requires an engine to handle network requests. This dependency integrates OkHttp as the underlying engine for handling HTTP requests and responses in Android applications. OkHttp supports WebSockets along with its robust HTTP client features, providing efficient network operations, connection pooling, and a powerful interface for making and intercepting requests.

Together, these dependencies allow our app to utilize WebSockets for real-time communication and leverage OkHttp's efficient networking capabilities. This combination is particularly powerful for applications needing to maintain persistent connections and manage high-frequency data exchange, such as messaging apps or live data feeds.

2. In your `AndroidManifest.xml` file, add the required permission to access the internet as we will need it to connect our WebSocket and receive/send messages:

```
<uses-permission android:name=
    "android.permission.INTERNET" />
```

We now have the library included in our project. As we will be using Ktor with Kotlin Flow, let's introduce it before diving into our WebSocket implementation.

Getting to know Kotlin Flow

Flow is part of Kotlin's coroutines library, and it's a type that can emit multiple values sequentially, as opposed to suspend functions that return only a single value. Flow builds upon the foundational concepts of coroutines to offer a declarative way to work with asynchronous streams of data.

Unlike sequences in Kotlin, which are synchronous and blocking, Flow is asynchronous and non-blocking. This makes Flow ideal for handling a continuous stream of data that can be observed and collected asynchronously, such as real-time messages from a WebSocket.

When integrating Flow with Ktor WebSockets, we can create a powerful combination where the WebSocket messages are emitted as a stream of data that can be processed using all the Flow operators. It allows for a clean, reactive-style approach to handling incoming and outgoing messages with WebSockets.

For example, in a chat application, incoming messages from a WebSocket can be represented as a flow of strings. The app can collect this flow to update the UI accordingly. Similarly, user actions that generate outgoing messages can be collected and sent through the WebSocket connection.

The Flow API is really simple and easy to use. As another example, imagine that we have a flow that emits three strings:

```
fun main() = runBlocking {
    // Define a simple flow that emits three strings
    val helloFlow = flow {
        emit("Hello")
        emit("from")
        emit("Flow!")
    }

    // Collect and print each value emitted by the flow
    helloFlow.collect { value ->
        println(value)
    }
}
```

In this code block, helloFlow is defined, using the flow builder to emit three strings one after another.

> **Note**
>
> There are several other builders apart from flow, such as flowOf, which creates a flow from a set of values, or toFlow(), which creates a flow from a collection.

The collect() function is then called on helloFlow. It acts as a subscriber that reacts to each emitted value by printing it.

If you run this code, you should see the following output:

```
Hello
from
Flow!
```

Now that we are a bit familiar with Kotlin Flow, we are ready to do the next step: build our implementation of a WebSocket using Ktor and Flow. As it is going to be one of the data sources that will provide messages to our app, we will call it WebsocketDataSource.

Implementing WebSocketDataSource

To implement the WebSocket data source, we are first going to create an `HttpClient` instance. `HttpClient` is a Ktor class that allows you to make HTTP requests and manage network connections. In the case of WebSockets, it is responsible for establishing and maintaining the connection between the client and server.

To create an `HttpClient` instance with WebSocket support, we are going to create a new file called `WebSocketClient` in the `feature.chat.data.network` package (you will need to create the data and network packages as they don't exist yet) and include the following code:

```
object WebsocketClient {
    val client = HttpClient(OkHttp) {
        install(WebSockets)
    }
}
```

Here, we're using the `OkHttp` engine to create an `HttpClient` instance, and then we're installing the `WebSockets` plugin to enable WebSocket support.

> **Note**
>
> In Ktor, **plugins** (also called features) are modular components that extend the functionality of Ktor applications. Plugins can be installed on both the client and server sides to provide additional features, such as authentication, logging, serialization, or custom behavior. Ktor's plugin-based architecture encourages a lightweight and modular approach, allowing you to include only the necessary components in your application.

Then, we will create our `MessagesSocketDataSource` class (in the same package).

To start creating our WebSocket, we will need a `WebSocketSession` instance. `WebSocketSession` represents a single WebSocket connection between the client and server, providing methods for sending and receiving messages, as well as managing the connection's lifecycle. In our implementation, we will create a `WebSocketSession` instance when we call the `connect()` method, like so:

```
class MessagesSocketDataSource @Inject constructor(
    private val httpClient: HttpClient,
) {

    private lateinit var webSocketSession:
        DefaultClientWebSocketSession

    suspend fun connect(url: String): Flow<Message>{
        return httpClient.webSocketSession { url(url) }
            .apply { webSocketSession = this }
```

```
            .incoming
            .receiveAsFlow()
            .map{ frame ->
                webSocketSession.handleMessage(frame) }
            .filterNotNull()
            .map { it.toDomain() }
    }
//...
}
```

Let's break down what this code is going to do:

- `suspend fun connect(url: String): Flow<Message>`: The connect function is defined as a suspending (`suspend`) function that takes a `url` parameter of type `String` and returns a `Flow<Message>` instance. `Flow` is a cold asynchronous stream used for processing data in a reactive way in Kotlin (a cold stream is one that will only emit messages when there is a consumer connected).

- `httpClient.webSocketSession { url(url) }`: This line uses `httpClient` to create a WebSocket session by calling the `webSocketSession` function and passing a lambda that sets the session's URL to the provided URL.

- `.apply { webSocketSession = this }`: This line stores the newly created WebSocket session using the `apply` function in the `webSocketSession` property. We also need to store it as we will need the session later for sending messages.

- `.incoming`: This line accesses the incoming property of `webSocketSession`. The incoming property is a channel that receives incoming `Frame` objects from the WebSocket server.

- `.receiveAsFlow()`: This line converts the incoming channel to a `Flow<Frame>` instance so that it can be processed using the Flow API.

- `.map { frame -> webSocketSession.handleMessage(frame) }`: This line maps each incoming `Frame` object to the result of calling the `handleMessage` function. We will define the `handleMessage` function later.

- `.filterNotNull()`: This line filters out any `null` values from the stream, ensuring that only non-`null` values are processed further.

- `.map { it.toDomain() }`: This line maps each non-`null` value to the result of calling the `toDomain()` function. This function will map the current data-related object to the domain `Message` model that we will create soon.

Before processing and handling the messages, we will also want to add two more functions to our WebSocket data source:

- We want one function to send messages, as we want our users to be able to send messages to their WhatsPackt friends
- We want another function to disconnect the WebSocket, as we should disconnect it from the server when it is not in use

We can add these like so:

```
suspend fun sendMessage(message: String) {
    webSocketSession.send(Frame.Text(message))
}

suspend fun disconnect() {
    webSocketSession.close(CloseReason(
        CloseReason.Codes.NORMAL, "Disconnect"))
}
```

When a WebSocket connection is closed, it's accompanied by a `CloseReason` class, which contains a code and an optional descriptive text. The code indicates the reason for the connection closure, such as normal closure, protocol error, or unsupported data. In our implementation, we use the `CloseReason` class to close the `WebSocketSession` with a normal closure.

Some common `CloseReason` codes include the following:

- `CloseReason.Codes.NORMAL`: Indicates a normal closure of the connection. This is the reason that will be provided when the user is no longer using the chat screen.
- `CloseReason.Codes.GOING_AWAY`: Indicates that the server is going away or shutting down.
- `CloseReason.Codes.PROTOCOL_ERROR`: Indicates that an error in the WebSocket protocol occurred.
- `CloseReason.Codes.UNSUPPORTED_DATA`: Indicates that the received data type is not supported.

Now that we know how to close our WebSocket connection, we need to define the `handleMessages` extension function to process all the messages while the connection is alive:

```
private suspend fun
DefaultClientWebSocketSession.handleMessage(frame: Frame):
WebsocketMessageModel? {
    return when (frame) {
        is Frame.Text -> converter?.deserialize(frame)
        is Frame.Close -> {
```

```
            disconnect()
            null
        }
        else -> null
    }
}
```

In the WebSocket protocol, data is transmitted in discrete units called frames. Ktor provides a `Frame` class to represent these units, with different subclasses for each frame type, such as `Frame.Text`, `Frame.Binary`, `Frame.Ping`, and `Frame.Close`.

In our case, we are only processing `Frame.Text` and `Frame.Close` messages. To receive a `Frame.Close` message, we will close the WebSocket (for now – in the future, maybe we would want to do a retry here or give feedback about the problem to the user). Then, to receive the `Frame.Text` messages, we are going to **deserialize** them from JSON (a lightweight data-interchange format that is commonly used for communication between systems) to the object we are going to work with. Here, `deserialize` just describes this conversion.

We can configure a converter in our WebSocket that allows us to easily deserialize our messages. First, we need to add new dependencies to our `build.gradle` file:

```
implementation("io.ktor:ktor-serialization-kotlinx-json:2.2.4)
```

Then, we are ready to set `contentConverter` in our WebSocket plugin:

```
object WebsocketClient {
    val client = HttpClient(OkHttp) {
        install(WebSockets) {
            contentConverter =
                KotlinxWebsocketSerializationConverter(Json)
        }
    }
}
```

In this case, we are configuring the `kotlinx.serialization` converter for the JSON format (there are also converters available for other standards, such as XML, Protobuf, and CBOR).

In addition, we must add the `@Serializable` annotation to those data classes that we want to be deserialized by the converter. In our case, we will create a `WebsocketMessageModel` class as follows:

```
@Serializable
class WebsocketMessageModel(
    val id: String,
    val message: String,
    val senderName: String,
    val senderAvatar: String,
```

```
    val timestamp: String,
    val isMine: Boolean,
    val messageType: String,
    val messageDescription: String
)
```

The last step in our flow chain is to convert the `WebsocketMessageModel` class to a domain. As we still don't have a domain model, we should create it first:

```
data class Message(
    val id: String,
    val senderName: String,
    val senderAvatar: String,
    val timestamp: String,
    val isMine: Boolean,
    val contentType: ContentType,
    val content: String,
    val contentDescription: String
) {
    enum class ContentType {
        TEXT, IMAGE
    }
}
```

Now, we can implement the mapper as a function of the `WebsocketMessageModel` class:

```
@Serializable
class WebsocketMessageModel(
    val id: String,
    val message: String,
    val senderName: String,
    val senderAvatar: String,
    val timestamp: String,
    val isMine: Boolean,
    val messageType: String,
    val messageDescription: String
) {

    companion object {
        const val TYPE_TEXT = "TEXT"
        const val TYPE_IMAGE = "IMAGE"
    }

    fun toDomain(): Message {
```

```
            return Message(
                id = id,
                content = message,
                senderAvatar = senderAvatar,
                senderName = senderName,
                timestamp = timestamp,
                isMine = isMine,
                contentDescription = messageDescription,
                contentType = toContentType()
            )
    }

    fun toContentType(): Message.ContentType {
        return when(messageType) {
            TYPE_IMAGE -> Message.ContentType.IMAGE
            else -> Message.ContentType.TEXT
        }
    }
  }
}
```

Here, we are adding the toDomain() function that maps the current WebsocketMessageModel class to the Message model. Note that almost all fields in the data model are similar to those in our domain Message model. The key exception is the messageType field, which we must convert to the enum we are using in the domain Message model. To simplify this conversion, we use the toContentType() function, which specifically transforms messageType from a String object to a ContentType enum.

We also would need to convert the domain Message object to the WebsocketMessageModel class. To do that, we need to add a new function to the WebsocketMessageModel class:

```
companion object {
    const val TYPE_TEXT = "TEXT"
    const val TYPE_IMAGE = "IMAGE"

    fun fromDomain(message: Message): WebsocketMessageModel {
        return WebsocketMessageModel(
            id = message.id,
            message = message.content,
            senderAvatar = message.senderAvatar,
            senderName = message.senderName,
            timestamp = message.timestamp,
            isMine = message.isMine,
            messageType = message.fromContentType(),
            messageDescription = message.contentDescription
```

```
        )
    }
}
```

Here, we are converting the `Message` domain object into a `WebsocketMessageModel` class.

Then, in the `send` function, we will proceed as follows:

```
suspend fun sendMessage(message: Message) {
    val websocketMessage =
        WebsocketMessageModel.fromDomain(message)
    webSocketSession.converter?
        .serialize(websocketMessage)?.let
    {
        webSocketSession.send(it)
    }
}
```

With these changes to the `sendMessage` function, we are now receiving a domain model object, converting it to `WebsocketMessageModel`, and finally serializing it into a `Frame` object and sending it through our WebSocket.

The next step is to connect this component (`MessagesWebsocketDataSource`) with `ViewModel`, which will be responsible for providing the view state to the view so that it can render accordingly.

Receiving messages in our ViewModel

Our app is ready to receive and send messages using a WebSocket. Now, we need to make them reach the UI we created in the previous chapter. We will do that in this section, but first, we need to think about the architecture and components needed to do that.

Understanding Clean Architecture implementation

In the previous chapter, we modularized our app and talked about using a Clean Architecture-based structure to organize our common and feature modules. We have already created our first component of this architecture, `MessagesWebsocketDataSource`, but it is important to understand the reasons behind this organization and which role every component plays in the architecture.

There are extensive books, articles, and videos about why and how to apply Clean Architecture principles to an Android app, even from official documentation by Google. Here, we are going to give you a short description and then break down into its layers.

Clean Architecture is an architectural pattern that promotes the organization of code into layers with well-defined responsibilities, making the application more modular, maintainable, testable, and scalable. The key benefits of using Clean Architecture are as follows:

- **Separation of concerns (SoC)**: Clean Architecture organizes code into distinct layers with specific responsibilities, ensuring that each layer handles a separate aspect of the application. This SoC leads to a more modular and maintainable code base, making it easier to understand, modify, and extend.

- **Testability**: By separating the different concerns into independent layers, it becomes easier to test each layer in isolation. This allows developers to write comprehensive unit and integration tests, ensuring that the application behaves correctly and is less prone to bugs.

- **Reusability**: The modular structure of Clean Architecture promotes reusability by encouraging the creation of components that can be easily shared across different parts of the application or even between different projects. This reduces code duplication and improves the overall efficiency of the development process.

- **Flexibility**: Clean Architecture decouples the various layers of the application, making it easier to change or update any of these layers independently without affecting the others. This provides more flexibility when refactoring, making changes to the application, or adapting to new requirements.

- **Scalability**: The modular nature of Clean Architecture makes it easier to scale the application as it grows in complexity or size. By organizing code into well-defined layers and components, developers can more easily add new features, update existing functionality, or improve performance without introducing unintended side effects or making the code base unmanageable.

- **Easier collaboration**: Clean Architecture helps teams work more effectively by providing a clear structure and guidelines for organizing code. This makes it easier for developers to understand the code base, find the components they need, and contribute to the project more efficiently.

- **Future-proofing**: By adhering to the principles of Clean Architecture, you ensure that the application is built on a solid foundation that can evolve and adapt over time. This makes it more resilient to changes in technology, requirements, or team members, improving the long-term viability of the project.

In summary, using Clean Architecture in your projects leads to better-organized, more maintainable, and scalable code bases. It improves the overall quality of the application, reduces technical debt, and makes it easier for teams to work together effectively.

Now, with the benefits of Clean Architecture firmly in mind, let's delve into the specifics. What follows are the layers and the components of code that we will incorporate within each layer:

- **Presentation layer**:

    - **View**: This consists of UI components, such as `Activity`, `Fragment`, `View`, and, in our case, `Composable` components. The view is responsible for displaying data and capturing user input.

    - **ViewModel**: The `ViewModel` serves as a bridge between the `View` components and the data layers. It handles the UI logic, exposes `LiveData` or `StateFlow` objects for data binding, and communicates with `UseCase` classes.

- **Domain layer**:

    - **UseCase**: This layer contains the business logic and coordinates the flow of data between the data layer and the presentation layer. `UseCase` implementations encapsulate specific actions that can be performed within the app, such as sending a message, fetching chat history, or updating user settings.

- **Data layer**:

    - **Repository**: The `Repository` component is responsible for managing the data flow and providing a clean API to request data from different sources (local database, remote API, and so on). It abstracts the underlying data sources and handles caching, synchronization, and data merging.

    - **Data source**: This layer contains the implementations for accessing specific data sources such as local databases (using Room or another **object-relational mapper** (**ORM**)) and remote APIs (using Retrofit or another networking library, as in our case where we are using Ktor).

In the following diagram, we can see the relationships between the different layers and the typical components every layer includes:

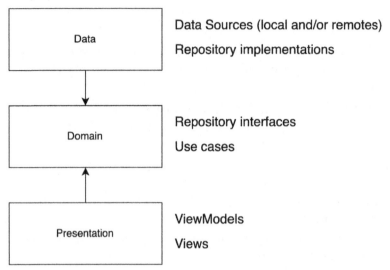

Figure 2.1: Clean Architecture in Android with the typical components per layer

Having this clear understanding of Clean Architecture's benefits and structure, let's now put these principles into practice.

Creating our Clean Architecture components

We have started building the data layer components, where we have created the `MessagesWebsocket DataSource` component. Now, it is time we build the rest of our Clean Architecture layers and components to reach the presentation layer.

In the end, this is what our app's Clean Architecture layers and components should look like:

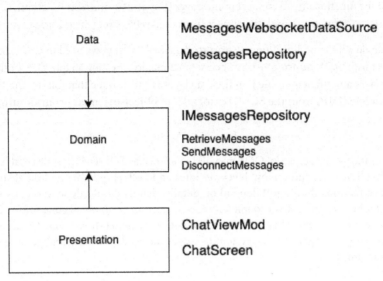

Figure 2.2: Layers and components that we will build in our project, following Clean Architecture principles

As we have already built the `MessagesWebsocketDataSource` component, the next component is the repository. The repository component will only connect with `MessagesWebsocketDataSource` (for now; we have bigger plans for it in the next chapter). We are going to call it `MessagesRepository`. Let's start building it:

```
class MessagesRepository @Inject constructor(
    private val dataSource: MessagesSocketDataSource
) {
    suspend fun getMessages(): Flow<Message> {
        return dataSource.connect()
    }

    suspend fun sendMessage(message: Message) {
        dataSource.sendMessage(message)
    }

    suspend fun disconnect() {
        dataSource.disconnect()
    }
}
```

MessagesRepository will just have one dependency (MessagesSocketDataSource) and will implement the functionality to connect to messages (the getMessages function), send messages (the sendMessage function), and disconnect from the WebSocket (the disconnect function).

Now, we need to do a little modification to MessagesRepository: we need to create an interface in the domain layer with the MessagesRepository functionality. Creating an interface for the repository in the domain layer and implementing it in the data layer is a technique that follows the **Dependency Inversion Principle (DIP)** from the SOLID principles of **object-oriented programming (OOP)**.

> **Note**
>
> DIP is one of the five principles of OOP and design known as SOLID. DIP states that high-level modules should not depend on low-level modules and both should depend on abstractions. Similarly, abstractions should not depend on details; details should depend on abstractions. The main idea behind DIP is to decouple modules, classes, or components in a software system, promoting flexibility, reusability, and maintainability. By depending on abstractions rather than concrete implementations, the system becomes more adaptable to changes and easier to test and maintain.

Let's create our IMessagesRepository interface:

```
interface IMessagesRepository {
    suspend fun getMessages(): Flow<Message>

    suspend fun sendMessage(message: Message)

    suspend fun disconnect()
}
```

Then, we will change our MessagesRepository class to implement this interface, adding the override in its functions:

```
class MessagesRepository @Inject constructor(
    private val dataSource: MessagesSocketDataSource
): IMessagesRepository {

    override suspend fun getMessages(): Flow<Message> {
        return dataSource.connect()
    }

    override suspend fun sendMessage(message: Message) {
        dataSource.sendMessage(message)
    }
```

```
    override suspend fun disconnect() {
        dataSource.disconnect()
    }
}
```

Now, we will continue in our journey to the presentation layer, implementing the domain layer.

The domain layer is not strictly mandatory, but it is highly recommended. While you can eliminate the domain layer and directly use repositories in your `ViewModel` instances, doing so would mix the responsibilities of the layers, which can lead to more complex and harder-to-maintain code. There may be cases where not implementing it could be considered; for example, if you are doing a **proof of concept** (**PoC**) or a simple app. Therefore, it is recommended to include the `UseCase` layer to maintain a clean and scalable architecture.

Following the **Single Responsibility Principle** (**SRP**), in this layer, we will create as many `UseCase` instances as different functions/responsibilities in our business logic. So, in our case, we will create three `UseCase` instances: one for retrieving messages, one for sending messages, and one for disconnecting or stopping message retrieval.

> **Note**
>
> SRP is one of the five principles of OOP and design known as SOLID. It states that a class, module, or function should have only one reason to change, meaning it should have only one responsibility. The principle aims to promote SoC by encouraging developers to break down their code into smaller, more focused components that handle a single task or aspect of the application. This leads to a more modular, maintainable, and easier-to-understand code base.

First, we will implement the `RetrieveMessages` use case:

```
class RetrieveMessages @Inject constructor(
    private val repository: IMessagesRepository
) {
    suspend operator fun invoke(): Flow<Message> {
        return repository.getMessages()
    }
}
```

Here, we have just one dependency: the repository. Note that we are declaring it using its interface. It is relevant because, as we detailed before, the domain shouldn't know anything about the data layer.

`RetrieveMessages` will have one function that will return a `Flow` instance with `Message` objects. For doing that, it will return `repository.getMessages()`. No mapping or alteration is needed as this function already returned a `Flow` instance of `Message` objects.

Second, we are going to implement the `SendMessage` use case:

```
class SendMessage @Inject constructor(
    private val repository: IMessagesRepository
) {
    suspend operator fun invoke(message: Message) {
        repository.sendMessage(message)
    }
}
```

Again, this use case will depend only on the `IMessagesRepository` interface. It will call its `sendMessage` function.

And finally, we will code the `DisconnectMessages` use case:

```
class DisconnectMessages @Inject constructor(
    private val repository: IMessagesRepository
) {
    suspend operator fun invoke() {
        repository.disconnect()
    }
}
```

The `DisconnectMessages` use case, as with the previous use cases implemented, depends on the `IMessagesRepository` interface and will call its `disconnect` function.

We are now done with the domain layer. Now, it's time to implement the `ViewModel` component that we will connect to the `ChatScreen` component, using `ChatViewModel`.

Implementing ChatViewModel

In Android, `ViewModel` is an architectural component introduced as part of the **Android Architecture Components** (**AAC**) library. It is designed to store and manage UI-related data in a lifecycle-conscious way. The primary responsibility of a `ViewModel` component is to hold and process the data required for a UI component (such as an `Activity`, `Fragment`, or `Composable` component) while properly handling configuration changes (such as device rotations) and surviving the lifecycle of the associated UI component.

Our `ChatViewModel` class will be responsible for handling the data required in our `ChatScreen` component (which we previously built in *Chapter 1*). This data will come and change from the use cases we have just created. So first, our `ChatViewModel` class will have those use cases as dependencies:

```
@HiltViewModel
class ChatViewModel @Inject constructor(
    private val retrieveMessages: RetrieveMessages,
```

```
        private val sendMessage: SendMessage,
        private val disconnectMessages: DisconnectMessages
) : ViewModel() {

    // ....
}
```

Then, we will need a property to hold the state. This property needs to be observable from the view but read-only (so that the view shouldn't be able to modify it). We will solve this by creating two different properties. The first property is _messages:

```
private val _messages =
MutableStateFlow<List<Message>>(emptyList())
```

This line creates a private mutable state flow that holds a list of Message objects. We will use it to manage and update messages internally within the ViewModel.

The second property will be messages:

```
val messages: StateFlow<List<Message>> = _messages
```

This line exposes the private mutable state flow as a public read-only state flow. This allows the UI components to observe messages without being able to modify them directly.

Now, we need to implement the loadAndUpdateMessages function that will call the RetrieveMessages use case:

```
private var messageCollectionJob: Job? = null
fun loadAndUpdateMessages() {
    messageCollectionJob =
    viewModelScope.launch(Dispatchers.IO) {
        retrieveMessages()
            .map { it.toUI() }
            .collect { message ->
                withContext(Dispatchers.Main) {
                    _messages.value = _messages.value +
                    message
                }
            }
    }
}
```

In the previous code block, it can be seen that we need to declare a `messageCollectionJob` variable. This variable is used to cancel the `messages` collection job when the `ViewModel` is cleared.

The `loadAndUpdateMessages` function is responsible for fetching and updating messages. It launches a coroutine with the `Dispatchers.IO` context for performing network or disk operations.

Inside the coroutine, the `retrieveMessages` function is called, and the resulting messages are mapped into the `Message` UI object and then collected using the `collect` function.

For each collected message, the `_messages` state flow is updated with the new message by switching the coroutine context to `Dispatchers.Main`.

Next, to make the mapping more readable, we are going to create two extension functions:

```
private fun DomainMessage.toUI(): Message {
    return Message(
        id = id,
        senderName = senderName,
        senderAvatar = senderAvatar,
        timestamp = timestamp,
        isMine = isMine,
        messageContent = getMessageContent()
    )
}

private fun DomainMessage.getMessageContent():
MessageContent {
    return when (contentType) {
        DomainMessage.ContentType.TEXT ->
            MessageContent.TextMessage(content)
        DomainMessage.ContentType.IMAGE ->
            MessageContent.ImageMessage(content,
            contentDescription)
    }
}
```

So, when retrieving and mapping messages, we just have to call the following:

```
retrieveMessages()
    .map { it.toUI() }
```

Then, we continue to process the `messages` collection job.

Then, we should add a function to send a new message. Basically, the idea is to launch the coroutine in the Dispatchers.IO context to send the message. As it is a network operation, it is recommended to use the I/O dispatcher and map the String object we are getting from the user to the domain object, as you can see in the following code block:

```
fun onSendMessage(messageText: String) {
    viewModelScope.launch(Dispatchers.IO) {
        val message = Message(messageText) // We will add
                                           here the rest
                                           of the fields
        sendMessage(message)
    }
}
```

Note that, to create the domain object, we are going to lack some information because, for example, we have no way to obtain the senderImage or the senderName properties that are mandatory to send a message. So, this function is not going to compile for now, but we will solve this problem in the following section.

Finally, we can use the onCleared function to disconnect from the message's retrieval:

```
override fun onCleared() {
    messageCollectionJob?.cancel()
    viewModelScope.launch(Dispatchers.IO) {
        disconnectMessages()
    }
}
```

This function is called when the ViewModel is no longer in use and will be disposed of by the system. This involves canceling the messageCollectionJob variable, provided it's not null, effectively halting the messages collection coroutine. Concurrently, in the context of Dispatchers.IO, a new coroutine is launched to execute the disconnectMessages function. This guarantees that any essential cleanup associated with disconnecting from the message source is carried out properly.

This is how the ChatViewModel component will look (for now):

```
import com.packt.feature.chat.domain.models.Message as
DomainMessage
// We are using this import with an alias to make it easier
    to identify the Message class from the domain layer

@HiltViewModel
class ChatViewModel @Inject constructor(
    private val retrieveMessages: RetrieveMessages,
    private val sendMessage: SendMessage,
```

```kotlin
    private val disconnectMessages: DisconnectMessages
) : ViewModel() {

    private val _messages =
        MutableStateFlow<List<Message>>(emptyList())
    val messages: StateFlow<List<Message>> = _messages

    private var messageCollectionJob: Job? = null

    fun loadAndUpdateMessages() {
        messageCollectionJob =
        viewModelScope.launch(Dispatchers.IO) {
            retrieveMessages()
                .map { it.toUI() }
                .collect { message ->
                    withContext(Dispatchers.Main) {
                        _messages.value = _messages.value +
                        message
                    }
                }
        }
    }

    private fun DomainMessage.toUI(): Message {
        return Message(
            id = id,
            senderName = senderName,
            senderAvatar = senderAvatar,
            timestamp = timestamp,
            isMine = isMine,
            messageContent = getMessageContent()
        )
    }

    private fun DomainMessage.getMessageContent():
    MessageContent {
        return when (contentType) {
            DomainMessage.ContentType.TEXT ->
                MessageContent.TextMessage(content)
            DomainMessage.ContentType.IMAGE ->
                MessageContent.ImageMessage(content,
                contentDescription)
        }
```

```
    }

    fun onSendMessage(messageText: String) {
        viewModelScope.launch(Dispatchers.IO) {
            val message = Message(messageText)
            sendMessage(message)
        }
    }

    override fun onCleared() {
        messageCollectionJob?.cancel()
        viewModelScope.launch(Dispatchers.IO) {
            disconnectMessages()
        }
    }
}
```

Now that we have our `ChatViewModel` component ready, we need to connect it to the view. We will make the changes needed in the `ChatScreen` component so that it connects to our `ChatViewModel` component. As the first step, we have added the `ViewModel` to the arguments:

```
@Composable
fun ChatScreen(
    viewModel: ChatViewModel = hiltViewModel(),
    chatId: String?,
    onBack: () -> Unit
) {
}
```

Then, we will also add a `LaunchEffect` composable that will start the messages' load:

```
LaunchedEffect(Unit) {
    viewModel.loadAndUpdateMessages()
}
```

Next, the `SendMessageBox` composable takes a lambda parameter, where we are going to send the message using the `ViewModel` function:

```
SendMessageBox { viewModel.onSendMessage(it) }
```

After that, we add the following new parameter to the `SendMessageBox` composable definition and call it in its `IconButton onClick` property:

```
@Composable
fun SendMessageBox(sendMessage: (String)->Unit) {
    Box(modifier = Modifier
        .defaultMinSize()
        .padding(top = 0.dp, start = 16.dp, end = 16.dp,
            bottom = 16.dp)
        .fillMaxWidth()
    ) {

        var text by remember { mutableStateOf("") }

        OutlinedTextField(
            value = text,
            onValueChange = { newText -> text = newText },
            modifier = Modifier
                .fillMaxWidth(0.85f)
                .align(Alignment.CenterStart)
                .height(56.dp),
        )

        IconButton(
            modifier = Modifier
                .align(Alignment.CenterEnd)
                .height(56.dp),
            onClick = {
                sendMessage(text)
                text = ""
            }
        ) {
            Icon(
                imageVector = Icons.Default.Send,
                tint = MaterialTheme.colors.primary,
                contentDescription = "Send message"
            )
        }
    }
}
```

Finally, we will inject the `messages` property to the `ListOfMessages` composable:

```
ListOfMessages(paddingValues = paddingValues, messages = messages)
```

This, of course, will also require a change in the composable definition and code:

```
@Composable
fun ListOfMessages(messages: List<Message>, paddingValues:
PaddingValues) {
    Box(modifier = Modifier
        .fillMaxSize()
        .padding(paddingValues)) {
        Row(modifier = Modifier
            .fillMaxWidth()
            .padding(16.dp)
        ) {
            LazyColumn(
                modifier = Modifier
                    .fillMaxSize(),
                verticalArrangement =
                    Arrangement.spacedBy(8.dp),
            ) {
                items(messages) { message ->
                    MessageItem(message = message)
                }
            }
        }
    }
}
```

Instead of using the `getFakeMessages()` function we were using when we built the `ListOfMessages` composable, we will use the `messages` list that we are now obtaining via properties.

And with that, we've covered almost everything, but there remain some challenges to address. For instance, we don't have the necessary information to display the correct avatar and name of the chat members or the necessary information to fill in the required properties for sending a message. While we will receive new messages once we connect to the WebSocket, the question of how to get historical messages remains. We will tackle these issues, along with other concerns related to error handling and synchronization, in the upcoming section.

Handling synchronization and errors

To make the chat messages functionality complete, we still have some issues we have to take into account: getting historical messages and receiver information and handling possible errors. We will go through them in this section.

Obtaining chat screen initialization data

Apart from the messages that we are going to be receiving or sending via the data source, we still need to get some additional information. This includes the following:

- Messages that have been sent and received before the WebSocket was connected (not all of them, though, because the conversation could have many messages, and it would take a long time to gather/load all of the information; instead we should prioritize fetching a certain number of the most recent messages)

- Receiver information, such as their name or avatar URL

There are several options to solve this – for example, we could have a different type of message with all this information when the WebSocket connection is established, or we could have a specific API call to retrieve this information. As we have already played with the Ktor WebSocket for the chat feature, we are going to use it to implement an API call to retrieve this information.

When we built `WebsocketMessagesDataSource`, we had to provide an `HttpClient` instance. Usually, these clients are shared within the same application, but we should create a new one to be used for our API requests. For that, we would need to add a new dependency:

```
implementation "io.ktor:ktor-client-content-negotiation:
$ktor_version"
```

Then, we can create the client like so (we can do it in the same file we defined the WebSocket client):

```
object RestClient {
    val client = HttpClient{
        install(ContentNegotiation) {
            json()
        }
    }
}
```

Next, we are going to create a `ChatRoomDataSource` class that will be in charge of handling this data retrieval:

```
class ChatRoomDataSource @Inject constructor(
    private val client: HttpClient,
    private val url: String
```

```
) {
    suspend fun getInitialChatRoom(id: String):
    ChatRoomModel {
        return client.get(url.format(id)).body()
    }
}
```

As seen here, we are going to inject the client and the URL as dependencies. Then, in the getInitialChatRoom function, we will call the client.get(url) function in order to make a request to the endpoint.

Using the Ktor client, you can use various HTTP methods. Here's a list of common ones:

- GET: Retrieves data from the specified endpoint. To use this method in Ktor, you can call the get function:

    ```
    val response: HttpResponse =
    client.get("https://api.example.com/data")
    ```

- POST: Sends data to the specified endpoint, usually for creating a new resource. To use this method in Ktor, you can call the post function:

    ```
    val response: HttpResponse =
    client.post("https://api.example.com/data") {
    body = yourData }
    ```

- PUT: Sends data to the specified endpoint, usually for updating an existing resource. To use this method in Ktor, you can call the put function:

    ```
    val response: HttpResponse =
    client.put("https://api.example.com/data") {
    body = yourUpdatedData }
    ```

- DELETE: Deletes a specified resource. To use this method in Ktor, you can call the delete function:

    ```
    val response: HttpResponse =
    client.delete("https://api.example.com/data/ID")
    ```

- PATCH: Applies partial modifications to a resource. To use this method in Ktor, you can call the patch function:

    ```
    val response: HttpResponse =
    client.patch("https://api.example.com/data") {
    body = yourPartialData }
    ```

In the case of our `getInitialChatRoom` function, we are using the `client.get(URL)` function (note that we have to provide the URL in a format such that we can then replace the ID of `ChatRoom`). We also need to return a new model, `ChatRoomModel`:

```
@kotlinx.serialization.Serializable
data class ChatRoomModel(
    val id: String,
    val senderName: String,
    val senderAvatar: String,
    val lastMessages: List<WebsocketMessageModel>
)
```

Now, in order to provide the dependencies that `ChatRoomDataSource` needs, we have to set our `ChatModule` class in the following way:

```
@InstallIn(SingletonComponent::class)
@Module
abstract class ChatModule {

    companion object {
        const val WEBSOCKET_URL =
            "ws://whatspackt.com/chat/%s"
        const val WEBSOCKET_URL_NAME = "WEBSOCKET_URL"
        const val WEBSOCKET_CLIENT = "WEBSOCKET_CLIENT"
        const val API_CHAT_ROOM_URL =
            "http://whatspackt.com/chats/%s"
        const val API_CHAT_ROOM_URL_NAME = "CHATROOM_URL"
        const val API_CLIENT = "API_CLIENT"
    }

    @Provides
    @Named(WEBSOCKET_CLIENT)
    fun providesWebsocketHttpClient(): HttpClient {
        return WebsocketClient.client
    }

    @Provides
    @Named(WEBSOCKET_URL_NAME)
    fun providesWebsocketURL(): String {
        return WEBSOCKET_URL
    }

    @Binds
    abstract fun providesMessagesRepository(
```

```
        messagesRepository: MessagesRepository
    ): IMessagesRepository

    @Provides
    @Named(API_CLIENT)
    fun providesAPIHttpClient(): HttpClient {
        return RestClient.client
    }

}
```

As both the `providesWebsocketClient` and `providesApiHttpClient` functions are returning the same type (`HttpClient`), we need them to be identifiable so that we can indicate to Hilt which dependency it should provide to `WebsocketDataSource` and which one goes to `ChatRoomDataSource`. That's the reason we are using qualifiers.

> **Note**
>
> Using qualifiers allows the **dependency injection (DI)** framework to determine the correct instance of a dependency to inject when there are multiple instances available of the same type. This ensures that the right instance is provided, preventing conflicts or ambiguity in your dependency management.

In the next code block, we are using a `WEBSOCKET_CLIENT` constant as the qualifier for the WebSocket `HttpClient` instance and `API_CLIENT` for the REST API `HttpClient` instance:

```
@Provides
@Named(WEBSOCKET_CLIENT)
fun providesWebsocketHttpClient(): HttpClient {
    return WebsocketClient.client
}

@Provides
@Named(API_CLIENT)
fun providesAPIHttpClient(): HttpClient {
    return RestClient.client
}
```

We should also use qualifiers to provide URLs for the WebSocket and for the API. Also, it is important to note that these URL values are now being provided by a companion object in `ChatModule` for simplification, but a better approach would be to have them defined as part of our Gradle file. That way, we will be able to override them depending on the build variant (release, debug, test, and so on) or flavor.

Regarding the qualifiers, we also need to indicate in the consumers of these dependencies which one should be injected. This will be done using the @Named annotation in the affected dependencies as follows:

```
class ChatRoomDataSource @Inject constructor(
    @Named(API_CLIENT) private val client: HttpClient,
    @Named(API_CHAT_ROOM_URL_NAME) private val url: String
) {
    suspend fun getInitialChatRoom(id: String):
    ChatRoomModel {
        return client.get(url.format(id)).body()
    }
}
```

Also, we have to modify the constructor in MessagesSocketDataSource so that Hilt knows which one it has to inject:

```
class MessagesSocketDataSource @Inject constructor(
    @Named(WEBSOCKET_CLIENT) private val httpClient:
        HttpClient,
    @Named(WEBSOCKET_URL_NAME) private val websocketUrl:
        String
) { ... }
```

Now that we have everything ready for our dependencies to be injected the correct way, it is time to implement the ChatRoomRepository component. We will implement it in a similar way that we implemented the MessagesRepository component.

First, we want to create an interface in our domain package:

```
package com.packt.feature.chat.domain

import com.packt.feature.chat.domain.models.ChatRoom
interface IChatRoomRepository {
    suspend fun getInitialChatRoom(id: String): ChatRoom
}
```

Then, we will create the actual implementation in the data.repository package:

```
package com.packt.feature.chat.data.network.repository

import com.packt.feature.chat.data.network.datasource
.ChatRoomDataSource
import com.packt.feature.chat.domain.IChatRoomRepository
import com.packt.feature.chat.domain.models.ChatRoom
```

```
import javax.inject.Inject

class ChatRoomRepository @Inject constructor(
    private val dataSource: ChatRoomDataSource
): IChatRoomRepository {
    override suspend fun getInitialChatRoom(id: String):
    ChatRoom {
        val chatRoomApiModel =
            dataSource.getInitialChatRoom(id)
        return chatRoomApiModel.toDomain()
    }
}
```

Here, we are obtaining the initial chat room information from the data source, and then we will map the obtained data model into the domain model.

Of course, this will not work unless we create the domain model, ChatRoom:

```
package com.packt.feature.chat.domain.models

data class ChatRoom(
    val id: String,
    val senderName: String,
    val senderAvatar: String,
    val lastMessages: List<Message>
)
```

Then, we should create the mapping from ChatRoomModel:

```
@Serializable
data class ChatRoomModel(
    val id: String,
    val senderName: String,
    val senderAvatar: String,
    val lastMessages: List<WebsocketMessageModel>
) {
    fun toDomain(): ChatRoom {
        return ChatRoom(
            id = id,
            senderName = senderName,
            senderAvatar = senderAvatar,
            lastMessages = lastMessages.map { it.toDomain() }
        )
    }
}
```

Here, we have just added the toDomain() function, which will map the data object (ChatRoomModel) to the domain object (ChatRoom).

Now, we need to bind the repository interface to its implementation. For that, we should add a binding declaration to our Hilt module:

```
@Binds
abstract fun providesChatRoomRepository(
    chatRoomRepository: ChatRoomRepository
): IChatRoomRepository
```

Here, we are saying to Hilt that every time it needs to provide an IChatRoomRepository dependency, it should provide ChatRoomRepository.

Now, we have the data source and the repository ready. We will need to implement a new use case whose responsibility will be to provide this initial information:

```
package com.packt.feature.chat.domain.usecases

import com.packt.feature.chat.domain.IChatRoomRepository
import com.packt.feature.chat.domain.models.ChatRoom
import javax.inject.Inject

class GetInitialChatRoomInformation @Inject constructor(
    private val repository: IChatRoomRepository
) {
    suspend operator fun invoke(id: String): ChatRoom {
        return repository.getInitialChatRoom(id)
    }
}
```

Here, we will be calling the repository getInitialChatRoom() function, to obtain it in the ChatRoom model.

We are now arriving at our destination: the ViewModel. We need to include GetInitial ChatRoomInformation as a dependency on the ViewModel, obtain this information when it is initialized, and make it available for the UI to observe it:

```
@HiltViewModel
class ChatViewModel @Inject constructor(
    private val retrieveMessages: RetrieveMessages,
    private val sendMessage: SendMessage,
    private val disconnectMessages: DisconnectMessages,
    private val getInitialChatRoomInformation:
        GetInitialChatRoomInformation
) : ViewModel() {...}
```

Next, we need to create a new `StateFlow` instance to be consumed by the UI. As it is going to hold the state of almost all the UI (except the messages; we will talk about this later), we are going to call it `uiState`:

```
private val _uiState = MutableStateFlow(Chat())
val uiState: StateFlow<Chat> = _uiState
```

Now, we are going to add a new function to be called upon view initialization:

```
fun loadChatInformation(id: String) {
    messageCollectionJob =
    viewModelScope.launch(Dispatchers.IO) {
        val chatRoom = getInitialChatRoomInformation(id)
        withContext(Dispatchers.Main) {
            _uiState.value = chatRoom.toUI()
            _messages.value = chatRoom.lastMessages.map {
                it.toUI()}
            updateMessages()
        }
    }
}
```

Here, we are using `messagesCollectionJob` (we could change its name to make it more generic as now it is going to be used by the `messages` collection job and the initial data retrieval).

Then, we retrieve the initial chat room information, update the `uiState` value, and set the messages we are receiving as the first messages in the `messages StateFlow` object (so that the chat will show the old messages).

Finally, we call the `updateMessages()` function, where we will connect to the WebSocket and start getting asynchronous messages.

Note that we will also need a `Chat` model that will be our `uiState` instance; this model is important as it will be the object consumed from the UI to configure it. Add this like so:

```
data class Chat(
    val id: String? = null,
    val name: String? = null,
    val avatar: String? = null
)

fun ChatRoom.toUI() = run {
    Chat(
        id = id,
        name = senderName,
```

```
        avatar = senderAvatar
    )
}
```

Now, we need to listen to this `uiState` instance from our screen composable and update the UI accordingly:

```
@Composable
fun ChatScreen(
    viewModel: ChatViewModel = hiltViewModel(),
    chatId: String?,
    onBack: () -> Unit
) {
    val messages by viewModel.messages.collectAsState()
    val uiState by viewModel.uiState.collectAsState()

    LaunchedEffect(Unit) {
        viewModel.loadChatInformation(chatId.orEmpty())
    }

    Scaffold(
        topBar = {
            TopAppBar(
                title = {
                    Text(stringResource(R.string.chat_title,
                    uiState.name.orEmpty()))
                }
            )
        },
        bottomBar = {
            SendMessageBox { viewModel.onSendMessage(it) }
        }
    ) { paddingValues->
        ListOfMessages(paddingValues = paddingValues,
        messages = messages)
    }
}
```

Here, we can see that we are calling the `loadChatInformation` function as soon as the `Composable` component is started. Then, once this information is obtained, we would show the name of the participant of the chat in the `TopAppBar` component, obtaining this info from the chat initialization. At the same time, the list of messages will be updated with the last messages.

Usually, it is desirable to encapsulate all the `uiState` properties in a single observable value as one of the advantages of Jetpack Compose is that it will handle the recomposition when it detects that the values related to a `Composable` component have changed. In this case, the criteria followed have been to separate them because in reality, the frequency of changes is very different between the two values:

- The `uiState` properties are not going to change for the same chat
- The `messages` list is likely to change with a high frequency (every time we send and receive a message)

During this section, we have set up our chat initialization, including all the components needed for the architecture, from the data source to the `ViewModel` changes. Now, it is time we take care of possible errors we could encounter and give some resilience to our chat screen.

Handling errors in the WebSocket

Errors are not unusual, especially in a long-lived connection such as a WebSocket, and in such a sensitive environment as a mobile one, it is important to take care of these errors because otherwise, our users could stop being able to send or receive messages and, in the worst case, have a fatal error that crashes the application.

There are several ways we can control these errors. One of them is to make every layer responsible for errors that could happen in its scope and only propagate to the UI (or the user knowledge) when the app cannot recover itself from them.

Here, we could have several errors:

- Connection errors that are recuperable errors and will be handled by a retry
- Parsing errors that are likely not recuperable as several retries will not change the way the app or the backend are formatting the messages (we cannot do much with these kinds of errors, apart from detecting them before deploying the app or having analytics tools to detect them)

In this section, we are going to focus on `MessagesSocketDataSource`. If we take a look at our `connect` function, we can see it could have some points of failure (for example, when initiating the session or when the message received is handled). The simplest way to solve this is to wrap those points with `try-catch` blocks:

```
suspend fun connect(): Flow<Message> {
    return flow {
        // Wrap the connection attempt with a try-catch
            block
        try {
            httpClient.webSocketSession { url(websocketUrl) }
                .apply { webSocketSession = this }
                .incoming
```

```
                    .receiveAsFlow()
                    .collect { frame ->
                        try {
                            // Handle errors while processing
                                the message
                            val message =
                                webSocketSession.handleMessage(
                                    frame)?.toDomain()
                            if (message != null) {
                                emit(message)
                            }
                        } catch (e: Exception) {
                            // Log or handle the error
                                gracefully
                            Log.e(TAG, "Error handling
                                WebSocket frame", e)
                        }
                    }
            } catch (e: Exception) {
                // Log or handle the connection error
                    gracefully
                Log.e(TAG, "Error connecting to WebSocket", e)
            }
        }.retryWhen { cause, attempt ->
            // Implement a retry strategy based on the cause
                and/or the number of attempts
            if (cause is IOException && attempt < MAX_RETRIES)
            {
                delay(RETRY_DELAY)
                true
            } else {
                false
            }
        }.catch { e ->
            // Handle exceptions from the Flow
            Log.e(TAG, "Error in WebSocket Flow", e)
        }
    }
```

We need to define also as constants TAG (to log messages in Logcat), MAX_RETRIES, which will be the number of retries we are going to use (because we cannot be eternally retrying), and RETRY_DELAY (the milliseconds we are going to wait between retries):

```
companion object {
    const val TAG = "MessagesSocketDataSource"
    const val RETRY_DELAY = 30000
    const val MAX_RETRIES = 5
}
```

Here, we are defining these values as constants, so if the WebSocket connection fails, we will retry the connection in another 30 seconds (30000 milliseconds). This will occur 5 times before giving up if it doesn't successfully connect.

Now that our users are receiving messages while using the app, we still need to provide a way of notifying them when they receive a new message but are not using the app. We can solve this problem by using push notifications.

Adding push notifications

Push notifications are messages that are sent to a user's device from a server, even when the user is not actively using the app. These messages appear as system notifications outside of the app and can be used to provide updates, alerts, or other relevant information to users.

To send push notifications, we need to decide which of the available options we want to use. The most popular is **Firebase Cloud Messaging** (**FCM**), but there are more push notification services such as OneSignal, Pusher, or **Amazon Simple Notification Service** (**SNS**). In our case, we are going to take the popular route and use FCM.

Firebase is a mobile and web application development platform provided by Google. It offers a suite of tools, services, and infrastructure designed to help developers build, improve, and grow their apps. Some of its features include authentication, push notifications, cloud databases, and so on. We are going to use it for the last two sections of this chapter.

To accomplish that, we first need to set up Firebase in our project.

Setting up Firebase

To set up Firebase in our project, we need to follow these steps:

1. Go to the Firebase console (`https://console.firebase.google.com/`) and click **Add project**. Then, follow the onscreen instructions to set up your project.

2. In the Firebase console, click on the Android icon to register your app. Enter your app's package name, and optionally, provide the SHA-1 fingerprint for Google Sign-In and other authentication features. Click **Register app** to proceed.

3. After registering our app, we'll be prompted to download a `google-services.json` file. Download it and place it in the app module of our Android project, at the root level.

4. Add Firebase SDK dependencies to your project's `build.gradle` files, like so:

```
classpath 'com.google.gms:google-services:
    $latest_version'
```

5. Then in the app module's `build.gradle` file where we are going to use it (in our case, `:common:data`), we should add these dependencies for the following specific Firebase services:

```
implementation platform('com.google.firebase:
    firebase-bom:$latest_version')
implementation 'com.google.firebase:firebase-auth'
implementation 'com.google.firebase:
    firebase-firestore'
implementation 'com.google.firebase:
    firebase-messaging'
```

Note that, as we did with Jetpack Compose dependencies, here we are going to use the **Bill of Materials (BoM)**. The advantage is that we don't need to specify the version of every dependency because the compatible ones will be provided by the BoM.

> **Note**
>
> A BoM is a mechanism used in dependency management systems to specify and manage the versions of multiple libraries and their transitive dependencies as a single entity. It helps simplify dependency management and ensures compatibility between different libraries that are part of the same ecosystem or suite.

6. Also, in order to facilitate the use of coroutines to handle Firebase tasks, we are going to add this extra dependency:

```
implementation 'org.jetbrains.kotlinx:
    kotlinx-coroutines-play-services:$latest_version'
```

Now, before we can receive a push notification, we need to identify our user. We do that by sending their token to Firebase.

Sending the FCM token to Firebase

To identify our users and send notifications specifically to them using FCM, we need to use FCM **tokens**. Each user is assigned a unique FCM token, which is used to send notifications to their devices. This token should be obtained and updated every time the user signs in or when the app starts.

We can obtain the FCM token by calling the getToken() method from the FirebaseMessaging class. To do that, we are going first to create a data source that will wrap the token-handling functionality:

```
package com.packt.data

import com.google.firebase.messaging.FirebaseMessaging
import kotlinx.coroutines.tasks.await
import javax.inject.Inject

class FCMTokenDataSource @Inject constructor(
    private val firebaseMessaging: FirebaseMessaging =
    FirebaseMessaging.getInstance()
) {
    suspend fun getFcmToken(): String? {
        return try {
            FirebaseMessaging.getInstance().token.await()
        } catch (e: Exception) {
            null
        }
    }
}
```

Here, we are injecting the FirebaseMessaging instance and obtaining the FCM token from Firebase.

Now, we need this FCM to be stored somewhere so that when a new message is sent to our users, we know which token is associated with them. There is no standard way to store it. Usually, this will be handled in the backend, which is far from the scope of this book. But we can prepare the app components needed. We are going to create a use case that would be the orchestrator of obtaining and then sending the FCM to be stored in the backend. This use case will need a repository to do both tasks: obtaining the token and storing it in our systems.

As always, create the interface for our repository in the domain layer (in this case, in the :common:domain module):

```
interface IFCMTokenRepository {
    suspend fun getFCMToken(): String
}
```

Then, we will create the repository implementation in the data layer (:common:data):

```
class FCMTokenRepository @Inject constructor(
    private val tokenDataSource: FCMTokenDataSource
) {
    suspend fun getToken(): String? {
        return tokenDataSource.getFcmToken()
    }
}
```

We will use this repository to obtain the token from Firebase. As said before, we also need to store the token somewhere, so we will create another repository for that:

```
interface IInternalTokenRepository {
    suspend fun storeToken(userId: String, token: String)
}
```

We will again leave the implementation empty as it is outside our scope. The relevant bit to understand here is that the token should be stored so that later, when our user receives a message, we can identify the token and send a push notification to the related device.

In the next code block, we can see how we are implementing the aforementioned interface, where you will provide the means to store the data source of your preference:

```
class InternalTokenRepository(): IInternalTokenRepository {
    override suspend fun storeToken(userId: String, token:
    String) {
        // Store in the data source of your choosing
    }
}
```

Now that we have the token sorted, we need to prepare our app to receive push notifications.

Preparing the app to receive push notifications

Push notifications are messages that pop up on a mobile device. They are especially useful when the user is not actively using the application and we need to call their attention. In this section, we are going to make our app capable of receiving them when a new message is received.

To start receiving push notifications, we need to make some modifications to our existing code first. For example, we have to think about what would we expect to happen if the user clicks on a notification: we may want it to open the ChatScreen component related to the message notification. Let's start with those changes.

To open the ChatScreen component directly, we will need to create a link that tells the system that it should open our application showing the ChatScreen component. This link is called a deep link.

A **deep link** is a type of link that directs a user to a specific piece of content or page within an Android application rather than just launching the application. Deep links are used to provide a more seamless user experience by allowing users to jump directly to a particular function, feature, or piece of content within an app from a website, another app, or even a simple text message or email.

To create our deep link, we are going to create an object called DeepLinks in the :common:framework module to organize all the deep links we are going to use in our application:

```
package com.packt.framework.navigation

object DeepLinks {
    const val chatRoute =
        "https://whatspackt.com/chat?chatId={chatId}"
}
```

Then, we need to modify our NavHost component– once the application receives an intent with this deep comlink, the app should navigate to the ChatScreen component. To accomplish that, we need to add a Deeplink instance as an option for the ChatScreen navigation graph in WhatsPacktNavigation:

```
private fun NavGraphBuilder.addChat(navController:
NavHostController) {

    composable(
        route = NavRoutes.Chat,
        arguments = listOf(
            navArgument(NavRoutes.ChatArgs.ChatId) {
                type = NavType.StringType }),
        deepLinks = listOf(
            navDeepLink {
                uriPattern = DeepLinks.chatRoute
```

```
            }
        )
    ) { backStackEntry ->
        val chatId = backStackEntry.arguments?.getString(
            NavRoutes.ChatArgs.ChatId)
        ChatScreen(chatId = chatId, onBack = {
            navController.popBackStack() })
    }
}
```

Here, we are adding the deep link pattern that we have in our DeepLinks object to be included as one of the route options for our ChatScreen component.

Then, we need to implement a FirebaseMessagingService function that will catch all the push notifications that we receive and will allow us to define a channel where notifications will be posted and handled by the Android system, ultimately showing them to the user (if the user has given our app permissions to do that):

```
class WhatsPacktMessagingService:
FirebaseMessagingService() {

    companion object {
        const val CHANNEL_ID = "Chat_message"
        const val CHANNEL_DESCRIPTION = "Receive a
            notification when a chat message is received"
        const val CHANNEL_TITLE = "New chat message
            notification"
    }

    override fun onMessageReceived(remoteMessage:
    RemoteMessage) {
        super.onMessageReceived(remoteMessage)

        if (remoteMessage.data.isNotEmpty()) {

            // We can extract information such as the
                sender, message content, or chat ID
            val senderName =
                remoteMessage.data["senderName"]
            val messageContent =
                remoteMessage.data["message"]
            val chatId = remoteMessage.data["chatId"]
            val messageId = remoteMessage.data["messageId"]
```

```
                    // Create and show a notification for the
                       received message
                    if (chatId != null && messageId != null) {
                        showNotification(senderName, messageId,
                        messageContent, chatId)
                    }
                }
            }
        }

        private fun showNotification(senderName: String?,
        messageId: String, messageContent: String?,
        chatId: String) {
            // Implement here the notification
        }
    }
```

Here, we are extracting some information from the message received, such as `senderName`, `messageContent`, `chatId`, and so on. Ideally, we could obtain the information we want to show in the notification.

This is just an example, though – the information structure would depend on the payload contract we already defined with the backend implementation.

Once we have extracted this information, we need to show the notification:

```
private fun showNotification(senderName: String?,
messageId: String, messageContent: String?, chatId: String)
{
    val notificationManager = getSystemService(
        Context.NOTIFICATION_SERVICE) as NotificationManager

    // Create a notification channel
    // (if you want to support versions lower than Android
       Oreo, you will have to check the version here)
    val channel = NotificationChannel(
        CHANNEL_ID,
        CHANNEL_TITLE,
        NotificationManager.IMPORTANCE_DEFAULT
    ).apply {
        description = CHANNEL_DESCRIPTION
    }
    notificationManager.createNotificationChannel(channel)
```

```kotlin
    // Create an Intent to open the chat when the
       notification is clicked. Here is where we are going
       to use our newly created deeplink
    val deepLinkUrl =
       DeepLinks.chatRoute.replace("{chatId}", chatId)

    val intent = Intent(Intent.ACTION_VIEW,
    Uri.parse(deepLinkUrl)).apply {
        flags = Intent.FLAG_ACTIVITY_NEW_TASK or
        Intent.FLAG_ACTIVITY_CLEAR_TASK
    }

    // Create a PendingIntent for the Intent
    val pendingIntent = PendingIntent.getActivity(this, 0,
       intent, PendingIntent.FLAG_IMMUTABLE)

    // Build the notification
    val notification = NotificationCompat.Builder(this,
       CHANNEL_ID)
       .setSmallIcon(R.drawable.our_notification_icon_for_
          whatspackt)
       .setContentTitle(senderName)
       .setContentText(messageContent)
       .setContentIntent(pendingIntent)
       .setAutoCancel(true)
       .build()

    // Show the notification
    notificationManager.notify(messageId.toInt(),
       notification)

}
```

First, we create a NotificationChannel instance, then the elements we need for our notification (such as PendingIntent, which will be used when the user clicks on the notification), and then the notification itself (using NotificationCompat). Finally, we use NotificationManager to notify our notification to the system.

> **Note**
>
> Creating a `NotificationChannel` instance is necessary for Android 8.0 (API level 26) and higher, as it provides users with better control over the app's notifications. Each `NotificationChannel` instance represents a unique category of notifications that an app can display, and users can modify the settings for each channel independently. This enables users to customize the behavior of your app's notifications based on their preferences.
>
> For example, users can set the importance level, enable/disable sound, or set a custom vibration pattern for each channel. They can also block an entire channel so that they no longer receive notifications from that specific category.
>
> When you create a `NotificationChannel` instance, you need to set an importance level, which determines how the system presents notifications from that channel to the user. The importance levels range from high (urgent and makes a sound) to low (no sound or visual interruption).

The last step is to add our service to the `AndroidManifest.xml` file, inside the `application` tag:

```xml
<application
    android:allowBackup = "true"
    android:dataExtractionRules =
        "@xml/data_extraction_rules"
    android:fullBackupContent = "@xml/backup_rules"
    android:icon = "@mipmap/ic_launcher"
    android:label = "@string/app_name"
    android:supportsRtl = "true"
    android:theme = "@style/Theme.WhatsPackt"
    tools:targetApi = "31">
    <activity
        android:name = ".MainActivity"
        android:exported = "true"
        android:label = "@string/app_name"
        android:theme = "@style/Theme.WhatsPackt">
        <intent-filter>
            <action android:name=
                "android.intent.action.MAIN" />

            <category android:name =
                "android.intent.category.LAUNCHER" />
        </intent-filter>
    </activity>
    <service
        android:name =
            "com.packt.data.WhatsPacktMessagingService"
        android:exported = "false">
```

```
        <intent-filter>
          <action android:name =
              "com.google.firebase.MESSAGING_EVENT" />
        </intent-filter>
      </service>
    </application>
```

And with that, we have our app ready to receive push notifications.

In the next section, we are going to see how after all the work we have done to keep our code scalable and decoupled, we can easily use Firebase instead of the WebSocket to send and receive messages.

Replacing the Websocket with Firestore

As we saw in the previous section, Firebase is a powerful product that simplifies the implementation of the backend for our apps. Now, we are going to see how we can use it also to simplify the chat messages feature.

What is Firestore?

Firestore, more formally known as Cloud Firestore, is a flexible, scalable, and real-time NoSQL database provided by Firebase. Firestore is designed to store and sync data for client-side applications, making it an ideal choice for building modern, data-driven applications.

One of its most important features is the real-time data synchronization. Firestore automatically synchronizes data in real time across all connected clients, ensuring that your application's data is always up to date. This is especially useful for applications requiring real-time collaboration or live updates, such as our chat app.

It is important to note that as a NoSQL database, we would have first to define the data structure. How are we to structure our documents? Well, let's start with that.

Chat data structure

To handle chat messages in Firestore NoSQL, we can use the following structure:

- Create a collection called `chats`. Each document in this collection will represent a chat room or conversation between users. The document ID can be generated automatically by Firestore or created using a custom method (for example, a combination of user IDs). Here, we can include common data that we need for the conversation (think about our `ChatRoom` model), such as the user's name, avatars, and so on...

- For each chat document, create a subcollection called `messages`. This subcollection will store the individual messages for that chat room or conversation.

- Each document in the `messages` subcollection will represent a single message. The structure of a message document might include fields such as `senderId`, `senderName`, `content`, and `timestamp`.

Following that, our structure will look like this:

```
chats (collection)
    |
    └── chatId1 (document)
          |
          ├── users (subcollection)
          |   |
          |   ├── userId1 (document)
          |   |    ├── userId: "user1"
          |   |    ├── avatarUrl:
          |   |         "https://example.com/avatar1.jpg"
          |   |    └── name: "John Doe"
          |   |
          |   └── userId2 (document)
          |        ├── userId: "user2"
          |        ├── avatarUrl:
          |             "https://example.com/avatar2.jpg"
          |        └── name: "Jane Smith"
          |
          └── messages (subcollection)
                |
                ├── messageId1 (document)
                |   ├── senderId: "user1"
                |   ├── senderName: "John Doe"
                |   ├── content: "Hello, how are you?"
                |   └── timestamp: 1648749123
                |
                └── messageId2 (document)
                    ├── senderId: "user2"
                    ├── senderName: "Jane Smith"
                    ├── content: "I'm doing great! How
                                    about you?"
                    └── timestamp: 1648749156
```

One important aspect is that, ideally, we should have authentication set up to identify our users. We will learn how to build it in *Chapter 7*, but for now, we are assuming that our users will be authenticated in Firebase.

Assuming that our chat will be used by authenticated users, we can limit and restrict access to the chat collection for modifications only for users who have already been authenticated. To accomplish that, we can define a set of rules in Firestore, using the Firebase console. Here is an example:

```
rules_version = '2';
service cloud.firestore {
  match /databases/{database}/documents {
    // Allow authenticated users to create chat documents,
       but not modify or delete them
    match /chats/{chatId} {
      allow create: if request.auth != null;
      allow read, update, delete: if false;
    }

    // Allow chat participants to read the chat's user data
    match /chats/{chatId}/users/{userId} {
      allow read: if request.auth != null &&
        request.auth.uid in resource.data.userId;
      allow write: if false;
    }

    // Allow authenticated users to create/modify messages
       in a chat they are participating in
    match /chats/{chatId}/messages/{messageId} {
      // Get chat participants
      function isChatParticipant() {
        let chatUsersDoc = get(
            /databases/$(database)/documents/chats/
                $(chatId)/users/$(request.auth.uid));
        return chatUsersDoc.exists();
      }

      // Check if the sender is the authenticated user
      function isSender() {
        return request.auth != null && request.auth.uid ==
          request.resource.data.senderId;
      }

      allow create: if isChatParticipant() && isSender();
      allow read: if isChatParticipant();
      allow update, delete: if false;
    }
  }
}
```

Now that we have defined these rules, we can switch to our Android app code and create a FirestoreMessagesDataSource class.

Creating a FirestoreMessagesDataSource class

The first step to creating the FirestoreMessagesDataSource class is to create the model that we are going to use to serialize the documents. This model has to include the same fields we included when we designed the Message document structure:

```
import com.google.firebase.Timestamp
import com.google.firebase.firestore.PropertyName
import com.packt.feature.chat.domain.models.Message
import java.text.SimpleDateFormat
import java.util.*

data class FirestoreMessageModel(

    @Transient
    val id: String = "",

    @get:PropertyName("senderId")
    @set:PropertyName("senderId")
    var senderId: String = "",

    @get:PropertyName("senderName")
    @set:PropertyName("senderName")
    var senderName: String = "",

    @get:PropertyName("senderAvatar")
    @set:PropertyName("senderAvatar")
    var senderAvatar: String = "",

    @get:PropertyName("content")
    @set:PropertyName("content")
    var content: String = "",

    @get:PropertyName("timestamp")
    @set:PropertyName("timestamp")
    var timestamp: Timestamp = Timestamp.now()
)
```

Note that we are including a field called `id` that has the `@Transient` annotation – this field will store the document `id` value (that for us will be the unique identification for the message as every message has its own document). The reason we have to put the `@Transient` annotation is to avoid this `id` field being stored in the document itself when writing in Firestore.

Now, as we did with the `MessagesSocketDataSource` class, we need to convert this data model into the domain model. We already have the `messages` domain model, so, in this case, we only have to implement the function to convert the `FirestoreMessageModel` data class into our `Message` domain model:

```
fun toDomain(userId: String): Message {
    return Message(
        id = id,
        senderName = senderName,
        senderAvatar = senderAvatar,
        isMine = userId == senderId,
        contentType = Message.ContentType.TEXT,
        content = content,
        contentDescription = "",
        timestamp = timestamp.toDateString()
    )
}

private fun Timestamp.toDateString(): String {
    // Create a SimpleDateFormat instance with the desired
        format and the default Locale
    val formatter = SimpleDateFormat("dd/MM/yyyy HH:mm:ss",
        Locale.getDefault())

    // Convert the Timestamp to a Date object
    val date = toDate()

    // Format the Date object using the SimpleDateFormat
        instance
    return formatter.format(date)
}
```

In this case, we are supposing we are only going to have text messages (no images) for simplification. However, it could have been easily done by including a field in the `Firestore` model indicating the type of message. Almost all the mapping between properties is straightforward, with the exception of the timestamp. In the `Message` model, we are expecting a `String` object with the date and time, and we are getting a `Timestamp` object from Firestore. So, we are using the `Timestamp.toDateString()` extension to obtain the formatted `String` object from the `Timestamp` object.

Also, as we would want to send messages too, we need to convert a domain `Message` object into the data object:

```
companion object {
    fun fromDomain(message: Message): FirestoreMessageModel
    {
        return FirestoreMessageModel(
            id = "",
            senderName = message.senderName,
            senderAvatar = message.senderAvatar,
            content = message.content
        )
    }
}
```

Note that we are not setting the timestamp (it will be created when the object is created), and the `id` field doesn't have a real value (as it won't be stored in Firestore).

Now, we can proceed with the `FirestoreMessagesDataSource` implementation. First, we define the class and its dependency:

```
class FirestoreMessagesDataSource @Inject constructor(
    private val firestore: FirebaseFirestore =
        FirebaseFirestore.getInstance()
) {
```

Then, we are going to add a `getMessages` function, to obtain chat messages:

```
    fun getMessages(chatId: String, userId: String):
    Flow<Message> = callbackFlow {
```

Inside this function, we will get a reference to the `messages` subcollection inside the specified chat:

```
        val chatRef =
            firestore.collection("chats").document(chatId)
                .collection("messages")
```

Now, we will create a query to get the messages ordered by timestamp (ascending):

```
        val query = chatRef.orderBy("timestamp",
            Query.Direction.ASCENDING)
```

In the next step, we add a snapshot listener to the query to listen for real-time updates. Every time a document in the messages is added, we will get a snapshot of the changed document there so that we can emit it through the flow to the consumers connected (in our case, `MessagesRepository`):

```
val listenerRegistration =
query.addSnapshotListener { snapshot, exception ->
    // If there's an exception, close the Flow with
        the exception
    if (exception != null) {
        close(exception)
        return@addSnapshotListener
    }
}
```

Just before sending the new messages through the flow, we need to map them to their domain counterpart and provide their ID. Also, `userId` will be needed to identify if the user has written the new message or if it is written by the other user in the conversation:

```
val messages = snapshot?.documents?.mapNotNull
{ doc ->
    val message =
        doc.toObject(FirestoreMessageModel::
        class.java)
    message?.copy(id = doc.id) // Copy the
                                  message with
                                  the document
                                  ID
} ?: emptyList()

val domainMessages = messages.map {
    it.toDomain(userId) }
```

Finally, we can send the list of messages to `Flow`:

```
domainMessages.forEach {
    try {
        trySend(it).isSuccess
    } catch (e: Exception) {
        close(e)
    }
}
}
```

In the case `Flow` is no longer needed, we should remove the snapshot listener:

```
        awaitClose { listenerRegistration.remove() }
    }
```

We also need to add a function to send messages. To send a message, we will simply add it to the `messages` collection in the document with the `chatId` value of the related conversation:

```
    fun sendMessage(chatId: String, message: Message) {
        val chatRef =
            firestore.collection("chats").document(chatId)
                .collection("messages")
        chatRef.add(FirestoreMessageModel
            .fromDomain(message))
    }
}
```

Next, we need to replace our previous `MessagesSocketDataSource` instance in `MessagesRepository` with `FirestoreMessagesDataSource`:

```
class MessagesRepository @Inject constructor(
    //private val dataSource: MessagesSocketDataSource
    private val dataSource: FirestoreMessagesDataSource
): IMessagesRepository {

    override suspend fun getMessages(chatId: String,
    userId: String): Flow<Message> {
        return dataSource.getMessages(chatId, userId)
    }

    override suspend fun sendMessage(chatId: String,
    message: Message) {
        dataSource.sendMessage(chatId, message)
    }

    override suspend fun disconnect() {
        // do nothing, Firestore data source is
           disconnected as soon as the flow has no
           subscribers
    }
}
```

And with some minor changes, we will have integrated this new provider. The good thing is that, as we have been working following a Clean Architecture, with mappings between layers, we don't have to change anything in other layers; for example, in `Usecases`, `ViewModel`, or the UI (apart from providing the `chatId` value and the `userId` value when calling the `getMessages` and `sendMessage` methods).

We could also have the two data sources living together in the same app (one as a fallback of the other), as the role of the repository is to serve as an orchestrator of the different data sources for a certain entity (in this case, the messages). We will see more about this in the next chapter as we will want to add local storage to our messages.

Summary

In this chapter, we explored various aspects of building a messaging app for Android. We discussed different approaches for sending and receiving messages, such as using WebSockets with Ktor or Firebase Firestore. We also covered how to structure the app using Clean Architecture principles, with separate layers for data, domain, and presentation, to ensure a well-organized and maintainable code base, and saw how easy is to introduce changes (for example, a change in the messages provider) if our architecture components are well decoupled.

Then, we delved into handling connection errors and synchronization issues using Kotlin coroutines and Flow, implementing error handling and retry mechanisms for a seamless user experience. Additionally, we examined the importance of push notifications in messaging apps and demonstrated their implementation using FCM, from setting up FCM in a project to handling incoming notifications.

By the end of this chapter, you should have a comprehensive understanding of the components and techniques required to build a robust real-time messaging app on Android.

Now, let's move on to learn how we can optimize our WhatsPackt app so that we can back up messages.

3

Backing Up Your WhatsPackt Messages

In any chat application, data handling is a significant concern – we need to ensure that messages sent and received are stored correctly, quickly retrieved when needed, and resilient to potential losses due to unforeseen circumstances such as device failures or accidental deletions. This requires a robust data persistence strategy. We also need to consider performance and user experience, which calls for effective caching mechanisms, as well as making sure that we have backups in the event of data loss or when the user changes devices.

In this chapter, we will start by introducing you to Room, a persistence library that provides an abstraction layer over SQLite and makes it easier to work with databases in Android. You'll learn about its architecture and components and how to use it to store and retrieve chat conversations and messages.

Next, we will tackle the creation of a cache mechanism orchestrating the use of Room locally and the use of the API to gather data from the backend.

Moving forward, we'll get you up to speed with Firebase Storage. You'll learn to set it up, understand its benefits, and how to secure data stored in it. We'll then use Firebase Storage to create a backup of our chat conversations, an essential feature for any chat application.

Finally, we'll explore how to use `WorkManager`, an API that makes it easy to schedule deferrable, asynchronous tasks even if the app exits or the device restarts. You'll learn how it can be used to schedule chat backups and how to upload these backups to **Amazon Simple Storage Service** (**Amazon S3**), ensuring data safety.

So, in this chapter, we will be covering the following topics:

- Understanding Room
- Implementing Room in WhatsPackt
- Getting to know Firebase Storage

- Scheduling `WorkManager` to send backups
- Using Amazon S3 for storage

Technical requirements

As in the previous chapter, you will need to have installed Android Studio (or another editor of your preference).

We are also going to assume that you followed along with the previous chapter. You can download this chapter's complete code from here: `https://github.com/PacktPublishing/Thriving-in-Android-Development-using-Kotlin/tree/main/Chapter-3`.

Understanding Room

When it comes to Android development, one of the most essential tasks is managing your application's data in a local database. The **Room** persistence library, part of Android Jetpack, is an abstraction layer over SQLite, a popular database that comes with Android. Room offers more robust database access while harnessing SQLite's full power.

Key features of Room

Before Room, developers primarily used **SQLite** directly or other **object-relational mapping** (**ORM**) libraries. While SQLite is powerful, it can be cumbersome to work with because it requires writing a lot of boilerplate code. Additionally, errors in SQL queries often aren't detected until runtime, which can lead to crashes.

Room solves these issues by providing a simpler and more robust API over the standard SQLite for managing local data storage. Here are some of its key features:

- **Compile-time verification of SQL queries**: Room verifies your SQL queries at compile time, not at runtime. This means if there's an error in one of your queries, you'll know as soon as you compile your app, not after you've shipped it to users. This leads to more robust and reliable code.

- **Reduced boilerplate code**: With Room, you don't need to write as much code to perform simple database operations. This leads to cleaner, more readable code.

- **Integration with other architecture components**: Room is designed to integrate seamlessly with other **Android Architecture Components** (**AAC**) library components, such as `LiveData` and `ViewModel`. This means you can create a well-architected, robust app that follows best practices for Android development.

- **Easy migration paths**: Room offers robust migration support, including migration paths and testing. As your app's data needs evolve, Room makes it easy to adapt your database structure to meet those needs.

- **Supports complex queries**: Despite simplifying interaction with SQLite, Room still allows you to perform complex SQL queries when you need more flexibility and power.

As you can see, Room offers an efficient and streamlined approach to managing your app's local data. It's a powerful tool that can make your Android development experience much more pleasant and productive.

Room's architecture and components

Room's architecture is based on three main components:

- `Database`

- `Entity`

- **Data Access Object (DAO)**

Here, you can see how every Room component interacts with the rest of the app:

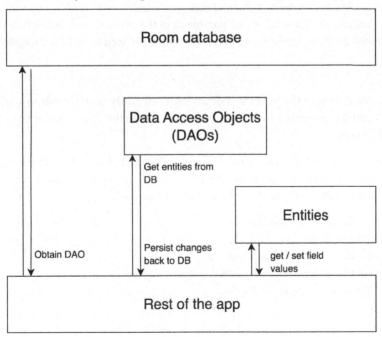

Figure 3.1: Diagram of Room architecture

Understanding these components is crucial when using Room effectively, so let's dive into them deeper.

Database

The `Database` class in Room is a high-level class that works as the main access point to your app's persisted data. It's an abstract class where you define an abstract method for each `@Dao` annotation in your app. When you create an instance of the `Database` class, Room generates the implementation code of these DAO methods (DAO will be explored in more detail in a moment).

The `Database` class is annotated with `@Database`, specifying the entities it comprises and the database version. If you modify the database schema, you need to update the version number and define a migration strategy, as in the following example:

```
@Database(entities = [Message::class, Conversation::class],
    version = 1)
abstract class ChatAppDatabase : RoomDatabase() {
    abstract fun messageDao(): MessageDao
    abstract fun conversationDao(): ConversationDao
}
```

Here, we've defined a `ChatAppDatabase` Room `Database` class with two entities, `Message` and `Conversation`. We've also defined abstract methods to access our DAOs – `messageDao()` and `conversationDao()`. The `entities` parameter in the `@Database` annotation takes an array of all entities in the database, while the `version` parameter is used for database migration purposes.

Entity

Entities in Room represent the tables in a database. Each entity corresponds to a table, and each instance of an entity represents a row in the table. Room uses the class fields in an entity to define the columns in a table.

You declare an entity by annotating a data class with `@Entity`. Each `@Entity` class represents a table in your database, and you can define the table name. If you don't define a table name, Room uses the class name as the table name, as in the following example:

```
@Entity(tableName = "messages")
data class Message(
    @PrimaryKey val id: String,
    @ColumnInfo(name = "conversation_id") val
        conversationId: String,
    // ...
)
```

Here, `Message` is an entity that represents a `"messages"` table in our database. Each instance of `Message` will represent a row within the `"messages"` table. Each property in the `Message` class represents a column in the table. The `@PrimaryKey` annotation is used to denote a primary key, and the `@ColumnInfo` annotation is used to specify the column name in the database. If not specified, Room uses the variable name as the column name.

DAO

DAOs are interfaces that define all the database operations that you want to perform. For each DAO, you can define methods for different operations such as insertion, deletion, and querying.

You should annotate an interface with @Dao, and then annotate each method with the corresponding operation you want to perform, such as `@Insert`, `@Delete`, `@Update`, or `@Query` for custom queries. Then, Room will autogenerate the necessary code to perform these operations at compile time. Here's an example:

```
@Dao
interface MessageDao {
    @Insert
    fun insert(message: Message)

    @Query("SELECT * FROM messages WHERE conversation_id =
        :conversationId")
    fun getMessagesForConversation(conversationId: String):
        List<Message>
}
```

In this `MessageDao` interface, we've defined two methods – `insert()` for inserting a `Message` object into our database and `getMessagesForConversation()` to retrieve all messages related to a specific conversation from our database. The `@Insert` annotation is a convenience annotation for inserting an entity into a table. The `@Query` annotation allows us to write SQL queries to perform complex reads and writes.

Understanding these components will allow us to leverage the power of Room effectively. The following sections will guide you through the process of implementing Room in our WhatsPackt application, starting from setting it up in Android Studio to creating entities and DAOs.

Implementing Room in WhatsPackt

In this section, you will be guided through the practical steps of implementing Room in our chat application. We will begin by setting up Room in Android Studio, followed by creating entities and DAOs and eventually using these components to interact with our database.

Adding dependencies

To start using Room, we first need to include the necessary dependencies in our project. Open your `build.gradle` file and add the following dependencies under `dependencies`:

```
dependencies {
    implementation "androidx.room:room-runtime:2.3.0"
    kapt "androidx.room:room-compiler:2.3.0"

    implementation "androidx.room:room-ktx:2.3.0"
    // optional - Test helpers
    testImplementation "androidx.room:room-testing:2.3.0"
}
```

The `room-runtime` dependency includes the core Room library, while the `room-compiler` dependency is required for Room's annotation-processing capabilities. Room's Kotlin extensions and coroutines support are provided by `room-ktx`, while `room-testing` provides useful classes for testing your Room setup.

After adding these lines, sync your project. You can do it using the **File** | **Sync Project with Gradle Files** option from the Android Studio menu or by selecting **Sync Now** in the automatic message that appears in the editor after adding the dependencies to the `build.gradle` file:

ⓘ Gradle files have changed since last project sync. A project sync may be...   Sync Now   Ignore these changes

Figure 3.2: The Sync Now option that appears in Android Studio when it detects any changes to Gradle files

We are ready now to create our database.

Creating the database

As discussed before, the `Database` component is the main access point for our app's data. So, let's create a `ChatAppDatabase` class:

```
@Database(entities = [Message::class, Conversation::class],
version = 1)
abstract class ChatAppDatabase : RoomDatabase() {
    abstract fun messageDao(): MessageDao
    abstract fun conversationDao(): ConversationDao

    companion object {
        @Volatile
        private var INSTANCE: ChatAppDatabase? = null
        fun getDatabase(context: Context): ChatAppDatabase {
```

```
        return INSTANCE ?: synchronized(this) {
            val instance = Room.databaseBuilder(
                context.applicationContext,
                ChatAppDatabase::class.java,
                "chat_database"
            ).build()
            INSTANCE = instance
            instance
        }
    }
  }
}
```

The `@Database` annotation marks this class as a Room database. It takes two parameters:

- `entities` is an array of classes that are annotated with `@Entity`, representing the tables within the database. In this case, the `Message` and `Conversation` classes are entities of `ChatAppDatabase`.

- `version` is the database version. If you make changes to the database schema, you'll need to increment this version number and define a migration strategy.

Next, `abstract fun messageDao(): MessageDao` and `abstract fun conversationDao(): ConversationDao` are abstract methods that return the respective DAOs. They do not have method bodies because Room generates their implementations.

Then, we declare a companion object to hold a singleton instance of `ChatAppDatabase`, by using the `@Volatile` annotation. This annotation means `INSTANCE` can be accessed by multiple threads at once but always in a consistent state, meaning a change made by one thread to `INSTANCE` is immediately visible to all other threads. `INSTANCE` is marked as nullable because it might not be initialized immediately.

In the `getDatabase()` function, we're implementing a common pattern for creating a singleton instance of a class in a thread-safe way. This pattern ensures that only one instance of `ChatAppDatabase` is ever created.

We use the `?:` operator to check whether `INSTANCE` is not `null`, and if it is, we enter the synchronized block. This block ensures that only one thread can enter this block of code at a time, preventing the creation of multiple instances of `ChatAppDatabase` if the function is called concurrently from multiple threads.

Within the synchronized block, we're calling `Room.databaseBuilder()` to create a new instance of `ChatAppDatabase`. We provide the application context to avoid memory leaks, the class of the database, and the name of the database.

Finally, we call `build()` to create the `ChatAppDatabase` instance.

After creating the new instance, we assign it to `INSTANCE` to cache it and then return the instance. The next time `getDatabase` is called, it will return the cached database instance instead of creating a new one. This is important because creating a Room database instance is an expensive operation, and having multiple instances would be a waste of resources.

This structure is essential for creating a database instance that will allow us to store messages and conversations.

The next step is to create entity classes.

Creating entity classes

The first entity class we are going to create is the `Message` class:

```
@Entity(
    tableName = "messages",
    foreignKeys = [
        ForeignKey(
            entity = Conversation::class,
            parentColumns = arrayOf("id"),
            childColumns = arrayOf("conversation_id"),
            onDelete = ForeignKey.CASCADE
        )
    ],
    indices = [
        Index(value = ["conversation_id"])
    ]
)
data class Message(
    @PrimaryKey(name = "id") val id: Int,
    @ColumnInfo(name = "conversation_id") val
        conversationId: Int,
    @ColumnInfo(name = "sender") val sender: String,
    @ColumnInfo(name = "content") val content: String,
    @ColumnInfo(name = "timestamp") val timestamp: Long
)
```

In this code, we are including quite a lot of instructions in the annotations, so let's go through them.

The @Entity annotation tells Room to treat this class as a table in the database. It comes with optional arguments, some of which are used here:

- tableName: This sets the name of the table as it will appear in the database. In this case, our table will be named "messages".

- foreignKeys: This sets up a foreign key relationship with another table. A ForeignKey instance takes four main arguments:

  - entity: This represents the class of the parent table that this entity has a relationship with. In this case, it's Conversation::class.

  - parentColumns: This specifies the column(s) in the parent entity that the foreign key references. Here, it's the id field of Conversation.

  - childColumns: This specifies the column(s) in the child entity that holds the foreign key. Here, it's the conversation_id field in Message.

  - onDelete: This represents the action that will be taken if the referenced row in the parent table is deleted. Here, ForeignKey.CASCADE is used, which means that if a Conversation instance is deleted, all messages that have a conversation_id value referencing the conversation's ID will be deleted as well.

- indices: This is used to create an index on conversation_id to speed up your queries. An index makes data retrieval faster at the cost of additional disk space and slower write speed. An index is particularly useful here because we will often perform operations related to a specific conversation, and indexing conversation_id will make these operations more efficient.

Then, we have also added annotations to the properties of the class:

- @PrimaryKey: This annotation indicates that the id field is the primary key for the Message table. A primary key uniquely identifies each row in the table. We could use here autoGenerate = true, which means that this field will be automatically filled with an incrementing integer for each new row.

- @ColumnInfo(name = "column_name"): This annotation lets you specify a custom column name in the database. If not specified, Room will use the variable name as the column name.

Now, let's create a Conversation entity:

```
@Entity(
    tableName = "conversations",
)
class Conversation(
    @PrimaryKey
    @ColumnInfo(name = "id") val id: String,
```

```
@ColumnInfo(name = "last_message_time") val
    lastMessageTime: Long
)
```

The Conversation entity is very simple – we will just store the Conversation ID and the time of the last message in the conversation.

Now that we have created and defined our entities, it's time to create DAOs in order to obtain and update data.

Creating DAOs

A DAO is an interface that serves as a communication layer between the application code and the database. It defines methods for each operation we might perform on the entities in our database.

Let's start with the DAO for the Message entity:

```
@Dao
interface MessageDao {
    @Query("SELECT * FROM messages WHERE conversation_id =
        :conversationId ORDER BY timestamp ASC")
    fun getMessagesInConversation(conversationId: Int):
        Flow<List<Message>>

    @Insert(onConflict = OnConflictStrategy.REPLACE)
    suspend fun insertMessage(message: Message): Long

    @Delete
    suspend fun deleteMessage(message: Message)
}
```

Breaking down the code, we have the following:

- @Dao: This annotation identifies the interface as a DAO.

- @Query: This annotation is used to specify SQL statements for complex data retrieval tasks.

- @Insert: This annotation is used to define a method that inserts its argument into the database. OnConflictStrategy.REPLACE means that if a message with the same primary key already exists, it will be replaced by a new one.

- @Delete: This annotation is used to define a method that deletes its argument from the database.

Now, let's create a DAO for the `Conversation` entity:

```
@Dao
interface ConversationDao {

    @Query("SELECT * FROM conversations ORDER BY
        last_message_time DESC")
    fun getAllConversations(): Flow<List<Conversation>>

    @Insert(onConflict = OnConflictStrategy.REPLACE)
    suspend fun insertConversation(conversation:
        Conversation): Long

    @Delete
    suspend fun deleteConversation(conversation:
        Conversation)
}
```

The annotations function the same way as they did in `MessageDao`. Here, we're retrieving all conversations ordered by the time of their last message, and we have methods for inserting and deleting conversations.

We now need to provide these DAOs for other app components so that they can be injected. With that in mind, we will create the following module:

```
@Module
@InstallIn(SingletonComponent::class)
object DatabaseModule {

    @Provides
    @Singleton
    fun provideDatabase(@ApplicationContext appContext:
    Context): ChatAppDatabase {
        return ChatAppDatabase.getDatabase(appContext)
    }

    @Provides
    fun provideMessageDao(database: ChatAppDatabase):
    MessageDao {
        return database.messageDao()
    }

    @Provides
    fun provideConversationDao(database: ChatAppDatabase):
```

```
    ConversationDao {
        return database.conversationDao()
    }
}
```

As we have previously covered the creation of Hilt modules in the previous chapters, we won't go over all the code again. Instead, here are the key parts of the code:

- We are using @Singleton to indicate that only a single instance of the object should be created and provided as a dependency.

- The @ApplicationContext qualifier tells Hilt that we want to inject the Application Context into the method. This is quite useful as, in Android, we have Application Context and Activity Contextwhich have different lifecycles. Remember that a Context in Android is an interface to global information about an application environment, offering access to resources and system services and existing in various scopes such as Application Context, which is tied to the lifecycle of the application, and Activity Context, which is associated with the lifecycle of an activity, among others.

  If we don't specify which Context we want to use, we can get confused or provide one that is not suitable for this situation. Using the @ApplicationContext qualifier will assure us that the Context injected will be the expected one (the Application Context, in this case).

Now, as we already did in the previous chapter for the API or WebSocket, we are going to create a data source to connect with the database: LocalMessagesDataSource.

Creating a LocalMessagesDataSource data source

We need to create a LocalMessagesDataSource data source that will wrap the DAO and expose the specific database operations our app needs. This way, if we decide to change the database in the future, we will only have to change it here (not in the rest of consumers). This class will serve as a DAO at a higher level of abstraction, simplifying the API for the rest of our app and making it easier to mock the database in tests.

In the following code, we are just calling the functions we already defined in the DAO:

```
class MessagesLocalDataSource @Inject constructor(private
val messageDao: MessageDao) {

    fun getMessagesInConversation(conversationId: Int):
    Flow<List<Message>> {
        return
            messageDao.getMessagesInConversation(
                conversationId)
    }
```

```
    suspend fun insertMessage(message: Message): Long {
        return messageDao.insertMessage(message)
    }

    suspend fun deleteMessage(message: Message) {
        messageDao.deleteMessage(message)
    }
}
```

As we said before, we will use this data source to wrap the database and provide an additional abstraction layer.

Now, it's time to combine this local data source with the remote one. This will force us to think about a caching strategy.

Handling two data sources in the MessagesRepository component

Up until now, we only had one data source (the WebSocket one), but we would like our users to be able to retrieve their messages even if they have no connection for a short time. That's the reason why we have just created a database and have it ready to be populated.

As our use case is to provide a fallback for the WebSocket so that the user can continue checking their messages, we will follow a strategy where the main source of truth will continue being the WebSocket, but we will store a copy of the messages in the app database. Also, we don't want the records of this database to grow infinitely, so we are setting a cap of 100 messages per conversation.

The component responsible for combining both data sources is MessagesRepository, which we already implemented to be connected to WebsocketDataSource in the previous chapter. Let's now modify it to include both data sources and to orchestrate the data retrieval and local storage:

```
class MessagesRepository @Inject constructor(
    private val dataSource: MessagesSocketDataSource,
    private val localDataSource: DatabaseDataSource
): IMessagesRepository {
```

Next, we will modify the getMessages() method to include the logic to store the information retrieved from MessagesSocketDataSource (remote data source) in DatabaseDataSource (local data source):

```
override suspend fun getMessages(chatId: String, userId:
String): Flow<Message> {
        return flow {
            try {
                dataSource.connect().collect { message ->
```

```
            localDataSource.insertMessage(message)
            emit(message)
            manageDatabaseSize()
        }
    } catch (e: Exception) {
        localDataSource.getMessagesInConversation(
        chatId.toInt()).collect {
            it.forEach { message -> emit(message) }
        }
    }
}
```

As can be seen, we have connected to the socket data source, but we have wrapped this action in a try-catch block. So, if everything goes correctly, we will store in our database every new message and then emit it in the flow.

At the same time, we call manageDatabaseSize(), which will check and keep the size of the database under the limit we have set (100 maximum messages per conversation). If the socket fails, we will retrieve messages from the database directly.

Now, we will also modify the sendMessage method, where we will also store every new message sent:

```
override suspend fun sendMessage(chatId: String,
message: Message) {
    dataSource.sendMessage(message)
    localDataSource.insertMessage(message)
}
```

The disconnect will be kept the same as we don't need to do anything related to the new data source:

```
override suspend fun disconnect() {
    dataSource.disconnect()
}
```

Finally, here is the mechanism that we will implement to keep the size of the database under the agreed number of messages per conversation:

```
private suspend fun manageDatabaseSize() {
    val messages =
        localDataSource.getMessagesInConversation(
            chatId.toInt()).first()
    if (messages.size > 100) {
        // Delete the oldest messages until we have 100
        left
```

```
        messages.sortedBy { it.timestamp
        }.take(messages.size - 100).forEach {
            localDataSource.deleteMessage(it)
        }
    }
  }
}
```

We will obtain all messages related to the conversation and check if the size is more than 100. Then, we will order them based on their timestamp and remove the oldest ones.

Now, we have the Room database integrated into our app. Our last messages will be available even if we lose the connection. In the following section, let's see how we can also send a backup of those messages to be stored in the cloud. For that, we will use Firebase Storage.

Getting to know Firebase Storage

Firebase Storage, also known as Cloud Storage for Firebase, is a powerful object storage service built for Google scale. It enables developers to store and retrieve user-generated content, such as photos, videos, or other forms of user data. Firebase Storage is backed by **Google Cloud Storage** (**GCS**), making it robust and scalable for any size of data, from small text files to large video files.

Here are some of the key features and capabilities of Firebase Storage:

- **User-generated content**: Firebase Storage allows your users to upload their own content directly from their devices. This could include anything from profile pictures to blog posts.

- **Integration with Firebase and Google Cloud**: Firebase Storage integrates smoothly with the rest of the Firebase ecosystem, including Firebase Authentication and Firebase Security Rules. It's also a part of the larger Google Cloud ecosystem, which opens up possibilities for using Google Cloud's advanced features, such as Cloud Functions.

- **Security**: Firebase Storage provides robust security features. Using Firebase Security Rules, you can control who has access to what data. You can restrict access based on a user's authentication state, identity, and claims, as well as data patterns and metadata.

- **Scalability**: Firebase Storage is designed to handle a large number of uploads, downloads, and storage of data. It automatically scales with your user base and traffic, meaning you don't need to worry about capacity planning.

- **Offline capabilities**: Firebase **software development kits** (**SDKs**) for Cloud Storage add Google security to file uploads and downloads for your Firebase apps, regardless of network quality. You can use it to pause, resume, and cancel transfers.

- **Rich media**: Firebase Storage supports rich media content. This means you can use it to store images, audio, video, or even other binary data.

- **Strong consistency**: Firebase Storage guarantees strong consistency, meaning that once an upload or download is completed, the data is immediately available from all Google Cloud Storage locations, and any subsequent reads will return the latest updated data.

In our context, a messaging application, Firebase Storage could be used to store and retrieve message history or backups, shared files, or even multimedia content within conversations. This could serve as a reliable backup solution or a means of synchronizing chat history across multiple devices. However, you need to ensure you handle privacy and security concerns, especially since chat conversations can contain sensitive data.

How Firebase Storage works

In Firebase Storage, data is stored as objects within a hierarchical structure. The full path to an object in Firebase Storage includes the project ID and the object's location within the storage bucket.

> **Note**
>
> In the context of cloud storage, a **bucket** is a basic container that holds data. It's the primary parent in the hierarchy of data organization. All data in cloud storage is stored in buckets. The concept of a bucket is used by many cloud storage systems, including GCS, Amazon S3, and Firebase Storage. These systems typically allow you to create one or more buckets in your storage space and then upload data as objects or files to these buckets. Each bucket has a unique name within the cloud storage system, and it contains data objects, or files, each of which is identified by a key or a name.

The object's location is defined by a path that you specify. This path is similar to a filesystem path and includes both the directories and the filename. For example, in the `images/profiles/user123.jpg` path, `images` and `profiles` are directories, and `user123.jpg` is the filename.

When you upload a file to Firebase Storage, you create a reference to the location where you're going to store the file. This reference is represented by a `StorageReference` object, which you create by calling the `child()` method on a reference to your Firebase Storage bucket and passing the path as an argument, as in the following example:

```
val storageRef = Firebase.storage.reference
val fileRef =
storageRef.child("images/profiles/user123.jpg")
```

Here, `fileRef` is a reference to the `user123.jpg` file in the profile's directory within the `images` directory.

You can use this reference to perform various operations, such as uploading a file, downloading a file, or getting a URL to the file. Each of these operations returns a `Task` object that you can use to monitor the operation's progress or get its result.

The paths in Firebase Storage are flexible, and you can structure them in a way that makes sense for your application. For instance, in a messaging application, you might store conversation logs in a chat_logs directory, with each log's filename being the chat's ID. The path to a chat log might look like this: chat_logs/chat123.txt.

Finally, it's worth noting that Firebase Storage uses rules to control who can read and write to your storage bucket. By default, only authenticated users can read and write data. You can customize these rules to suit your application's needs.

Let's start setting up Firebase Storage in our project.

Setting up Firebase Storage

To start using Firebase Storage, we'll first need to add the Cloud Storage for Firebase Android library to our app. This can be done by adding the following line to our module's build.gradle file:

```
implementation 'com.google.firebase:firebase-storage-ktx'
```

As for the chat messages, one approach would be to save the chat logs as text files in Firebase Storage. Each conversation could have its own text file, and each message would be a line in that file. So, we are going to create a data source to upload those files:

```
class StorageDataSource @Inject constructor(private val
firebaseStorage: FirebaseStorage) {
    suspend fun uploadFile(localFile: File, remotePath:
    String) {
        val storageRef =
            firebaseStorage.reference.child(remotePath)
        storageRef.putFile(localFile.toUri()).await()
    }

    suspend fun downloadFile(remotePath: String, localFile:
    File) {
        val storageRef =
            firebaseStorage.reference.child(remotePath)
        storageRef.getFile(localFile).await()
    }
}
```

Here, we've added the Firebase storage instance as a parameter to the constructor, allowing it to be injected when the class is instantiated using Hilt. The uploadFile and downloadFile methods suspend the coroutine until the upload or download operation completes, using the await() extension function.

To be able to use the Firebase storage instance, we would need to provide the `FirebaseStorage` dependency. For that, we will need to create the following module so that Hilt is aware of how it can obtain it:

```
@Module
@InstallIn(SingletonComponent::class)
object StorageModule {
    @Singleton
    @Provides
    fun provideFirebaseStorage(): FirebaseStorage =
        FirebaseStorage.getInstance()
}
```

Now, we need to create those files, to then be uploaded using this data source. We are going to do it in a newly created repository: `BackupRepository`.

The `BackupRepository` repository will serve as an intermediary between different data sources (such as local databases via DAOs and remote data sources such as Firebase Storage) and the rest of the application. It retrieves data from the sources, processes it if necessary, and provides it to the calling code in a convenient form.

Here is the code for this repository:

```
class BackupRepository @Inject constructor(
    private val messageDao: MessageDao,
    private val conversationDao: ConversationDao,
    private val storageDataSource: StorageDataSource
) {
    private val gson = Gson()

    suspend fun backupAllConversations() {
        // Get all the conversations
        val conversations =
            conversationDao.getAllConversations()

        // Backup each conversation
        for (conversation in conversations) {
            val messages =
                messageDao.getMessagesForConversation(
                    conversation.conversationId)

            // create a JSON representation of the messages
            val messagesJson = gson.toJson(messages)

            // create a temporary file and write the JSON
```

```
                to it
            val tempFile = createTempFile("messages",
                ".json")
            tempFile.writeText(messagesJson)

            // upload the file to Firebase Storage
            val remotePath =
                "conversations/${conversation.conversationId
                }/messages.json"
            storageDataSource.uploadFile(tempFile,
                remotePath)

            // delete the local file
            tempFile.delete()
        }
    }

    private fun createTempFile(prefix: String, suffix:
    String): File {
        // specify the directory where the temporary file
            will be created
        val tempDir =
            File(System.getProperty("java.io.tmpdir"))

        // create a temporary file with the specified
            prefix and suffix
        return File.createTempFile(prefix, suffix, tempDir)
    }
}
```

As can be seen in the code, it uses `ConversationDao` to fetch all conversations in the local database. Each conversation represents a distinct chat thread.

Then, for each conversation, it fetches the associated messages using `MessageDao`, converts the messages to a JSON string using the Gson library, writes this JSON string to a temporary file, and then uploads the file to Firebase Storage through `StorageDataSource`.

Once the upload to Firebase Storage is complete, it deletes the local temporary file to clean up the storage space on the device.

`BackupRepository` handles all the details of data retrieval, processing, and storage. Other parts of the application don't need to know how the data is stored or retrieved. They only interact with `BackupRepository`, which provides a simple interface for these operations. This makes the code easier to maintain, understand, and test.

Finally, we will create `UploadMessagesUseCase`, which will be the use case or domain interactor responsible for executing the upload action.

Creating UploadMessagesUseCase

The responsibility of `UploadMessagesUseCase` will be to execute the backup using `BackupRepository`. As most of the logic is already in the repository, the code will be simpler and will look like this:

```
class UploadMessagesUseCase @Inject constructor(
    private val backupRepository: BackupRepository
) {
    suspend operator fun invoke() {
        backupRepository.backupAllConversations()
    }
}
```

Now, we are ready to retrieve and upload these backups. As it can be a time- and resource-consuming task, the idea will be to do it periodically, once per week or once per day. This is where `WorkManager` comes in handy.

Scheduling WorkManager to send backups

WorkManager is a component of Android Jetpack designed to manage and schedule deferrable background tasks. It ensures these tasks run even if the app exits or the device restarts, and effectively handles retries and backoff strategies. As it also takes care of compatibility issues, alongside upholding best practices for battery and system health, `WorkManager` is the recommended tool for tasks that require guaranteed and efficient execution.

`WorkManager` uses an underlying job dispatching service based on the following criteria:

- It uses `JobScheduler` for devices with API 23 and above

- For devices with API 14 to 22, it uses a combination of `BroadcastReceiver` (for system broadcasts) and `AlarmManager`

- If the app includes the optional `WorkManager` dependency on Firebase `JobDispatcher` and Google Play services are available on the device, `WorkManager` uses Firebase `JobDispatcher`

`WorkManager` chooses the appropriate way to schedule a background task, depending on the device API level and included dependencies. To use `WorkManager`, we need first to understand how we can create `Worker` and `WorkRequest` instances.

Introducing the Worker class

A **Worker** is a class where you define the task or job that needs to be executed. It is the core class that defines the work that needs to be performed and how to perform that work. You extend the `Worker` class (or `CoroutineWorker` if you're using Kotlin coroutines) and override the `doWork()` method to define what the task should do.

The `doWork()` method is where you put the code that needs to be executed in the background. This is where you define the operation that needs to be performed, such as fetching data from the server, uploading a file, processing an image, and so on.

Each `Worker` instance is given a maximum of 10 minutes to finish its execution and return a `Result` instance. The `Result` instance can be one of three types:

- `Result.success()`: Indicates that the work completed successfully. You can optionally return a `Data` object that can be used as the output data of this work.

- `Result.failure()`: Indicates that the work failed. You can optionally return a `Data` object that can describe the failure.

- `Result.retry()`: Indicates that the work failed and should be tried at another time according to its retry policy.

A unique feature of `Worker` is that it's **lifecycle-aware**. If the task in a `Worker` instance is running and the app goes to the background, the `Worker` instance can continue to run, whereas if the device restarts while the `Worker` instance is running, the task can resume when the device is back up. This ensures that the work will be performed under the constraints specified when creating a `WorkRequest` instance, even if your app process is not around.

Here is an example of a basic `Worker` class:

```
class ExampleWorker(appContext: Context, workerParams:
WorkerParameters)
    : Worker(appContext, workerParams) {
    override fun doWork(): Result {
        // Code to execute in the background
        return Result.success()
    }
}
```

In the example, we extend the `Worker` class and override the `doWork()` method to specify the task to be performed. In this case, we are just returning the result as successful, but the code to do the actual work would be where the `// Code to execute in the background` comment is placed.

To make our `Worker` instances work, we need another component: `WorkRequest`. Let's see how we can configure and use it.

Configuring the WorkRequest component

WorkRequest is the class that defines an individual unit of work. It encapsulates your Worker class, along with any constraints that must be satisfied for the work to run and any input data it needs.

There are two concrete implementations of WorkRequest that you can use:

- OneTimeWorkRequest: As the name suggests, this represents a one-off job. It will only be executed once.

- PeriodicWorkRequest: This is used for repeating jobs that run periodically. The minimum repeat interval that can be defined is 15 minutes. This constraint is discussed further in the official documentation: https://developer.android.com/reference/androidx/work/PeriodicWorkRequest.

WorkRequest has several options for setting conditions for the execution of work and for scheduling multiple pieces of work to run in a particular order:

- **Constraints**: A WorkRequest instance can have a Constraints object set on it, which allows you to specify conditions that must be met for the work to be eligible to run. For example, you might require that the device is idle or charging, or that it has a certain type of network connectivity. We will learn about these conditions in detail in a few paragraphs.

- **Input data**: You can attach input data to a WorkRequest instance using the setInputData() method, providing your Worker instance with all the information it needs to do its work.

- **Backoff criteria**: You can set backoff criteria for the WorkRequest instance to control retry timing when the work fails.

- **Tags**: You can also add tags to your WorkRequest instance, which will make it easier to track, observe, or cancel specific groups of work.

- **Chaining work**: WorkManager allows you to create dependent chains of work. This means that you can ensure certain pieces of work are executed in a certain order. You can create complex chains that run a series of WorkRequest objects in a specific order.

WorkManager offers several types of constraints that you can set on a WorkRequest object to specify when your task should run. This is done using the Constraints.Builder class. Here are the available constraints you can set:

- **Network type** (setRequiredNetworkType): This constraint specifies the type of network that must be available for the work to run. Options include NetworkType.NOT_REQUIRED, NetworkType.CONNECTED, NetworkType.UNMETERED, NetworkType.NOT_ROAMING, and NetworkType.METERED.

- **Battery not low** (setRequiresBatteryNotLow): If this constraint is set to true, the work will only run when the battery isn't low.

- **Device idle** (`setRequiresDeviceIdle`): If this constraint is set to `true`, the work will only run when the device is in idle mode. This is usually when the user hasn't interacted with the device for a period of time.

- **Storage not low** (`setRequiresStorageNotLow`): If set to `true`, the work will only run when the storage isn't low.

- **Device charging** (`setRequiresCharging`): If set to `true`, the work will only run when the device is charging.

Here is an example of how we can configure a `WorkRequest` instance:

```
val constraints = Constraints.Builder()
    .setRequiresCharging(true)
    .setRequiredNetworkType(NetworkType.CONNECTED)
    .setRequiresBatteryNotLow(true)
    .build()

val workRequest = OneTimeWorkRequestBuilder<MyWorker>()
    .setConstraints(constraints)
    .addTag("myWorkTag")
    .build()
```

In this example, `MyWorker` will only run when the device is charging, connected to a network, and the battery level is not low. It will also have a tag, which will allow us to identify it easily.

Here is a diagram with the flow followed for the `Worker` and `WorkRequest` instances to be executed:

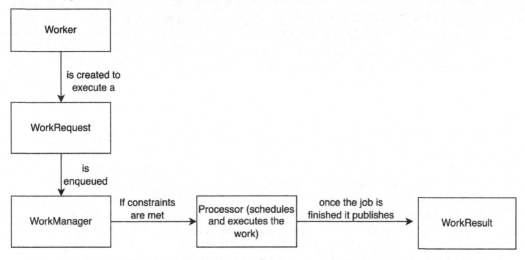

Figure 3.3: Diagram of WorkManager flow to execute a WorkRequest instance

We now have the tools to build our own `Worker` instance and configure the `WorkRequest` instance to retrieve and upload the backup. So, let's actually create them.

Creating our Worker instance

First, to support the `WorkManager` API, we need to include the related dependencies in our code:

```
dependencies {
    implementation "androidx.work:work-runtime-ktx:$2.9.0"
    // Hilt AndroidX WorkManager integration
    implementation 'androidx.hilt:hilt-work:$2.44
    ...
}
```

As we have seen before, the `Worker` class will execute the task that can run in the background even when the app is not being used. In other words, it's a unit of work that can be scheduled to run under certain conditions. In our case, we have just created the logic for that (in `UploadMessagesUseCase`), so our `Worker` class will need to have access to that class.

That's the reason we will start adding **HiltWorker** annotation to our worker. `HiltWorker` is an annotation provided by Hilt's `androidx.hilt` extension library. This annotation tells Hilt that it should create an injectable Worker instance (that is, Hilt should manage the dependencies of this `Worker` instance).

Here's the complete code for our `Worker` class:

```
@HiltWorker
class UploadMessagesWorker @AssistedInject constructor(
    @Assisted appContext: Context,
    @Assisted workerParams: WorkerParameters,
    private val uploadMessagesUseCase:
        UploadMessagesUseCase
) : CoroutineWorker(appContext, workerParams) {

    override suspend fun doWork(): Result = coroutineScope
    {
        try {
            uploadMessagesUseCase.execute()
            Result.success()
        } catch (e: Exception) {
            if (runAttemptCount < MAX_RETRIES) {
                Result.retry()
            } else {
                Result.failure()
            }
        }
```

```
        }
    }

    companion object {
        private const val MAX_RETRIES = 3
    }
}
```

We are also using a new annotation: `AssistedInject`. Now, `AssistedInject` is a Dagger Hilt feature that helps with scenarios where you need to inject some dependencies but also need to provide some arguments at runtime. Here, the `appContext` and `workerParams` arguments to the constructor are provided at runtime (when the `Worker` instance is created by `WorkManager`), while `uploadMessagesUseCase` is a dependency that should be injected.

The `doWork()` function is where the work that this `Worker` instance should perform is defined. This function is a suspend function and runs within a coroutine scope. This means it can perform long-running operations such as network requests or database operations without blocking the main thread.

In `doWork()`, `uploadMessagesUseCase.execute()` is called to perform the actual work of uploading messages. If this operation is successful, `Result.success()` is returned. If an `Exception` error is thrown, `Result.retry()` is returned if `runAttemptCount` is less than `MAX_RETRIES`, which means the work should be retried. If `runAttemptCount` equals or exceeds `MAX_RETRIES`, `Result.failure()` is returned, which means the work should not be retried.

As we want it to only retry three times, we are using `runAttemptCount`, which is a property provided by `ListenableWorker` (the superclass of `CoroutineWorker`) that keeps track of how many times the work has been attempted.

Finally, `MAX_RETRIES` is a constant that defines the maximum number of retries. It is set to 3 in this example.

To summarize, this `Worker` instance uploads messages by calling `uploadMessagesUseCase.execute()`, and it can retry the operation up to three times in case of failure. The actual dependencies of this `Worker` instance (`UploadMessagesUseCase`) are provided via **dependency injection** (**DI**) using Dagger Hilt. Now, we need to set up the `WorkRequest` class.

Setting up the WorkRequest class

In the case of the `WorkRequest` class, we will have to think about how frequently we want our messages to be backed up; for example, we can do a backup once per week. Also, we are going to configure the `WorkRequest` class to be only called when the user has a Wi-Fi connection. Here is how we do it:

```
val constraints = Constraints.Builder()
    .setRequiredNetworkType(NetworkType.UNMETERED)
    .build()
```

```
val uploadMessagesRequest =
PeriodicWorkRequestBuilder<UploadMessagesWorker>(7,
TimeUnit.DAYS)
    .setConstraints(constraints)
    .setBackoffCriteria(BackoffPolicy.LINEAR,
        PeriodicWorkRequest.MIN_PERIODIC_INTERVAL_MILLIS,
        TimeUnit.MILLISECONDS)
    .build()

WorkManager.getInstance(this).enqueue(
    uploadMessagesRequest)
```

We use `PeriodicWorkRequestBuilder` to create a `WorkRequest` instance that runs `UploadMessagesWorker` once every week. The `WorkRequest` instance has a constraint that requires an unmetered network connection (Wi-Fi). It also specifies a linear backoff policy for retries – this means that each retry attempt is delayed by a fixed amount of time, increasing linearly with each subsequent retry.

The `enqueue()` method schedules the `WorkRequest` instance to run. If the constraints are met and there's no other work ahead of it in the queue, it will start running immediately. Otherwise, it will wait until the constraints are met and it's the `WorkRequest` instance's turn in the queue.

Please note that due to OS restrictions, a `PeriodicWorkRequest` instance may not run exactly when the period elapses; it may have some delay, but it will run at least once within that time period.

We can call this code and enqueue the `WorkRequest` instance from any place in our app, but to ensure it gets scheduled, the most convenient place is when we start up the app, in the `WhatsPacktApplication.onCreate` method:

```
@HiltAndroidApp
class WhatsPacktApp: Application() {

    override fun onCreate() {
        super.onCreate()
        //Include WorkRequest initialization here
    }
}
```

With all this, we would have our app ready to periodically back up messages, and our work well could have finished here. However, to explore a different approach, let's see what happens if we need to integrate another storage provider – for example, Amazon S3.

Using Amazon S3 for storage

Amazon S3 is a scalable, high-speed, web-based cloud storage service designed for online backup and archiving of data and applications on **Amazon Web Services** (**AWS**). It's a well-known alternative to Firebase Storage.

Here's a brief overview of some key features and capabilities of Amazon S3:

- **Storage**: Amazon S3 can store any amount of data and access it from anywhere on the web. It provides virtually limitless storage.

- **Durability and availability**: Amazon S3 is designed for 99.999999999% (11 9s) of durability, and it stores redundant copies of data across multiple geographically separated data centers. It also provides 99.99% availability of objects over a given year.

- **Security**: Amazon S3 provides advanced security features such as encryption for data at rest and in transit, and fine-grained access controls to resources using AWS **Identity and Access Management** (**IAM**), **access control lists** (**ACLs**), and bucket policies.

- **Scalability**: Amazon S3 is designed to scale storage, requests, and users to support an unlimited number of web-scale applications.

- **Performance**: AWS storage makes sure that when you add or delete files, you can immediately read the latest version of your files. If you overwrite a file or delete it, there might be a short delay before these changes are fully updated everywhere.

- **Integration**: Amazon S3 integrates well with other AWS services, such as AWS CloudTrail for logging and monitoring, Amazon CloudFront for content delivery, AWS Lambda for serverless compute, and many more.

- **Management features**: S3 provides functionalities for management tasks such as organizing data and configuring finely-tuned access controls to meet specific business, organizational, and compliance requirements.

- **Data transfer**: S3 Transfer Acceleration enables fast, easy, and secure transfers of files over long distances between your client and your Amazon S3 bucket.

- **Storage classes**: Amazon S3 provides several storage classes for different types of data storage needs, such as S3 Standard for general-purpose storage of frequently accessed data, S3 Intelligent-Tiering for data with unknown or changing access patterns, S3 Standard-IA for long-lived but infrequently accessed data, and S3 Glacier for long-term archive and digital preservation.

- **Query-in-place functionality**: S3 Select enables applications to retrieve only a subset of data from an object by using simple SQL expressions.

These features make Amazon S3 a robust and versatile choice for various use cases, ranging from web applications to backup and restore, archive, enterprise applications, IoT devices, and big data analytics.

To implement our storage solution based on Amazon S3, we first need to integrate the AWS SDK into our app.

Integrating the AWS S3 SDK

We can integrate the AWS S3 SDK into our Android project by adding the following dependencies in our `build.gradle` file:

```
implementation 'com.amazonaws:aws-android-sdk-s3:
$latest_version'
implementation 'com.amazonaws:aws-android-sdk-
cognitoidentityprovider:$latest_version'
```

We have added here dependencies for the AWS SDK and the dependency needed to use Amazon Cognito.

We'll also need to provide our AWS credentials (access key ID and secret access key) to the SDK. For mobile applications, it is recommended to use Amazon Cognito for credential management.

Setting up Amazon Cognito

Amazon Cognito is a service that provides user sign-up and sign-in services, as well as access control for mobile and web applications. When you use Amazon Cognito for your user pool, you have the option to secure your data in AWS services (such as Amazon S3 for file storage) without having to embed AWS keys in your application code, which is a significant security risk.

Here are the instructions to set up Amazon Cognito in our Android application:

1. First, go to the Amazon Cognito console: `https://console.aws.amazon.com/cognito/home`.
2. From there, click **Identity Pools**, then **Create new identity pool**.
3. Check **Guest Access** under the **Authentication** section, and click **Next**.
4. Select **Create a New IAM Role**, create a name for it, and click **Next**.
5. Then create a new name for the identity pool and click **Next**.
6. Review the summary (as in *Figure 3.4*), then click **Create identity pool**:

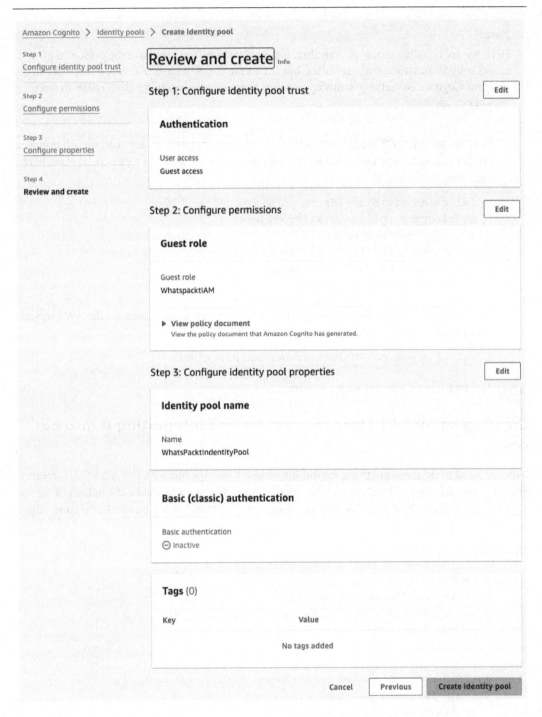

Figure 3.4: New identity pool configuration

> **Note**
>
> Here, we are enabling access to unauthenticated identities. You also have the option to give access only to authenticated identities, but note that you will have to create every user in Amazon Cognito. Nevertheless, this approach is more secure than using the S3 SDK to store keys in our app code.

7. Next, in our app, we'll need to obtain the AWS credentials provider. For that, we will initialize `CognitoCachingCredentialsProvider` with our `IdentityPoolId` class, in the region we configured it:

    ```
    val credentialsProvider =
    CognitoCachingCredentialsProvider(
        applicationContext,
        "IdentityPoolId", // Identity Pool ID
        Regions.US_EAST_1 // Region
    )
    ```

8. Now, we can use the credentials provider instance while creating a client for the AWS service. For example, to use it with Amazon S3, use this code:

    ```
    val s3 = AmazonS3Client(credentialsProvider)
    ```

Now, it is time to create a new storage provider.

Creating an AWS S3 Storage provider and integrating it into our code

Now, we need to do the same thing we did for Firebase Storage but with the AWS SDK: create a provider. This provider will be `AWSS3Provider` and will be used to handle the upload of files to AWS S3. It will take a `Context` object and a `CognitoCachingCredentialsProvider` object as constructor parameters.

This is how we can implement it:

```
class AWSS3Provider(
    private val context: Context,
    private val credentialsProvider:
        CognitoCachingCredentialsProvider
) {

    suspend fun uploadFile(bucketName: String, objectKey:
    String, filePath: String) {
        withContext(Dispatchers.IO) {
            val transferUtility = TransferUtility.builder()
```

```
                .context(context)
                .awsConfiguration(AWSMobileClient
                    .getInstance().configuration)
                .s3Client(AmazonS3Client(
                    credentialsProvider))
                .build()

        val uploadObserver = transferUtility.upload(
            bucketName,
            objectKey,
            File(filePath)
        )

        uploadObserver.setTransferListener(object :
        TransferListener {
            override fun onStateChanged(id: Int, state:
            TransferState) {
                if (TransferState.COMPLETED == state) {
                    // The file has been uploaded
                    successfully
                }
            }

            override fun onProgressChanged(id: Int,
            bytesCurrent: Long, bytesTotal: Long) {
                val progress = (bytesCurrent.toDouble()
                    / bytesTotal.toDouble() * 100.0)
                Log.d("Upload Progress", "$progress%")
            }

            override fun onError(id: Int, ex:
            Exception) {
                throw ex
            }
        })
    }
  }
}
```

The `uploadFile` function is a suspending function, meaning it can be called from any coroutine scope. The `withContext(Dispatchers.IO)` function is used to switch the coroutine context to the I/O dispatcher, which is optimized for I/O-related tasks, such as network calls or disk operations.

Let's delve into the `uploadFile` function, which is the core of this class.

The `TransferUtility` class simplifies the process of uploading and downloading files to/from Amazon S3. Here, we're building a `TransferUtility` instance, providing it with the Android context, AWS configuration, and an `AmazonS3Client` instance initialized with the provided `CognitoCachingCredentialsProvider` class.

The `transferUtility.upload()` method is used to upload a file to the specified bucket in S3. We provide the name of the bucket (`bucketName`), the key under which to store the new object (`objectKey`), and the file we want to upload (`File(filePath)`). This function returns a `UploadObserver` instance.

`UploadObserver` is used to monitor the progress of the upload.

We attach `TransferListener` to the observer to get callbacks when the upload state changes, the upload makes progress, or an error occurs.

The `onStateChanged()` method is called when the state of the transfer changes. If the state is `TransferState.COMPLETED`, it means the file has been uploaded successfully.

The `onProgressChanged()` method is called when more bytes have been transferred. Here, we calculate the progress as a percentage and log it.

The `onError()` method is called if an error occurs during the transfer. We will throw an error when it happens, to be handled by the consumers or this provider.

The `uploadFile` function is called from within a coroutine, and since the actual upload operation is a network I/O operation, it's wrapped in `withContext(Dispatchers.IO)`. This ensures the operation doesn't block the main thread, as the I/O dispatcher uses a separate thread pool that's optimized for disk and network I/O.

Now, we will need to create a data source to connect our `BackupRepository` instance to this new provider. The best way to do it is by implementing `IStorageDataSource`, a common interface for both data sources. This way, you're able to swap the underlying implementation (Firebase Storage, AWS S3, and so on) without changing the rest of your code. (This is an application of the **Dependency Inversion Principle** (**DIP**), one of the SOLID principles of **object-oriented** (**OO**) design, which helps make your code more flexible and easier to maintain.)

This is how we will implement `S3StorageDataSource`:

```
class S3StorageDataSource @Inject constructor(
    private val awsS3Provider: AWSS3Provider
) : IStorageDataSource {

    override suspend fun uploadFile(remotePath: String,
    file: File) {
        awsS3Provider.uploadFile(BUCKET_NAME, remotePath,
        file.absolutePath)
    }
```

```
    companion object {
        private const val BUCKET_NAME = "our-bucket-name"
    }
}
```

In this code, we are implementing the `uploadFile` function calling the `awsProvider.` `uploadFile` function, which will upload the file to the bucket with the `our-bucket-name` name.

This new `S3StorageDataSource` class can be provided via Hilt in a similar way to the previous `FirebaseStorageDataSource` class:

```
@Module
@InstallIn(SingletonComponent::class)
object StorageModule {
    @Provides
    @Singleton
    fun provideStorageDataSource(awsS3Provider:
    AWSS3Provider): IStorageDataSource {
        return S3StorageDataSource(awsS3Provider)
    }
}
```

Here, we create a `@Module` annotation that includes a `@Provides` or `@Binds` method for `IStorageDataSource`, and Hilt will take care of injecting the right implementation based on your configuration. If you want to switch from Firebase Storage to AWS S3, you'd modify this module to provide `S3StorageDataSource` instead of `FirebaseStorageDataSource`.

Finally, we need to integrate it into our `BackupRepository` class. It is as easy as replacing the `StorageDataSource` dependency for the `IStorageDataSource` dependency:

```
class BackupRepository @Inject constructor(
    private val messageDao: MessageDao,
    private val conversationDao: ConversationDao,
    private val storageDataSource: IStorageDataSource
) {
    // The rest of the class as it was before
    ...
}
```

And that's all. Depending on what we are providing in our Hilt module to satisfy the `IStorageDataSource` dependency, it will use the Firebase Storage one or the AWS S3 one.

And with this change, we finish this chapter and also our work in the WhatsPackt application!

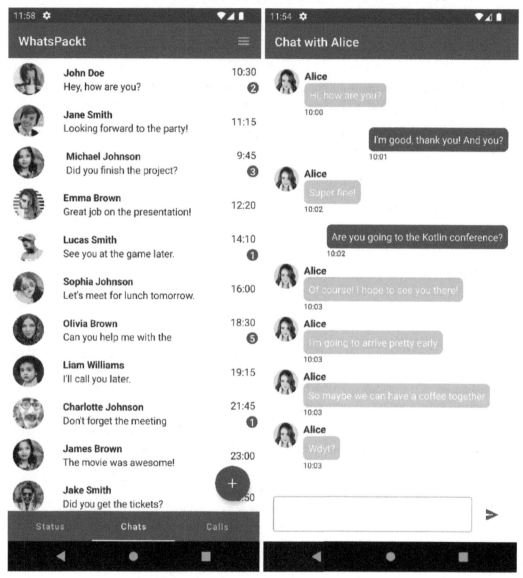

Figure 3.5: WhatsPackt's final appearance

Summary

In this chapter, we centered our efforts on creating a good offline experience for our user (storing the messages in a local database using Room) and providing a mechanism to store the messages backup, in case something fails. We have also learned how to use different providers to store our files in the cloud using Firebase Firestore and AWS S3.

Now, we have finished our work in the WhatsPackt app. In the next chapter, we will start building a new app: Packtagram. It will be an app to share photos and videos with our friends that will provide new and different challenges when creating it, such as capturing video. These are challenges that we will learn to overcome.

Part 2:
Creating Packtagram,
a Photo Media App

In this second part, you will learn to create an Instagram-like social networking app, Packtagram, by setting up its structure, developing user interfaces for stories and news feeds, and implementing data retrieval and caching. You will then explore integrating CameraX to enhance photo capturing and editing functionalities, including using machine learning to generate hashtags. Finally, you will add video capabilities to the app, learning to capture, edit with FFmpeg, and upload videos to Cloud Storage for Firebase, transforming Packtagram into a comprehensive multimedia platform.

This part includes the following chapters:

- *Chapter 4, Building the Packtagram UI*

- *Chapter 5, Creating a Photo Editor Using CameraX*

- *Chapter 6, Adding Video and Editing Functionality to Packtagram*

4
Building the Packtagram UI

As we leave the exciting world of chat applications behind, it's time to take on another interesting challenge – social networking. Social networking apps have seen an exponential rise in popularity over the last decade, becoming integral to our daily lives. These platforms have changed the way we communicate, share, and interact with each other on a global scale. Among them, Instagram stands out with its simplicity, its emphasis on visuals, and its engaging features, such as its newsfeed and stories.

The next few chapters are dedicated to the process of creating an Instagram-like social networking application while leveraging Android's powerful features and capabilities. We will call it Packtagram!

To start this journey, we'll begin by setting up a solid foundation and structuring our project. The structure of an Android application has a significant impact on the ease of development and the application's scalability over time. This chapter will cover various aspects of project structuring, such as defining the file hierarchy, segregating modules, and choosing the right architecture pattern for our needs.

Once our project structure is robust and scalable, we'll transition into the realm of UI development. In the case of Instagram, the primary components that catch our attention are its newsfeed and stories. We'll dive into the process of implementing these critical features, focusing on their user-friendly interfaces and seamless navigation flow.

After the UI, we'll move on to the heart of any dynamic application: data retrieval. We'll learn how to interact with servers to fetch data, focusing on the newsfeed.

In the final part of this chapter, we will venture into the world of data caching. Social media apps often involve a large amount of data transfer, and to provide a seamless and efficient user experience, effective data management strategies, including caching, are necessary. We will explore how to store stories and news items locally, thus reducing network calls and improving the app's performance.

This chapter will cover the following topics:

- Setting up Packtagram's modules and dependencies
- Creating the stories screen
- Creating the newsfeed screen and its components
- Using Retrofit and Moshi to retrieve newsfeed information
- Implementing pagination to the newsfeed

Technical requirements

As in the previous chapter, you will need to have Android Studio (or another editor of your preference) installed.

We are going to start a new project in this chapter, so it isn't necessary to download the changes that you made in the previous chapter.

Nonetheless, you can have the complete code that we are going to build through this chapter in this book's GitHub repository: `https://github.com/PacktPublishing/Thriving-in-Android-Development-using-Kotlin/tree/main/Chapter-4`.

Setting up Packtagram's modules and dependencies

To set up our app structure, we are going to create a new project. We could do this by following the same instructions that we covered in *Chapter 1*, but we are going to introduce a variation here: our Gradle files will be written in Kotlin, and we will also use version catalogs.

Setting up a version catalog

A **version catalog** is a feature that was introduced in Gradle 7.0 to centralize the declaration of dependencies in a project. This feature provides an organized way to manage dependencies, making it easier to control and update the different versions of libraries across different modules of a project.

With a version catalog, you define all the dependencies and their versions in a **Tom's Obvious, Minimal Language** (**TOML**) file, usually named `libs.versions.toml`. This file resides in the Gradle folder of your project.

A version catalog offers several benefits:

- It simplifies dependency management by providing a single place to define and update the dependencies
- It minimizes errors caused by discrepancies in dependency versions across modules

- It improves the readability of build scripts by removing the need to declare each dependency individually as the declaration is centralized in a unique file

To use version catalogs, in Android Studio, fill out the details for a new project, including **Name** – here, I chose **Packtagram**. For the **Build configuration language** field, select **Kotlin DSL (build.gradle.kts)**:

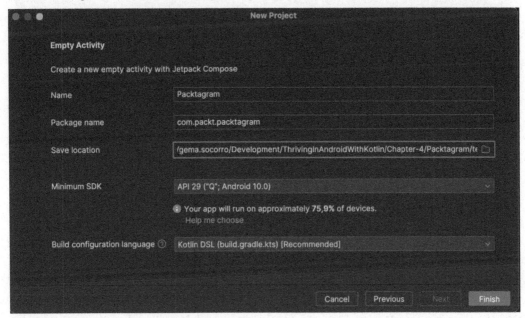

Figure 4.1: Creating a new project in Android Studio Jellyfish (2023.3.1)

With this option, Android Studio will automatically create the file needed to specify the versions. This file is called `libs.versions.toml` and its default content will look like this:

```
[versions]
agp = "8.1.0-beta01"
org-jetbrains-kotlin-android = "1.8.10"
core-ktx = "1.9.0"
...

[libraries]
core-ktx = { group = "androidx.core", name = "core-ktx", version.ref =
"core-ktx" }
junit = { group = "junit", name = "junit", version.ref = "junit" }
...

[plugins]
```

```
com-android-application = { id = "com.android.application", version.
ref = "agp" }
org-jetbrains-kotlin-android = { id = "org.jetbrains.kotlin.android",
version.ref = "org-jetbrains-kotlin-android" }
```

```
[bundles]
```

As shown in the following code (and in the `libs.version.toml` file generated by Android Studio in your project), the file is composed of several sections:

- `versions`: This section contains the versions of the dependencies that will be used in your project. You simply assign a reference name to each version number. This is useful to centralize versioning, particularly when the same version of a library is used in multiple places.

- `libraries`: In this block, you define your actual dependencies by assigning them an alias and linking them to the correct version defined in the `versions` block. This alias can then be used throughout your project to refer to the dependency.

- `bundles`: Bundles are groups of dependencies that are commonly used together. By creating a bundle, you can include multiple dependencies in your build scripts with a single alias. This can simplify your build scripts and make them easier to read and manage.

- `plugins`: This section is where Gradle plugins that are used in the project are defined. Similar to libraries, each plugin is given an alias and linked to a version number from the `versions` block. This feature makes managing plugins as straightforward as managing other dependencies.

Now, if we open the `gradle.build.kts` file of our app module, we'll see how the version catalog declarations are used. For example, here, we can see how the plugins are now applied:

```
plugins {
    alias(libs.plugins.com.android.application)
    alias(libs.plugins.org.jetbrains.kotlin.android)
}
```

The term `alias` is used here to refer to a predefined plugin dependency that has been specified in the `libs.versions.toml` file.

Here, we can see how the dependencies are declared:

```
dependencies {

    implementation(libs.core.ktx)
    implementation(libs.lifecycle.runtime.ktx)
    implementation(libs.activity.compose)
    implementation(platform(libs.compose.bom))
    implementation(libs.ui)
    implementation(libs.ui.graphics)
```

```
    implementation(libs.ui.tooling.preview)
    implementation(libs.material3)
    ...
}
```

As you can see, every dependency is referred to by the name we have given them in the version catalog file (`libs.versions.toml`). It is now easier to have all the project dependencies synchronized and included in the modules.

Talking about modules, it's time we also structure our app using modularization. We already learned about the different strategies to modularize our app in *Chapter 1*, so this is a good time to review that information.

Modularizing our app

In this case, we will segment Packtagram into several feature modules, each encapsulating distinct functionalities:

- **Newsfeed module**: The newsfeed module is dedicated to the main feed and is where users see and interact with posts from those they follow. We'll isolate this functionality because it's the core user experience and likely the first screen users will see. This module will need to handle rendering posts, managing likes and comments, and refreshing the feed.

- **Stories module**: We'll separate the stories functionality into its own module because it's a distinct user experience that requires specific UI elements and data handling. The stories module needs to manage how different user stories are rendered, track the view status, and manage story creation.

- **Profile module**: User profiles are a central part of the Instagram experience, so we'll house this functionality in the profile module. This module will handle displaying user information, managing posts specific to a user, and editing profile details.

- **Search module**: Search functionality is complex enough to justify its own module. This module will deal with user queries, display search results, and manage interactions with search results.

- **Messaging module**: Direct messaging is a separate feature in Instagram, so we'll also isolate it in a dedicated module. This module will manage creating and displaying chats, sending and receiving messages, and notifications of new messages.

- **Core module**: This module will contain shared utilities, network interfaces, and other common components used across the application. This prevents code duplication and provides a central point for managing shared resources.

By choosing this modularization strategy, we've effectively separated our app into logical components that can be developed, tested, and debugged independently. This also aligns well with the idea of **separation of concerns**, ensuring that each part of our app has a clear, singular purpose. In the following sections, we'll explore each of these modules in detail, building the functionalities one by one, culminating in our completed social networking app.

So, let's create the modules while following the same instructions provided in *Chapter 1*. Our module structure will look like this:

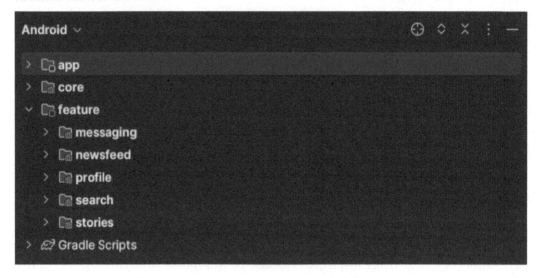

Figure 4.2: The modules structure for Packtagram

As we can see, we should have a module called `:app` (already created when creating the project), a module called `:core` for the core functionality, and a module called `:feature` that contains all of the feature modules (`:messaging`, `:newsfeed`, `:profile`, `:search`, and `:stories`).

As part of this project, we will focus on the `newsfeed` and `stories` modules (we already know how to create messaging functionality as that was covered in the last three chapters, so we don't need to cover that again).

In the case of the feature modules, we will structure them internally using the same approach we already followed in the WhatsPackt project: organizing the code and dependencies in layers. For example, we could structure the `:newsfeed` module like so:

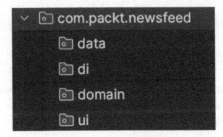

Figure 4.3: Internal structure for the feature modules

Here, we can see that we have created four internal packages:

- `data`: This is where we will place the logic for the data layer, including the components needed to retrieve the information from the backend and the data sources
- `di`: This is where we will place the logic needed to define the dependency injection instructions
- `domain`: This is where we will place the domain logic, including the repositories and use cases
- `ui`: This is where we will place all the logic related to the user interface, including ViewModels, composables, and other Android View components

We will implement the necessary components that will be part of the modules in this and the following chapters.

As part of our module structure, we've included an internal module specifically for dependency injection. Previously, in our WhatsPackt project, we used the Dagger Hilt framework for dependency injection. However, in this project, we will take a different approach by using Koin.

Getting to know Koin

Koin was mentioned briefly in *Chapter 1*, but let's learn about its main features here:

- **Simplicity**: It offers an easy setup process and is easy to learn
- **Efficiency**: It is lightweight as it doesn't rely on reflection
- **Kotlin-centric**: Designed specifically for Kotlin, it leverages Kotlin-specific features such as extension functions, **domain-specific languages** (**DSLs**), and property delegation
- **Scope management**: It has a clear way to manage the life cycle of injected instances
- **Integration**: It provides seamless integration with popular frameworks, such as ViewModel, Coroutines, and others
- **Testing**: It includes tools to simplify testing by allowing dependencies to be mocked or overridden
- **DSL configuration**: Koin uses a more readable and concise form of configuration

Let's prepare Koin for this project so that we can use it in the following sections and chapters.

Setting up Koin

To start setting up Koin, we need to add the necessary dependency to our version catalog. To do that, you will add the necessary Koin dependencies to the `libs.versions.toml` file. Be sure to use the latest version of Koin and replace `latest-version` with the actual version number:

```
[versions]
...
koin = "latest-version"

[libraries]
...
koin-core = { group = "io.insert-koin", name = "koin-core", version.
ref = "koin" }
koin-android = { group = "io.insert-koin", name = "koin-android",
version.ref = "koin" }
koin-androidx-navigation = { group = "io.insert-koin", name = "koin-
androidx-navigation", version.ref = "koin" }
koin-androidx-compose = { group = "io.insert-koin", name = "koin-
androidx-compose", version.ref = "koin" }
koin-test = { group = "io.insert-koin", name = "koin-test", version.
ref = "koin" }
koin-test-junit4 = { group = "io.insert-koin", name = "koin-test-
junit4", version.ref = "koin" }
```

As we can see, we have added the `koin` version in the `versions` block and the packages we might need in the `libraries` block.

Now, we need to add the dependencies to our module's Gradle files. To do this, add the following lines to the dependency Lambda:

```
dependencies {
    ...
    implementation(libs.koin.core)
    implementation(libs.koin.android)
    implementation(libs.koin.androidx.compose)
    implementation(libs.koin.androidx.navigation)
    ...
}
```

Adding these dependencies will allow us to use Koin in our modules. As a start, you should add them to the :app, :feature:newsfeed, and :feature:stories modules, which are the modules we are going to work with in this and the following two chapters.

Next, we need to create our Application class. Koin is typically initialized in your Application class. As we don't have one already, we will create one as part of the :app module and add the following code:

```
class PacktagramApplication : Application() {
    override fun onCreate() {
        super.onCreate()
        startKoin {
            androidLogger()
            androidContext(this@PacktagramApplication)
            modules(appModule)
        }
    }
}
```

In the startKoin block, we've specified that we want to use the Android logger (androidLogger()). The androidLogger() function is a part of Koin's API and configures Koin to use Android's native logging mechanism. Essentially, it enables Koin to print logs to Logcat.

When you initialize Koin with androidLogger(), you will be able to see important information about Koin's behavior and operations in Logcat while debugging your application. This includes details such as which dependencies are being created, if any errors occur during the creation of a dependency, the life cycle of scopes, and more.

After that, we provided the Android context (androidContext(this@MyApplication)) to the framework in case we need it to create any of our dependencies.

The next line is modules(appModule). This function is where you'll list the modules that contain your project's dependencies and the instructions to provide them. To start, we will only have appModule, which we can create like so:

```
import org.koin.dsl.module

val appModule = module {
    ...
}
```

Inside the `module` block, we should define our dependencies once we start building them. Here's an example:

```
val exampleModule = module {
    single { MyDataSource(get()) }
    single { MyRepository(get()) }
    factory { MyUseCase(get()) }
    viewModel { MyViewModel(get()) }
}
```

The `module` function in Koin is used to define a module where you specify how to create your various dependencies. Inside a module, you can use functions such as `single`, `factory`, and `viewModel` to create instances of your dependencies.

Here's a breakdown of these functions:

- `single`: This function creates a singleton object of the specified type. Once this object is created, the same instance will be provided every time this type of object is needed. For example, `single { MyDataSource(get()) }` defines how to create a single instance of `MyDataSource`. The `get()` function inside the curly braces is a Koin function that fetches any required dependencies for creating the `MyDataSource` instance.

- `factory`: This function is used when you want to create a new instance every time the dependency is needed, instead of reusing the same instance. For instance, `factory { MyUseCase(get()) }` creates a new `MyUseCase` object every time a `MyUseCase` instance is requested.

- `viewModel`: This function is used to create instances of `ViewModel` classes. It works like `single` but is specialized for Android's `ViewModel` instances. All `ViewModel` instances are tied to an activity or fragment life cycle and can survive configuration changes, such as screen rotation. For instance, `viewModel { MyViewModel(get()) }` defines how to create an instance of `MyViewModel`.

- `bind`: This function is used alongside `single`, `factory`, or `scoped` to provide additional interfaces this class can fulfill. For example, if the `MyImplementation` class implements `MyInterface`, you could enter the following:

  ```
  single { MyImplementation() } bind MyInterface::class
  ```

  The `get()` function that you can see in the definitions is a Koin function that automatically fetches the required dependencies. For example, if `MyDataSource` has a dependency on a `MyApi` instance, then `get()` will fetch that `MyApi` instance, provided that it has been defined somewhere in the Koin modules.

Returning to our project, we are going to leave the `appModule` empty for now – we will complete it once we start creating new components.

Talking of components, let's start with the UI we need to show the stories screen.

Creating the stories screen

In this section, we'll focus on developing a feature for creating and editing new stories within our stories feature. We'll begin by writing a `StoryEditorScreen` composable, along with its corresponding `ViewModel`, aptly named `StoryEditorViewModel`. Although this `ViewModel` will initially have limited functionality, we'll expand upon it in subsequent chapters.

Let's start creating our `ViewModel`, as follows:

```
class StoryEditorViewModel: ViewModel() {
    private val _isEditing = MutableStateFlow(true)
    val isEditing: StateFlow<Boolean> = _isEditing
}
```

In the preceding code, we are declaring `StoryEditorViewModel` and adding a property that will indicate if our screen is in edit mode or not. Edit mode will be used when the user has taken a photo or a video and wants to add more components to it.

Now, we need to take care of the dependency injection of this `ViewModel` as it must be accessible from the screen we are about to create. We can create `storyModule` in `:feature:story` to be able to provide it, as follows:

```
val storyModule = module {
    viewModel<StoryEditorViewModel>()
}
```

Here, we are just telling Koin that it needs to provide `StoryEditorViewModel` where it is needed.

We also need to add this new module to the `PacktagramApplication` Koin initialization:

```
class PacktagramApplication : Application() {
    override fun onCreate() {
        super.onCreate()
        startKoin {
            androidLogger()
            androidContext(this@PacktagramApplication)
            modules(appModule, storyModule)
        }
    }
}
```

In the `modules(appModule, storyModule)` line, we have included `storyModule` to provide all the dependencies that we'll need in the stories feature.

Now, we are ready to start with the Jetpack Compose magic and create `StoryEditorScreen`. This screen will have `viewModel` as a dependency and handle `TopAppBar` and a new composable, `StoryContent`, that will hold the main functionality of the story creation and edition. We can create `StoryEditorScreen` as follows:

```
@Preview
@OptIn(ExperimentalMaterial3Api::class)
@Composable
fun StoryEditorScreen(
    viewModel: StoryEditorViewModel = koinViewModel()
) {
    val isEditing = viewModel.isEditing.collectAsState()
    Column(modifier = Modifier.fillMaxSize()) {
        if (isEditing.value) {
            TopAppBar(title = { Text(text = "Create Story") })
        }
        StoryContent(isEditing.value)
    }
}
```

As we can see, the `StoryEditorScreen` composable receives `StoryEditorViewModel` as a parameter, which provides data and functionality for this screen. This `ViewModel` is provided by Koin, using the `koinViewModel` function.

Next, `isEditing` is a state derived from the `isEditing` state flow of `ViewModel`. This state will represent whether the user is in the process of editing a story or not. The `collectAsState()` function collects the latest value from the state flow and represents it as a state in Compose. Whenever the `isEditing` state flow emits a new value, the UI will recompose to reflect the new state.

Inside `StoryEditorScreen`, there's a `Column` composable that takes up the maximum size of the screen. A `Column` composable allows us to arrange its children vertically. Inside this `Column`, there's a condition to check the `isEditing` state. If `isEditing` is true, `TopAppBar` will be shown with **Create Story** as its title. Here, `TopAppBar` is a composable that represents a Material Design App Bar and is generally placed at the top of the screen – this App Bar will only be shown when the user is in the editing state.

The `StoryContent` composable is then included in `Column`, outside of the condition for `isEditing`. This means that `StoryContent` will always be shown, regardless of whether the user is in editing mode or not. The `isEditing` state is passed to `StoryContent` to inform it of the current editing status. Let's work on this composable now.

This composable should have a background that will be the image or the video the user wants to include in the story and will take all the space on the screen. By doing this, the options on the screen will be different, depending on whether we're capturing the media or editing it. Here's the code for this composable:

```
@Composable
fun StoryContent(
    isEditing: Boolean = false,
    modifier: Modifier = Modifier
) {
    Box(modifier = Modifier.fillMaxSize().padding(20.dp)) {
        Box(
            modifier = Modifier
                .fillMaxWidth()
                .wrapContentHeight()
        ) {
            Button(
                onClick = { /*Handle back*/},
                modifier =
                    Modifier.align(Alignment.TopStart)
            ) {
                Image(
                    painter = painterResource(id =
                        R.drawable.ic_arrow_back),
                    contentDescription = "Back button")
            }
            if (isEditing) {
                Button(
                    onClick =
                        { /* Handle create caption */ },
                    modifier =
                        Modifier.align(Alignment.TopEnd)
                ) {
                    Image(
                        painter = painterResource(id =
                            R.drawable.ic_caption),
                        contentDescription = "Create label"
                    )
                }
            }
        }

        Image(
            painter = painterResource(id =
```

```
                    R.drawable.ic_default_image),
            modifier = Modifier.fillMaxSize(),
            contentDescription = "Default image"
        )


        Row(
            modifier = Modifier
                .wrapContentHeight()
                .align(Alignment.BottomCenter)
        ) {
            if (isEditing) {
                Button(
                    onClick =
                        { /* Handle create caption */ }
                ) {
                    Text(stringResource(id =
                        R.string.share_story))
                }
            } else {
                OutlinedButton(
                    onClick =
                        { /* Handle take a photo */ },
                    modifier= Modifier.size(50.dp),
                    shape = CircleShape,
                    border= BorderStroke(4.dp,
                        MaterialTheme.colorScheme.primary),
                    contentPadding = PaddingValues(0.dp),
                    colors =
                        ButtonDefaults.outlinedButtonColors(
                        contentColor =
                        MaterialTheme.colorScheme.primary)
                ) {
                }
            }
        }
    }
}
```

Let's break down this code:

- The outermost Box is the main container, which takes up the maximum size of its parent and adds a padding of 20.dp.

- The first child of Box is another Box that is set to take up the full width and wrap the content height.

- Inside this Box, there is a Button component aligned to the top-start corner of its parent Box. This button is used to handle a back navigation action. Inside this button is an Image component with an arrow icon.

> **Note**
>
> The terms "start" and "end" are used for layout positioning to ensure better support for both **left-to-right** (**LTR**) and **right-to-left** (**RTL**) languages. When you use the "start" and "end" attributes in your layout, Android automatically adjusts the orientation based on the text direction of the current locale. In LTR languages such as English, "start" maps to "left" and "end" maps to "right," while in RTL languages such as Arabic, "start" maps to "right" and "end" maps to "left." This approach simplifies the process of localizing your app for multiple languages and text directions.

- If the isEditing flag is true, an additional Button is added to Box. This button, which is aligned to the top end (the right, in LTR layouts) of its parent Box, allows users to create a caption for their story. The button uses an image of a caption icon to communicate its function.

- The next child of the outermost Box is Image, which displays a default image. This Image takes up the maximum size of Box, signifying that this image will be the main focus of this screen.

- The last child of the outermost Box is a Row that's aligned to the bottom center of Box. This Row contains two different buttons that are displayed conditionally, based on the isEditing flag.

- If isEditing is false, OutlinedButton is shown. This button, styled to look like a circular button with a border, allows the user to take a photo. Note that the actual implementation for taking a photo is not included in the provided code and should be handled in the onClick function.

- If isEditing is true, a Button component appears instead. This button, labeled **Share Story**, is intended to allow the user to share the created story. As you can see, it is using stringResource with a key of R.string.share_story, so we should add it to string.xml. Again, the actual implementation of the share functionality should be handled in the onClick function.

With the previous code, when the screen is in editing mode, it should look like this:

Figure 4.4: The story screen in edit mode

Otherwise, when it is not in editing mode, it will look like this:

Figure 4.5: The story screen when it is not in edit mode

As we can see, it is easy and intuitive to add or remove composables conditionally from a view.

With that, we've finished the story screen, until we add more functionality in the next chapters to capture photos and video. Let's continue with the newsfeed user interface.

Creating the newsfeed screen and its components

The newsfeed is the main screen of our Packtagram app and is where the user will see the latest posts from their friends. It is structured using several components:

- **Title bar**: This is where the user can access the messaging feature

- **List of posts**: The list of posts shown in our app

- **Bottom bar**: This is used to navigate to different sections in the app

We are going to start structuring our newsfeed screen by creating a `MainScreen` composable. Here, we will define the user interface for the main view in our Packtagram app.

This `MainScreen` composable will have a `Scaffold` composable as its main component. Here, we will define the title bar and the bottom bar with the different options for navigation:

```
@Composable
fun MainScreen(
    modifier: Modifier = Modifier,
){
    val tabs = generateTabs()
    val selectedIndex = remember { mutableStateOf(0) }
    val pagerState = rememberPagerState(initialPage = 0)
```

Here, we are starting with the composable declaration and the properties we need to handle the tabs that we are going to use in the `bottomBar` navigation.

Now, it's time to add the `Scaffold` composable. This is where we will add the `title` and `bottomBar`. Let's start with the `title`:

```
Scaffold(
    topBar = {
        TopAppBar(
            title = {
                Text(stringResource(R.string.app_name))
            },
            actions = {
                IconButton(onClick =
                { /* Menu action */ }) {
                    Icon(Icons.Rounded.Send,
                    contentDescription = "Messages")
                }
            }
        )
    },
```

With that, we have created the `Scaffold` composable and added `TopAppBar`. We used this in *Chapter 1*, but it is important to remember that a container is generally used to hold the title of the screen and any actions relevant to the screen's context. Here, `TopAppBar` takes in two important lambdas:

- `title`: This is where you define the title of the App Bar. In this case, it's displaying a `Text` composable that fetches a string resource – that is, the name of the app (Packtagram).

- `actions`: This is where we define the actions that will appear on the right-hand side of the App Bar. Actions are typically represented with icons and are used to perform functions relevant to the current screen. In this case, there's a single `IconButton` with an envelope icon (which, when clicked, would navigate the user to the messaging screen).

The next step is to add the `BottomBar`:

```
bottomBar = {
    TabRow(selectedTabIndex = selectedIndex.value)
    {
        tabs.forEachIndexed { index, _ ->
            Tab(
                icon = { Icon(tabs[index].icon,
                    contentDescription = null) },
                selected = index ==
                    selectedIndex.value,
                onClick = {
                    selectedIndex.value = index
                }
            )
        }
    }
},
```

Here, `BottomBar` is usually where navigation controls for the app are placed. In this case, `TabRow` is used, which is a container for `Tab` composables. The main Lambda of `TabRow` is used to generate the `Tab` elements. It iterates through each `TabItem` in tabs (which is a list of `TabItem` objects generated by `generateTabs()`), and for each one, it creates a `Tab` element. The `Tab` element is provided with an icon from `TabItem`, regardless of whether it's selected (based on if its index matches `selectedIndex.value`), and an `onClick` function that sets `selectedIndex.value` to the index of the clicked `Tab`.

Now, we need to add the content to the `Scaffold` composable:

```
content = { innerPadding ->
    HorizontalPager(
        modifier = Modifier.padding(innerPadding),
        pageCount = tabs.size,
        state = pagerState
    ) { index ->
        when (index) {
            0 -> {
                NewsFeed()
            }
            1 -> {
                //Search
            }
            2 -> {
                // New publication
            }
            3 -> {
                // Reels
            }
            4 -> {
                // Profile
            }
        }
    }
    LaunchedEffect(selectedIndex.value) {
        pagerState.animateScrollToPage(
        selectedIndex.value)
    }
},
)
}
```

The `content` section is where the main content of your app goes. In this case, the content is a `HorizontalPager` composable with pages corresponding to the tabs in the bottom bar.

The main Lambda in `HorizontalPager` is used to generate each page. The content of the page is determined by the index provided to the Lambda: when `index` is 0, `NewsFeed()` is displayed, and placeholders are left for the rest of the navigation options.

There's another Lambda inside the `content` section: the `LaunchedEffect` block. This is essentially a side effect that is performed when `selectedIndex.value` changes. In this case, it triggers an animation that scrolls `HorizontalPager` to the page that corresponds to the selected index.

Now that `MainScreen` is ready, we can work on the `NewsFeed` list.

Creating the NewsFeed list

First, we need to create the `ViewModel` class that we are going to use in our `NewsFeed` composable. We will call it `NewsFeedViewModel` and add the following code:

```
class NewsFeedViewModel : ViewModel() {
    private val _posts =
        MutableStateFlow<List<Post>>(emptyList())
    val posts: StateFlow<List<Post>> get() = _posts
}
```

Here, we are initializing `NewsFeedViewModel`. For now, we will only have a public property. We'll use this to gather information so that we can render the posts in the user interface.

Now, it is time to handle the dependency injection for this `NewsFeedViewModel`. We are creating a dependency injection module per app module. So, in this case, since we are working on the newsfeed module, we will create a new dependency injection module to provide `NewsFeedViewModel`:

```
val newsFeedModule = module {
    viewModel<NewsFeedViewModel>()
}
```

Then, we will add it to the modules list in `PacktagramApplication`:

```
class PacktagramApplication : Application() {
    override fun onCreate() {
        super.onCreate()
        startKoin {
...

            modules(
                appModule,
                storyModule,
                newsFeedModule
            )
        }
    }
}
```

Here, we've added `newsFeedModule` to the already existing modules list in `PacktagramApplication`.

Now, we need to create the NewsFeed composable, which will include the list of posts:

```
@Composable
fun NewsFeed(
    modifier: Modifier = Modifier,
    viewModel: NewsFeedViewModel = koinViewModel()
) {
    LazyColumn{
        itemsIndexed(viewModel.posts){ _, post ->
            PostItem(post = post)
        }
    }
}
```

Here, we can use LazyColumn to render the list of posts. As we can see, we will need a PostItem composable to draw every list item. We will build this in the following section.

Creating the PostItem composable

Our PostItem composable will include all the components needed to render a post. We will need the following:

- A title bar with the picture and name of the author

- The media content (a picture initially but this could also be a video)

- An action bar with several actions (like, share, and so on)

- A label with the likes count

- A caption written by the author

- The timestamp of the post's publication

Following those requirements, this is what our PostItem composable will look like:

```
@Composable
fun PostItem(
    post: Post
){
    Column{
        Spacer(modifier = Modifier.height(2.dp))
        TitleBar(post = post)
        MediaContent(post = post)
        ActionsBar()
        LikesCount(post = post)
        Caption(post = post)
```

```
            Spacer(modifier = Modifier.height(2.dp))
            CommentsCount(post = post)
            Spacer(modifier = Modifier.height(4.dp))
            TimeStamp(post = post)
            Spacer(modifier = Modifier.height(10.dp))
        }
    }
```

As you can see, it is very readable and almost self-explanatory. We will create a `Column` composable and place every one of the composables we need vertically, leaving some spaces between as needed.

Now, let's create the composables we'll need. We will start in order, with `TitleBar`:

```
@Composable
fun TitleBar(
    modifier: Modifier = Modifier,
    post: Post
){
    Row(
        modifier = modifier
            .fillMaxWidth()
            .height(56.dp)
        ,
        verticalAlignment = Alignment.CenterVertically
    ) {
        Spacer(modifier = modifier.width(5.dp))
        Image(
            modifier = modifier
                .size(40.dp)
                .weight(1f),
            painter = painterResource(id =
                post.user.image),
            contentDescription =
                "User ${post.user.name} avatar"
        )
        Text(
            text = post.user.name,
            modifier = modifier
                .weight(8f)
                .padding(start = 10.dp),
            fontWeight = FontWeight.Bold
        )
        IconButton(onClick = { /* Menu options */}) {
            Icon(
```

```
                    Icons.Outlined.MoreVert,
                    "More options"
                )
            }
        }
    }
}
```

The base for this composable will be a Row composable as it will arrange its children in a horizontal sequence. The verticalAlignment parameter is set to Alignment.CenterVertically to align the items in the row vertically in the center.

Here's a description of the children composables that were used:

- Spacer: This is used to provide some space on the interface. Here, it provides a width of 5.dp at the start of the row.

- Image: This is an image composable that is being used to display the user's profile picture. The image source is taken from the Post object that was passed in.

- Text: This displays the user's name and takes the name from the Post object that was passed in. The fontWeight parameter is set to FontWeight.Bold to make the text bold.

- IconButton: This is a button with an icon. The onClick parameter is a Lambda function that gets called when the button is clicked. In this case, the function is empty, but this is where you would put code to handle the button press. The Icon element inside is used to display the more-options icon.

Now that TitleBar is ready, it's time for the MediaContent composable, which will display the content that the user has posted:

```
@Composable
fun MediaContent (
    modifier: Modifier = Modifier,
    post: Post
) {
    Box (
        modifier = modifier
            .fillMaxWidth()
            .height(300.dp),
        contentAlignment = Alignment.Center,

    ) {
        Image (
            modifier = Modifier
                .fillMaxSize(),
            painter = rememberImagePainter(post.image),
```

```
                contentDescription = null
            )
        }
    }
}
```

The preceding code generates a box that contains an image as this composable is used to display the main image content of a post. These are the main components:

- Box: This is a layout composable that stacks its children. In this case, it's used to hold an Image component. The contentAlignment parameter is set to Alignment.Center to center the image in the box and has a modifier applied to it to fill the maximum width and to set a height of 300.dp.

- Image: This is an Image composable that's used to display an image. The image source is taken from the Post object passed in. The modifier is used to ensure the image fills the maximum size of the Box composable. Here, rememberImagePainter is used to load and display the image from a source (such as a URL or a local file), and it's remembered across recompositions.

Now that we've completed the MediaContent composable, we will consider ActionsBar, which will provide the instructions to render the action buttons:

```
@Composable
fun ActionsBar(
    modifier: Modifier = Modifier,
){
    Column(
        modifier = modifier
            .fillMaxWidth()
            .height(40.dp),
        horizontalAlignment = Alignment.CenterHorizontally,
    ) {
        Row(
            modifier = modifier
                .fillMaxSize()
        ) {
            Row(
                modifier = modifier
                    .fillMaxHeight()
                    .weight(1f)
                ,
                verticalAlignment =
                    Alignment.CenterVertically,
            ) {
                IconButton(onClick = { }) {
                    Icon(
```

```
            imageVector =
                Icons.Outlined.Favorite,
            contentDescription = "like",
            modifier = modifier
        )
    }
    IconButton(onClick = { }) {
        Icon(
            imageVector = Icons.Outlined.Edit,
            contentDescription = "comment",
            modifier = modifier
        )
    }
    IconButton(onClick = { }) {
        Icon(
            imageVector = Icons.Outlined.Share,
            contentDescription = "share",
            modifier = modifier
        )
    }
    Row(
        modifier = modifier
            .fillMaxHeight()
            .weight(1f)
    ) {

    }
    Row(
        modifier = modifier
            .fillMaxHeight()
            .weight(1f),
        verticalAlignment =
            Alignment.CenterVertically,
        horizontalArrangement = Arrangement.End
    ) {
        IconButton(onClick = { }) {
            Icon(
                imageVector =
                    Icons.Outlined.Star,
                contentDescription =
                    "bookmark",
            )
        }
```

```
                        }

                    }

                }

            }

    }
```

The preceding code generates a UI that represents the action buttons under a post, similar to those on Instagram where you can like, comment, share, and bookmark a post. Here's what each part of the function does:

- `Column`: This creates a column in which you can place other UI elements vertically. The `horizontalAlignment` parameter is set to `Alignment.CenterHorizontally`, which centers the elements horizontally in the column.

- `Row`: This creates a row in which other UI elements can be placed horizontally. It fills the maximum size of the parent, which is `Column`.

- The first group of three `IconButton` composables are in a `Row` composable and are for the `Like`, `Comment`, and `Share` actions. Each `IconButton` takes a Lambda for the `onClick` event, which currently does nothing.

- There are then two additional `Row` composables, both with `fillMaxHeight().weight(1f)`, that appear to be placeholders, perhaps for adding additional icons in the future.

- The final `Row` composable has an `IconButton` composable for the `Bookmark` action. It has `verticalAlignment` set to `Alignment.CenterVertically` and `horizontalArrangement` set to `Arrangement.End` to position the icon in the center vertically and at the end (right-hand side in LTR layouts) of the available space horizontally.

- `Icon`: Each `Icon` displays an image and has a `contentDescription` composable for accessibility purposes. The `modifier` parameter can be used to adjust the layout or other visual properties of the icon.

Having configured the `ActionsBar` composable to provide a flexible UI layout featuring a range of interactive buttons, our next focus will be the likes count. It's very straightforward to implement:

```
@Composable
fun LikesCount(
    modifier: Modifier = Modifier,
    post: Post
){
    Row(
        modifier = modifier
            .fillMaxWidth()
            .height(30.dp)
```

```
                .padding(horizontal = 10.dp)
            ,
            verticalAlignment = Alignment.CenterVertically
    ) {
        Text(
            text = post.likesCount.toString().plus(
                «likes"),
            fontWeight = FontWeight.Bold,
            fontSize = 16.sp
        )
    }
}
```

The `LikesCount` function is a `Composable` function that creates a row to display the number of likes that a post has received. Here's what each part of the function does:

- `Row`: This creates a row in which other UI elements can be placed horizontally. It uses the provided modifier to fill the maximum width of the parent container, setting its height to `30.dp` and adding a padding of `10.dp` horizontally. The `verticalAlignment` parameter is set to `Alignment.CenterVertically`, which centers the elements vertically in the row.

- `Text`: This creates a text element that displays the number of likes that the post has received. It gets the `likesCount` field from the `Post` object, converts it into a string, and appends the word **likes** to the end. It also sets the font weight to bold and the font size to `16.sp`.

The next composable is the caption, which is the text that the user adds to the post:

```
@Composable
fun Caption(
    modifier: Modifier = Modifier,
    post: Post
) {
    Row(
        modifier = modifier
            .fillMaxWidth()
            .wrapContentHeight()
            .padding(horizontal = 10.dp)
        ,
        verticalAlignment = Alignment.CenterVertically
    ) {
        Text(
            text = buildAnnotatedString {
                val boldStyle = SpanStyle(
                    fontWeight = Bold,
                    fontSize = 14.sp
```

```
        )
        val normalStyle = SpanStyle(
            fontWeight = FontWeight.Normal,
            fontSize = 14.sp
        )
        pushStyle(boldStyle)
        append(post.user.name)
        append(" ")
        if (post.caption.isNotEmpty()){
            pushStyle(normalStyle)
            append(post.caption)
        }
      }
    }
  )
 }
}
```

Here's what each part of the function does:

- Row: This creates a row in which other UI elements can be placed horizontally. It uses the provided modifier to fill the maximum width of the parent container, wrap its height to its content, and add a padding of 10.dp horizontally. The verticalAlignment parameter is set to Alignment.CenterVertically, which centers the elements vertically in the row.

- Text: This creates a text element that displays the caption of the post, preceded by the user's name. The buildAnnotatedString function is used to build a string with different text styles for different parts. Thanks to that, the user's name is styled with a bold font weight, and the caption is styled with a normal font weight.

Upon completing the Caption composable, let's tackle the CommentsCount composable:

```
@Composable
fun CommentsCount(
    modifier: Modifier = Modifier,
    post: Post
) {
    Row(
        modifier = modifier
            .fillMaxWidth()
            .wrapContentHeight()
            .padding(horizontal = 10.dp),
        verticalAlignment = Alignment.CenterVertically
    ) {
        Text(
            text = stringResource(R.string.comment_count,
```

```
                    post.commentsCount),
            fontWeight = FontWeight.Normal,
            fontSize = 14.sp
        )
    }
}
```

The CommentsCount composable creates a layout to display the number of comments on a post. Here's what each part of the function does:

- Row: This creates a row in which other UI elements can be placed horizontally. It uses the provided modifier to fill the maximum width of the parent container, wrap its height to its content, and add a padding of 10.dp horizontally. The verticalAlignment parameter is set to Alignment.CenterVertically, which centers the elements vertically in the row.

- Text: This creates a text element that displays the number of comments. The stringResource function is used to get a string resource, which is a format string that takes a number and inserts it into the correct place to form a string that says **Read 3 comments**. The string format is then filled in with the number of comments from the Post object.

Now that we've finished implementing the CommentsCount composable, we will create the TimeStamp composable:

```
fun TimeStamp(
    modifier: Modifier = Modifier,
    post: Post
) {
    Row(
        modifier = modifier
            .fillMaxWidth()
            .wrapContentHeight()
            .padding(horizontal = 10.dp),
        verticalAlignment = Alignment.CenterVertically
    ) {
        Text(
            text = "${post.timeStamp} hours ago ",
            fontSize = 10.sp,
            fontWeight = FontWeight.Light
        )
    }
}
```

The `TimeStamp` function is a composable that creates a layout to display the timestamp of a post. Here's what each part of the function does:

- `Row`: This creates a row in which other UI elements can be placed horizontally. It uses the provided `Modifier` value to fill the maximum width of the parent container, wrap its height to its content, and add a padding of `10.dp` horizontally. The `verticalAlignment` parameter is set to `Alignment.CenterVertically`, centering the elements vertically in the row.

- `Text`: This creates a text element that displays the timestamp. The `text` parameter of this function is set to a string that includes the `timeStamp` attribute from the `Post` object. The `fontSize` and `fontWeight` parameters set the size and weight of the font to `10.sp` and `FontWeight.Light`, respectively.

With this composable, we have finished the `Post` composable components. If we do a preview with fake data, we'll see the following screen:

Figure 4.6: Newsfeed screen

Now, it is time to implement a way to populate the information needed from the backend.

Using Retrofit and Moshi to retrieve newsfeed information

In this section, we're going to prepare our app so that it can retrieve the newsfeed information from the backend. To do that, we'll need to create an HTTP client that handles the calls to the backend services. Since we used `ktor` in our first project, we are going to take a different approach for this one and use **Retrofit**.

Retrofit is a type-safe HTTP client for Android and Java (which is completely compatible with Kotlin). Retrofit makes it easy to connect to a REST web service by translating the API into Kotlin or Java interfaces. Here are some of its main features:

- **Easy to use**: Retrofit turns your HTTP API into a Kotlin or Java interface. All you have to do is define the API's URL and method (`GET`, `POST`, and so on) using annotations. Retrofit will automatically convert the HTTP responses into data objects.

- **Type conversion**: By default, Retrofit can only deserialize HTTP bodies into OkHttp's `ResponseBody` type and it can only accept its `RequestBody` type for `@Body`. Converters can be added to support other types. For example, a JSON converter can be used to convert the API's responses into Kotlin or Java objects automatically.

- **HTTP methods annotations**: You can use annotations to describe HTTP methods such as `GET`, `POST`, `DELETE`, `UPDATE`, and others. You can also use other annotations, such as `Headers`, `Body`, `Field`, `Path`, and more, to make your request exactly as needed.

- **URL parameter replacement and query parameter support**: Add parameters to your request with annotations. For example, you can add a path parameter by setting the specific value in the URL, or you can add a query parameter at the end of the URL.

- **Synchronous and asynchronous calls**: Retrofit supports both synchronous (blocking) calls and asynchronous (non-blocking) calls. For Android, asynchronous calls are more important as network operations on the main thread are discouraged.

- **Support for coroutines and RxJava**: Retrofit provides out-of-the-box support for coroutines and RxJava. This makes it easy to use with these popular libraries for handling asynchronous operations.

- **Interceptors**: Retrofit also allows you to use OkHttp's interceptors. You can add headers to every request or log the request and response data for debugging purposes.

We also need to use a converter to parse the backend responses into objects. We will use **Moshi** (`https://github.com/square/moshi`) for that. Moshi is a modern JSON library for Android and Java, also built by Square. It aims to be easy to use and efficient, and its design is inspired by the well-regarded Gson library, but it seeks to improve upon several design aspects. Here are some of its main features:

- **Easy to use**: Moshi provides simple `toJson()` and `fromJson()` methods to convert Java and Kotlin objects into JSON and vice versa.

- **Built-in and custom converters**: Moshi has built-in support for converting many common types and can encode any object graph of these. For other classes, you can write custom converters, called **adapters**, that define how these types are converted to and from JSON.

- **Kotlin support**: Moshi supports Kotlin and provides the `moshi-kotlin-codegen` module, which leverages annotation processing to generate adapters for your Kotlin classes automatically.

- **Null safety**: Moshi handles `null` values in the JSON input and can be configured to allow or disallow `null` values in your Java or Kotlin objects.

- **Annotation-based**: Much like Retrofit, Moshi uses annotations to denote special behavior for certain fields (for example, custom names and transient values).

- **Fault-tolerant**: Moshi is fault-tolerant and will not fail the entire operation if it encounters unknown properties or incompatible types in the JSON data. This can be beneficial when dealing with APIs that may occasionally change.

- **Efficient**: Moshi is designed to be efficient in its operation, minimizing object allocation and garbage collection overhead.

Now that we know the advantages of using Retrofit with Moshi, let's start integrating them into our project.

Adding the Retrofit and Moshi dependencies

To use both the Retrofit and Moshi libraries, we need to configure their dependencies. First, we will add them to the versions catalog file:

```
[versions]
...
retrofit = "2.9.0"
moshi = "1.12.0"
coroutines = "1.5.1"
moshi-converter = "0.8.0"

...


[libraries]
...
```

```
retrofit = { group = "com.squareup.retrofit2", name = "retrofit",
version.ref="retrofit"}
retrofitMoshiConverter = { group = "com.squareup.retrofit2", name =
"converter-moshi", version.ref="retrofit"}
moshi = { group = "com.squareup.moshi", name = "moshi", version.ref =
"moshi" }
moshiKotlin = { group = "com.squareup.moshi", name = "moshi-kotlin",
version.ref = "moshi" }
moshiKotlinCodegen = { group = "com.squareup.moshi", name = "moshi-
kotlin-codegen", version.ref = "moshi" }
moshiKotlinCodegen = { group = "com.squareup.retrofit2", name =
"retrofit-kotlinx-serialization-converter", version.ref = "moshi-
converter" }
coroutinesCore = {  group = "org.jetbrains.kotlinx", name = "kotlinx-
coroutines-core", version.ref = "coroutines" }
coroutinesAndroid = {  group = "org.jetbrains.kotlinx", name =
"kotlinx-coroutines-android", version.ref = "coroutines" }

[plugins]
...
kotlin-kapt = { id = "org.jetbrains.kotlin.kapt", version.ref = "org-
jetbrains-kotlin-android" }
```

Then, we will include the dependencies in our module's `build.gradle.kts` file, making them available to use in our module:

```
dependencies {

    implementation(libs.retrofit)
    implementation(libs.retrofitMoshiConverter)
    implementation(libs.moshiConverter)
    implementation(libs.moshi)
    implementation(libs.moshiKotlin)
    kapt(libs.moshiKotlinCodegen)
    implementation(libs.coroutinesCore)
    implementation(libs.coroutinesAndroid)

...
}
```

After adding these dependencies, we should be ready to work with both libraries. Let's start creating our data source so that we can obtain the data for the newsfeed.

Creating the data source for the newsfeed

At this point, we're ready to create our data source. We will do this in the `:feature:newsfeed` module. First, we need to create an interface to define our API endpoints using Retrofit. We can use `@GET`, `@POST`, and others to define what kind of HTTP request we want to make:

```
interface NewsFeedService {
    @GET("feed")
    suspend fun getNewsFeed(): List<PostApiData>
}
```

This is an interface for the Retrofit library that's used to turn the HTTP API into a Kotlin interface. It also defines an endpoint for your API:

- `interface NewsFeedService`: This is declaring a new interface named `NewsFeedService`.
- `@GET("feed")`: This is an annotation that describes an HTTP GET request. The `"feed"` parameter is the endpoint where the request will be sent. So, the full URL for this request would be something like `https://packtagram.com/feed` if the base URL of your Retrofit client is `https://packtagram.com/`.
- `suspend fun getNewsFeed(): List<PostApiData>`: This is declaring a function named `getNewsFeed` that is expected to return a list of `Post` objects. The `suspend` keyword means that this function is a suspending function, which is a type of function that can be paused and resumed at a later time. This will be called later from a coroutine.

So, to put it all together, when `getFeed` is called, it will make a GET request to the `https://packtagram.com/feed` URL and expect to receive a JSON array of `PostApiData` objects, which are then parsed into a list of `Post` objects in your Kotlin code.

To see an example of a JSON file that contains the expected fields, check out `https://api.mockfly.dev/mocks/09e4e43e-7992-4dd7-b99f-e168667a240e/feed`.

Now, we need to generate a client from this interface. For that, we will use the Retrofit builder:

```
object RetrofitInstance {

    private const val BASE_URL = "https://packtagram.com/"

    fun getNewsFeedApi(): NewsFeedService = run {
        Retrofit.Builder()
            .baseUrl(BASE_URL)
            .addConverterFactory(
                MoshiConverterFactory.create())
            .build()
            .create(NewsFeedService::class.java)
```

```
        }
    }
```

Here, we are creating a function called `getNewsFeedApi()` that will build the `NewsFeedService` client. For that, we need a `BASE_URL` function that we can hardcode in this same file. The recommendation is to store this information in a configuration file so that we can easily change it if we need to have different `buildTypes` of the app, for example.

We are also adding the Moshi converter using the `.addConverterFactory` `(MoshiConverterFactory.create())` function. This will allow Retrofit to deserialize the backend responses using Moshi.

Now, we need to create `NewsFeedRemoteDataSource`:

```
class NewsFeedRemoteDataSource(private val api:
NewsFeedService) {
    suspend fun getNewsFeed(): List<PostApiData> {
        return api.getNewsFeed()
    }
}
```

As we can see, we have created a `NewsFeedRemoteDataSource` composable. Here, we will have one function, `getNewsFeed()`. This function will call `NewsFeedService` to obtain the newsfeed.

Now, let's create the repository for this newsfeed.

Creating the repository

The next step is to define the repository that will orchestrate the information gathering and storage using the different data sources (for now, we only have one, `NewsFeedRemoteDataSource`). It will also map the information into the new layer: the domain layer.

First, we'll define its interface as part of the domain layer:

```
interface NewsFeedRepository {
    suspend fun getNewsFeed():List<Post>
}
```

Second, we'll implement its functionality as part of the data layer:

```
class NewsFeedRepositoryImpl(
    private val remoteDataSource: NewsFeedRemoteDataSource
): NewsFeedRepository {
    override suspend fun getNewsFeed(): List<Post> {
        return remoteDataSource
            .getNewsFeed()
```

```
        .map { it.toDomain() }
    }
}
```

As we can see, for now, it will only have a `getNewsFeed()` function that will obtain a list of `Post`. objects It will obtain the newsfeed from the remote data source and map the `PostApiData` objects into `Post` objects.

Now, let's create the use case to obtain this data.

Creating the GetTheNewsFeedUseCase

As we progress through the layers, the next step will be to create the use cases needed. In this case, we will create a use case to obtain the newsfeed – that is, `GetTheNewsFeedUseCase`:

```
class GetTheNewsFeedUseCase(
    private val repository: NewsFeedRepository
) {
    suspend operator fun invoke(): List<Post> {
        return repository.getNewsFeed()
    }
}
```

Here, we are using `repository` to get the newsfeed in the `invoke` function.

Before continuing, we need to create the data classes that we will be using in the data and domain layers. In the case of the domain layer, we will create the `Post` data class:

```
data class Post(
    val id: String,
    val user: UserData,
    val imageUrl: String,
    val caption: String,
    val likesCount: Int,
    val commentsCount: Int,
    val timeStamp: Long
) {
    data class UserData(
        val id: String,
        val name: String,
        val imageUrl: String
    )
}
```

Here, we are declaring all the fields that we need for the `Post` object in the domain layer.

In the case of the data layer, we will create the `PostApiData` data class and mapping functions that we'll need to map to the domain object:

```
data class PostApiData(
    @Json(name = "id")
    val id: String,

    @Json(name = "author")
    val user: UserApiData,

    @Json(name = "image_url")
    val imageUrl: String,

    @Json(name = "caption")
    val caption: String,

    @Json(name = "likes_count")
    val likesCount: Int,

    @Json(name = "comments_count")
    val commentsCount: Int,

    @Json(name = "timestamp")
    val timeStamp: Long
) {
    data class UserApiData(

        @Json(name = "id")
        val id: String,

        @Json(name = "name")
        val name: String,

        @Json(name = "image_url")
        val imageUrl: String
    ) {
        fun toDomain(): Post.UserData {
            return Post.UserData(
                id = id,
                name = name,
                imageUrl = imageUrl
            )
```

```
        }
    }

    fun toDomain(): Post {
        return Post(
            id = id,
            user = user.toDomain(),
            imageUrl = imageUrl,
            caption = caption,
            likesCount = likesCount,
            commentsCount = commentsCount,
            timeStamp = timeStamp
        )
    }
}
```

Here, we should include the fields that the response from the backend will return to our app. Note that we are using the `@Json(name = "")` annotation in the properties to specify the name of the field in the JSON that the backend will return.

Before jumping to consume the use case in `ViewModel`, we have to sort out the dependency injection for all the components we have just created. We will do so in `newsFeedModule`:

```
val newsFeedModule = module {
    single { RetrofitInstance.getNewsFeedApi() }
    single { NewsFeedRemoteDataSource(get()) }
    single<NewsFeedRepository> {
        NewsFeedRepositoryImpl(get()) }
    factory { GetTheNewsFeedUseCase(get()) }
    viewModel<NewsFeedViewModel>()
}
```

Now, it is time to integrate this use case into `NewsFeedViewModel`.

Integrating the use case into our ViewModel

For the ViewModel, we will need to create a new function to obtain the posts. We will call it `loadPosts()`:

```
    init {
        loadPosts()
    }

    private fun loadPosts() {
```

```
        viewModelScope.launch {
            val newPosts = getTheNewsFeedUseCase()
            _posts.value = newPosts
        }
    }
```

Here, we are loading the posts as soon as the app shows the view and the ViewModel is created.

The changes to the `posts` property are already being consumed by our `NewsFeed` composable, so it will update the UI when it receives any posts.

We could also add some error handling here, but as we already worked on that topic in the first project, we will leave it here.

Now, it wouldn't be realistic (and performant) to load all the existing posts initially. As we did with the messaging project, we'll need to paginate so that we can obtain the posts gradually, following the user scroll. We will see how in the next section.

Implementing pagination in the newsfeed

To implement pagination in our app, we will start by modifying the Retrofit service. Typically you're required to add parameters to your API endpoint that control the "page" of data you're requesting. For instance, we might have a `pageNumber` parameter and a `pageSize` parameter (though this will depend on the design of your backend endpoints).

First, let's adjust `NewsFeedService` so that it includes the two parameters we just mentioned:

```
interface NewsFeedService {
    @GET("/feed")
    suspend fun getNewsFeed(
        @Query("pageNumber") pageNumber: Int,
        @Query("pageSize") pageSize: Int
    ): List<PostApiData>
}
```

Now, we will need to change the signature of the data source function so that it includes those fields. In the data source, we will change the following function:

```
suspend fun getNewsFeed(pageNumber: Int, pageSize:
Int): List<PostApiData> {
    return api.getNewsFeed(pageNumber, pageSize)
}
```

In the repository, we will handle storing the current page and keeping the desired size of pages (this could also be a constant somewhere):

```
class NewsFeedRepositoryImpl(
    private val remoteDataSource:
    NewsFeedRemoteDataSource): NewsFeedRepository
{

    private var currentPage = 0
    private val pageSize = 20 // Or whatever page size we
                                         prefer

    override suspend fun getNewsFeed(): List<Post> {
        return remoteDataSource
            .getNewsFeed(currentPage, pageSize)
            .map { it.toDomain() }
            .also { currentPage++ }
    }

    fun resetPagination() {
        currentPage = 0
    }
}
```

Here, we are storing the current page so that when we call the data source, we can specify if we want the next one. We have also added a function called resetPagination() that will reset the current page so that we can start again.

Next, we are going to use resetPagination() in UseCase when the user navigates to the top and wants to get the first of the publications:

```
suspend operator fun invoke(fromTheBeginning: Boolean):
List<Post> {
    if (fromTheBeginning) {
        repository.resetPagination()
    }
    return repository.getNewsFeed()
}
```

The next step is to handle when we should load the next page and load the next posts. To do so, we'll need to modify our NewsFeed composable and NewsFeedViewModel.

First, we are going to implement the `NewsFeedViewModel` part:

```
init {
        loadInitialPosts()
    }

    private fun loadInitialPosts() {
        viewModelScope.launch {
            val newPosts = withContext(dispatcher) {
                getTheNewsFeedUseCase(fromTheBeginning =
                    true)
            }
            _posts.value = newPosts
        }
    }

    fun loadMorePosts() {
        viewModelScope.launch {
            val newPosts = withContext(dispatcher) {
                getTheNewsFeedUseCase(fromTheBeginning =
                    false)
            }
            val updatedPosts = (_posts.value +
                newPosts).takeLast(60)
            _posts.value = updatedPosts
        }
    }
```

Here, we've renamed our initial function `loadInitialPosts()` so that it indicates that it will load the first posts. Then, we created a new function called `loadMorePosts()` that will load the new page. It will add it to the existing post list.

Now, we need to make a few modifications to our `NewsFeed` composable so that it will call the ViewModel when a new page is needed. For that reason, we need to create a `LazyListState` extension that we will invoke whenever the user reaches the end of the list:

```
fun LazyListState.OnBottomReached(
    loadMore : () -> Unit
){
    val shouldLoadMore = remember {
        derivedStateOf {
            val lastItemInView =
                layoutInfo.visibleItemsInfo.lastOrNull()
                    ?: return@derivedStateOf true
```

```
                lastItemInView.index ==
                    layoutInfo.totalItemsCount - 1
        }
    }
    LaunchedEffect(shouldLoadMore){
        snapshotFlow { shouldLoadMore.value }
            .collect {
                if (it) loadMore()
            }
    }
}
```

This extension function observes the scrolling state of LazyColumn or LazyRow. When the user has scrolled to the bottom, it calls the provided loadMore function to load more items. This pattern is common in implementing "infinite scrolling" or "pagination," which is what we are currently implementing.

Now, we need to use it in our LazyColumn layout. For that, we need to remember LazyListState in the NewsFeed composable:

```
@Composable
fun NewsFeed(
    modifier: Modifier = Modifier,
    viewModel: NewsFeedViewModel = koinViewModel()
) {
    val posts = viewModel.posts.collectAsState()
    val listState = rememberLazyListState()
    LazyColumn{
        itemsIndexed(posts){ _, post ->
            PostItem(post = post)
        }
    }

    listState.OnBottomReached {
        viewModel.loadMorePosts()
    }
}
```

With this change, every time our user reaches the bottom of the list, we will call the function to load more posts and get the next page.

Now that we've finished our paging implementation, our user experience will be more performant and smoother when navigating the newsfeed.

Summary

In this chapter, we primarily focused on structuring and modularizing our Packtagram app while enhancing maintainability. Leveraging Jetpack Compose, we designed the components and screens for some of the features of the interface that we are going to be working on in the next chapters.

Additionally, this chapter delved into the intricacies of connecting the developed UI to the backend, which is pivotal for data management and operation handling. We implemented Retrofit for network operations and Moshi for JSON parsing, bridging the gap between the user interface and the data source. Moreover, we introduced the concept of paging to efficiently manage large datasets. By doing so, we ensured smoother data load, faster response times, and enhanced app performance overall, significantly improving the user's experience.

In the next chapter, we will dive into the photo functionality of our app. We will use an incredible library called CameraX and take advantage of some of its capabilities. We will also learn how to apply machine learning to our camera preview using ML Kit.

5

Creating a Photo Editor Using CameraX

In the smartphone era, taking and sharing photos has become second nature, and platforms such as Instagram have shown us how powerful a single photo can be. For apps like these, it's not just about snapping a picture; it's about enhancing and personalizing that image to tell a story. But have you ever wondered what lies behind those in-app camera buttons and filters?

Enter CameraX, Android's go-to tool for everything camera-related. This tool doesn't just make capturing photos seamless; it's also the bridge to editing and refining them. In this chapter, we'll get hands-on with CameraX, discovering how it can transform the Packtagram photography experience. We'll also design an interactive space for users to tweak and enhance their shots, adding that personal touch. And for the cherry on top? We'll dive into a bit of smart tech, teaching our app to recognize photo themes and suggest relevant hashtags.

Building on our prior work – crafting the screens and feed for our Instagram-inspired app – we're now diving deeper into the app's features. With CameraX, intuitive editing tools, and some clever features, we're set to elevate our app's photo-sharing game.

In this chapter, we will cover the following topics:

- Getting to know CameraX
- Integrating CameraX into our Packtagram app
- Adding photo-editing functionalities
- Using **machine learning** (**ML**) to categorize photos and generate hashtags

Technical requirements

As in the previous chapter, you will need to have Android Studio (or another editor of your preference) installed.

You can find the complete code that we will be using in this chapter in this book's GitHub repository: `https://github.com/PacktPublishing/Thriving-in-Android-Development-using-Kotlin/tree/main/Chapter-5`.

Getting to know CameraX

Since the inception of the Android platform, cameras have played a pivotal role in defining the feature set of smartphones. From capturing moments to enabling augmented reality experiences, the camera has evolved from a mere hardware component to a powerful tool for developers. This evolution, however, has not been without its complexities.

The evolution of camera libraries in Android

Since the first version of Android, developers interacted with the camera hardware through the Camera API; this was Android's first attempt at giving developers the power to harness the capabilities of onboard cameras.

As devices proliferated and features such as more advanced photo hardware grew, the need for a more robust API became evident. Consequently, Camera2 API was introduced in API level 21 (Lollipop). While this offered more granular control over camera capabilities and supported the expanding features of new hardware, its steep learning curve made camera development challenging for many in terms of complexity and performance overhead.

Given the intricacies of Camera2 and the variances in camera hardware across different devices, developers found it increasingly difficult to provide a consistent camera experience to end users. This fragmentation, alongside the complexity of Camera2, made it imperative for a more streamlined, developer-friendly solution.

Enter CameraX.

The importance and advantages of CameraX

CameraX is Android's modern solution for camera app development that was developed with the primary goal of simplifying the process while reducing the fragmentation between devices. Here's why it has quickly become indispensable:

- **Consistency across devices**: CameraX abstracts the differences between device-specific camera behaviors, ensuring that most features work consistently across a wide range of devices.

- **Life cycle awareness**: Gone are the days of tedious life cycle management. CameraX is integrated with Android's life cycle libraries, meaning less boilerplate code and more focus on core camera functionality.

- **Use case-based approach**: Instead of dealing with low-level tasks, developers can now focus on specific use cases, such as image preview, image capture, and image analysis. This makes development faster and less error-prone.

- **Extensions for enhanced capabilities**: With the CameraX Extensions API, developers can access device-specific features such as portrait mode, HDR, and more, further enriching the camera experience.

- **Backward compatibility**: CameraX offers compatibility with devices running Android 5.0 (API level 21) and beyond, ensuring a wider reach than Camera2.

- **Performance and quality**: CameraX provides optimized performance out of the box, delivering high-quality images and videos without the need for extra tuning.

In summary, CameraX has not only simplified camera app development but also bridged the gap that's caused by hardware discrepancies. As we delve deeper into this chapter, you'll come to appreciate the nuances and capabilities that CameraX brings to the table, setting the stage for powerful, consistent, and high-quality camera applications on Android.

Now, let's start using CameraX and configuring its dependencies in our project.

Setting up CameraX

To set up CameraX, we need to add the necessary dependencies to our version catalog file, `libs.versions.toml`, as follows:

```
[versions]
...
camerax = "1.2.1"
accompanist = "0.31.1-alpha"

[libraries]
...
cameraCore = { module = "androidx.camera:camera-core", version.ref =
"camerax" }
cameraCamera2 = { module = "androidx.camera:camera-camera2", version.
ref = "camerax" }
cameraView = { module = "androidx.camera:camera-view", version.ref =
"camerax" }
cameraExtensions = { module = "androidx.camera:camera-extensions",
version.ref = "camerax" }
accompanist = { group = "com.google.accompanist", name = "accompanist-
permissions", version.ref = "accompanist"}
```

In this code block, we are adding the dependencies that are needed to use CameraX, plus a library called Accompanist.

Accompanist is a collection of extension libraries that are designed to complement Jetpack Compose. It fills the gaps by offering utilities for specific use cases and easing the integration of Compose with other Android capabilities. The features of Accompanist include image loading integrations, useful components such as ViewPager, tools to manage system UI insets, Compose navigation enhancements, and permissions handling. To learn more and expand on this information, please refer to the official documentation: https://google.github.io/accompanist/.

In our case, we are going to use it to simplify the process of checking and asking the user for camera permissions.

Regarding the dependencies to use CameraX, we are adding the following:

- cameraCore: This dependency provides the core functionality of CameraX, including the ability to manage camera devices, configure capture sessions, and receive frames from the camera. It is the foundation for all other CameraX dependencies.

- cameraCamera2: This dependency provides the Camera2 implementation of CameraX, which is the most powerful and flexible way to access the camera on Android devices. It provides low-level access to the camera's hardware and allows for custom capture configurations and processing pipelines.

- cameraView: This dependency provides a pre-built view component that integrates with CameraX to simplify the process of displaying camera preview frames. It takes care of the layout and setup of the view so that you can focus on capturing and processing the camera data.

- cameraExtensions: This dependency provides a set of extensions for CameraX that add additional features, such as support for focus peaking, image stabilization, and panorama capture. It also includes extensions for working with ML models on camera frames.

> **Note**
> The versions in the previous code are the latest stable ones at the time of writing this book, but there will likely be new ones by the time you are reading this.

After adding these dependencies to the version catalog, we need to add them to the build.gradle. kts file of the :feature:stories module, as follows:

```
implementation(libs.cameraCore)
implementation(libs.cameraCamera2)
implementation(libs.cameraView)
implementation(libs.cameraExtensions)
implementation(libs.androidx.camera.lifecycle)
implementation(libs.accompanist)
```

Now that our project is ready to use CameraX, let's learn more about the library.

Learning about CameraX's core concepts

In this section, we'll learn about some of CameraX's most important concepts.

View life cycle

CameraX, a Jetpack support library, simplifies camera development across Android devices, and its life-cycle-aware nature seamlessly integrates with Jetpack Compose, empowering developers to create resilient and efficient camera applications. At the core of CameraX's design philosophy lies its inherent support for Android's life cycle, which eliminates the complexities of managing camera resources. CameraX automatically handles camera start, stop, and resource release based on life cycle events, streamlining the development process.

Jetpack Compose, the declarative UI toolkit for Android, is also deeply rooted in life cycle concepts. Composables inherently possess life cycle states, such as onActive and onDispose, that get triggered during their existence within the UI hierarchy. Combining the powers of CameraX and Compose offers a harmonized approach to managing the camera's life cycle within Composable UI components.

Image analysis

CameraX goes beyond just capturing images. With **image analysis**, developers can process live camera feeds in real time. This is perfect for features such as barcode scanning, face detection, or even applying live filters. Here is an example:

```
@Composable
fun CameraPreviewWithImageAnalysis() {
    val cameraProvider = rememberCameraProvider()
    val preview = remember { Preview.Builder().build() }
    val text = remember { mutableStateOf("Analyzing...") }

    val imageAnalyzer = ImageAnalysis.Builder()
        .setAnalyzer { image ->
            // Process the image data here
            text.value = "Detected image to analyze..."
        }
        .build()

    LaunchedEffect(cameraProvider) {
        val useCaseBinding = UseCaseBinding.Builder()
            .addUseCases(preview, imageAnalyzer)
            .build()
```

```
        val camera =
            cameraProvider.bindToLifecycle(useCaseBinding)
        camera.close()
    }

    Box(modifier = Modifier.fillMaxSize()) {
        Preview(preview)
        Text(text.value)
    }
}
```

The preceding code defines a composable function called `CameraPreviewWithImageAnalysis` that displays a camera preview and analyzes the live camera feed, utilizing Jetpack Compose and CameraX to achieve this.

First, the `rememberCameraProvider` function is used to retrieve the camera provider instance, which is responsible for managing the camera's life cycle and providing access to camera controls. Then, a `Preview` instance is created using `Preview.Builder` to define the camera preview surface. This preview will display the live camera feed on the screen.

After that, an `ImageAnalysis` instance is created using `ImageAnalysis.Builder` to process the live camera feed. The `setAnalyzer` method is used to specify an analyzer function that will be called whenever a new image frame is available.

A `LaunchedEffect` block is used to start a coroutine that binds the camera preview and image analyzer to the camera's life cycle. The `bindToLifecycle` method is used to connect the use cases to the camera's life cycle, ensuring that they start and stop automatically when the app starts and stops.

A `mutableStateOf` variable text is used to store the current state of the analysis. The text variable is updated within the analyzer function to reflect the results of the image analysis.

Finally, the `Box` composable is used to lay out the camera preview and the text. The `fillMaxSize` modifier is used to make `Box` occupy the entire screen. The `Preview` composable is placed inside `Box` to display the camera preview. The `Text` composable is also placed inside `Box` to display the current state of the analysis.

This is a basic example of how to apply image analysis, but there are some already existing image analyzers, such as `BarcodeScanner`. The following code is built upon the previous one, adding this analyzer:

```
@Composable
fun BarcodeScannerPreview() {
    val cameraProvider = rememberCameraProvider()
    val preview = remember { Preview.Builder().build() }
    val barcodeText = remember { mutableStateOf("") }
```

```
    val barcodeScanner = BarcodeScanner.Builder()
        .setBarcodeFormats(BarcodeScannerOptions.
            BarcodeFormat.ALL_FORMATS)
        .build()

    LaunchedEffect(cameraProvider) {
        val imageAnalyzer = ImageAnalysis.Builder()
            .setAnalyzer { image ->
                val rotation =
                    image.imageInfo.rotationDegrees
                val imageProxy =
                    InputImage.fromMediaImage(image.image,
                        rotation)

                barcodeScanner.processImage(imageProxy)
                    .addOnSuccessListener { barcodes ->
                        if (barcodes.isNotEmpty()) {
                            val barcode = barcodes[0]
                            barcodeText.value =
                                barcode.displayValue
                        } else {
                            barcodeText.value = "No barcode
                                detected"
                        }
                    }
                    .addOnFailureListener { e ->
                        barcodeText.value = "Barcode
                            scanning failed: ${e.message}"
                    }
            }
            .build()

        val useCaseBinding = UseCaseBinding.Builder()
            .addUseCases(preview, imageAnalyzer)
            .build()

        val camera =
            cameraProvider.bindToLifecycle(useCaseBinding)
        camera.close()
    }

    Box(modifier = Modifier.fillMaxSize()) {
        Preview(preview)
```

```
        Text(barcodeText.value)
    }
}
```

Similar to the previous example, this code defines a composable function called `BarcodeScannerPreview` that displays a camera preview and analyzes the live camera feed for barcodes. However, this code specifically focuses on barcode scanning and utilizes the ML Kit `BarcodeScanner` library to achieve this functionality.

First, the `rememberCameraProvider` and `Preview` functions are used in the same way as they were in the previous example to retrieve the camera provider instance and create a preview instance for displaying the live camera feed.

Then, a `BarcodeScanner` instance is created using `BarcodeScanner.Builder`, specifying the barcode formats to be detected. In this case, all barcode formats are specified using `BarcodeScannerOptions.BarcodeFormat.ALL_FORMATS`.

Following this, an `ImageAnalysis` instance is created using `ImageAnalysis.Builder`, and the analyzer function is defined to process each image frame. First, the analyzer function retrieves the image rotation from the `imageInfo` object. Then, it converts the `ImageProxy` instance into an `InputImage` format that's compatible with ML Kit's `BarcodeScanner`.

The `BarcodeScanner.processImage` method is called on the `InputImage` instance to detect barcodes. Here, `OnSuccessListener` is used to handle the successful barcode detection, while `OnFailureListener` is used to handle any errors that occur during barcode scanning.

If barcodes are detected, the `displayValue` value of the first barcode is extracted and stored in the `barcodeText` mutable state variable. This variable is used to update the text field with the detected barcode information.

With this, we have created our first image analyzer to get barcode information. Let's move on to the next feature: `CameraSelector`.

CameraSelector

When dealing with cameras, it's not always about just one camera – many modern devices come with multiple camera lenses. This is where `CameraSelector` comes to the rescue, allowing developers to programmatically choose between, say, the front or rear camera. Whether you're building a selfie app or a more standard photo application, `CameraSelector` ensures consistent behavior across the board. Let's see how we can allow a user to select which camera they want to use:

```
@Composable
fun CameraSelectorExample() {
    val cameraProvider = rememberCameraProvider()
    val preview = remember { Preview.Builder().build() }
    val isUsingFrontCamera = remember {
```

```
            mutableStateOf(true) }
    val cameraSelector = remember {
        if (isUsingFrontCamera.value) {
            CameraSelector.DEFAULT_FRONT_CAMERA
        } else {
            CameraSelector.DEFAULT_BACK_CAMERA
        }
    }

    val imageAnalyzer = ImageAnalysis.Builder()
        .setAnalyzer { image ->
            // Process the image data here
        }
        .build()

    LaunchedEffect(cameraProvider) {
        val useCaseBinding = UseCaseBinding.Builder()
            .addUseCases(preview, imageAnalyzer)
            .build()

        val camera =
            cameraProvider.bindToLifecycle(useCaseBinding)
        camera.close()
    }

    Box(modifier = Modifier.fillMaxSize()) {
        Preview(preview)
        Column {
            Button(onClick = {
                isUsingFrontCamera.value =
                    !isUsingFrontCamera.value
            }) {
                Text("Switch Camera")
            }
        }
    }
}
```

The preceding code will display a camera preview and a button. Clicking the button will switch between the front and rear cameras. The isUsingFrontCamera mutable state variable is used to keep track of which camera is currently being used. Then, cameraSelector is updated whenever the isUsingFrontCamera variable changes. The camera preview is automatically updated to reflect the new camera selection.

It's also possible to provide your users with more control over the camera functionality. So, let's talk about `CameraControls`.

CameraControls

A comprehensive camera experience isn't just about capturing or analyzing an image. It's also about control. With `CameraControls`, developers gain access to an array of functions that allow them to manipulate the camera feed. From zooming into a subject and adjusting focus for that crystal-clear shot to toggling the torch for those night-time snaps, `CameraControls` ensures users always get the perfect shot.

Here is an example of how to use `CameraControls` to zoom, adjust focus, and toggle the torch, starting with the first part of the code:

```
@Composable
fun CameraControlsExample() {
    val cameraProvider = rememberCameraProvider()
    val preview = remember { Preview.Builder().build() }
    val zoomLevel = remember { mutableStateOf(1.0f) }
    val focusPoint = remember { mutableStateOf(0.5f, 0.5f) }
    val isTorchEnabled = remember { mutableStateOf(false) }

    val imageAnalyzer = ImageAnalysis.Builder()
        .setAnalyzer { image ->
            // Process the image data here
        }
        .build()
```

In the preceding code, we are defining the `rememberCameraProvider` function, which is used to retrieve the camera provider instance. It manages the camera's life cycle and provides access to camera controls. Then, `Preview.Builder()` is used to create a `Preview` instance, which defines the surface on which the live camera feed will be displayed.

Three `mutableStateOf` variables are used to store the state of the zoom level, focus point, and torch status:

- `zoomLevel`: This stores the current zoom level, ranging from 1.0f (no zoom) to 5.0f (maximum zoom)

- `focusPoint`: This stores the current focus point, represented as a pair of coordinates (x, y) within the preview frame

- `isTorchEnabled`: This stores the current torch status, indicating whether the torch is enabled or disabled

Let's continue with the next part of the code:

```
LaunchedEffect(cameraProvider) {
    val cameraControl =
        cameraProvider.getCameraControl(preview)

    cameraControl.setZoomRatio(zoomLevel.value)
    cameraControl.setFocusPoint(focusPoint.value)
    cameraControl.enableTorch(isTorchEnabled.value)

    val useCaseBinding = UseCaseBinding.Builder()
        .addUseCases(preview, imageAnalyzer)
        .build()

    val camera =
        cameraProvider.bindToLifecycle(useCaseBinding)
    camera.close()
}
```

Here, the `cameraControl.getCameraControl(preview)` method retrieves the `CameraControl` instance associated with the preview. This instance provides access to various camera controls:

- `cameraControl.setZoomRatio(zoomLevel.value)`: This control sets the zoom level using the value stored in the `zoomLevel` variable
- `cameraControl.setFocusPoint(focusPoint.value)`: This control sets the focus point using the coordinates stored in the `focusPoint` variable
- `cameraControl.enableTorch(isTorchEnabled.value)`: This control enables or disables the torch based on the value stored in the `isTorchEnabled` variable

Now, let's move on to the last chunk of code:

```
Box(modifier = Modifier.fillMaxSize()) {
    Preview(preview)
    Column {
        Slider(
            value = zoomLevel.value,
            onValueChange = { zoomLevel.value = it },
            valueRange = 1.0f..5.0f,
            steps = 10
        ) {
            Text("Zoom")
        }
```

```
Button(onClick = {
    val newFocusPoint = if (focusPoint.value ==
    0.5f) {
        0.1f to 0.1f
    } else {
        0.5f to 0.5f
    }
    focusPoint.value = newFocusPoint
    cameraControl.setFocusPoint(newFocusPoint)
}) {
    Text("Adjust Focus")
}

Button(onClick = {
    isTorchEnabled.value =
        !isTorchEnabled.value
    cameraControl.enableTorch(
        isTorchEnabled.value)
}) {
    Text("Toggle Torch")
}
        }
    }
}
```

In this last code block, the controls are configured and used within the Column layout:

- A Slider component is used to adjust the zoom level. The valueRange property defines the range of zoom levels (1.0f to 5.0f), and the onValueChange callback updates the zoomLevel variable with the selected zoom level.

- A Button component triggers a change in the focus point. When clicked, it updates the focusPoint variable between two predefined locations (0.5f to 0.5f and 0.1f to 0.1f).

- Another Button component toggles the torch status. When clicked, it updates the isTorchEnabled variable and calls cameraControl.enableTorch to set the torch accordingly.

In conclusion, CameraX provides a robust and versatile platform for developing high-quality camera applications on Android. It offers a simplified API, streamlined use cases, and a comprehensive set of features, making it an ideal choice for building modern camera-centric apps. Now, we are ready to use it in our app.

Integrating CameraX into our Packtagram app

Now that we know more about CameraX, let's start integrating it into our app. First, we will need to deal with the camera permissions, providing a way for the user to accept them. Then, we will set up our camera preview and add the camera capture functionality to our code.

Setting up the permissions checker with Accompanist

There are several ways to check if the camera permissions have been granted, and if not, to request them: we could do this manually or use a library. In this case, we will use the Accompanist library, as we introduced at the beginning of this chapter.

Before requesting any permission at runtime, it's fundamental to declare the same permissions in the app's `AndroidManifest.xml` file. This declaration informs the Android operating system of the app's intentions. For the camera permission, you need to add the following line within the `<manifest>` tag:

```
<uses-permission android:name="android.permission.CAMERA" />
```

While the manifest informs the system of the app's needs, runtime permissions are about seeking the user's explicit consent. Ensure you always have both in place when accessing protected features or user data.

Now, let's go into the permissions checker code. Our aim here is to create a reusable composable function that can handle the camera permission elegantly. It should be able to request the permission, handle user decisions, and, if necessary, explain why the app needs this permission.

First, we need to import the required libraries:

```
import com.google.accompanist.permissions.ExperimentalPermissionsApi
import com.google.accompanist.permissions.PermissionState
import com.google.accompanist.permissions.rememberPermissionState

@OptIn(ExperimentalPermissionsApi::class)
@Composable
fun CameraPermissionRequester(onPermissionGranted: () -> Unit) {
    // ... code ...
}
```

Here, the `@OptIn` annotation indicates that we're using an experimental API from the Accompanist permissions library.

Now, inside `CameraPermissionRequester`, we need to add the following:

```
val cameraPermissionState = rememberPermissionState(Manifest.
permission.CAMERA)
```

Here, `rememberPermissionState` is a helper function that recalls the current state of the camera permission. It provides information such as whether the permission is granted, if we've already asked the user, or if we should show a rationale.

With the permission state in hand, we can create a UI flow that responds to this state:

- **Permission granted**: If permission is already granted, the user can directly proceed to use the camera.

- **Show rationale**: Sometimes, if a user denies a certain permission, it's helpful to explain why the app needs that permission. This is where the rationale comes into play.

- **Permission not yet requested**: If the app hasn't asked for the permission yet, we want to provide a button to initiate the request.

- **Permission denied without rationale**: In some cases, users deny permissions and opt not to be asked again. It's good practice to guide them to the app settings if they change their mind.

Let's learn how to handle all these possible flows. First, we will create a new composable called `CameraPermissionRequester`. The `onPermissionGranted` callback is provided to handle the scenario when the camera permission has been granted:

```
@OptIn(ExperimentalPermissionsApi::class)
@Composable
fun CameraPermissionRequester(onPermissionGranted:
@Composable () -> Unit) {
```

Next, we will retrieve `cameraPermissionState`:

```
    // Camera permission state
    val cameraPermissionState = rememberPermissionState(
        android.Manifest.permission.CAMERA
    )
```

The `rememberPermissionState(permission)` function retrieves the current state of the specified permission. In this case, we're checking the status of the CAMERA permission, which is necessary for accessing the device's camera. The result is stored in the `cameraPermissionState` variable.

Now, let's evaluate the different values it could have:

```
        if (cameraPermissionState.status.isGranted) {
            OnPermissionGranted.invoke()
```

In the previous code block, we are starting to evaluate the `status.isGranted` property of the `cameraPermissionState` object, which indicates whether the permission has been granted. If it's true, it means the permission is available, and we can call the `onPermissionGranted` callback to proceed with using the camera features.

If it is false, this means that the permission hasn't been granted, so we will have to communicate that situation to the user and give them the option to grant it:

```
        } else {
                Surface(
                    modifier = Modifier
                        .fillMaxWidth()
                        .padding(16.dp)
                        .padding(top = 24.dp),
                    color =
                      MaterialTheme.colorScheme.background,
          ) {
            Column(
                modifier = Modifier.padding(16.dp),
                verticalArrangement =
                    Arrangement.spacedBy(12.dp),
                horizontalAlignment =
                    Alignment.CenterHorizontally
            ) {
                val textToShow = if
                (cameraPermissionState.shouldShowRationale)
                {
                    "The camera and record audio are
                    important for this app. Please grant
                    the permissions."
                } else {
                    "Camera permission is required for this
                    feature to be available. Please grant
                    the permission."
                }

                Text(
                    text = textToShow,
                    style =
                    MaterialTheme.typography.bodyLarge.copy
                    (
                        fontSize = 16.sp,
                        fontWeight = FontWeight.Medium
                    ),
```

```
            color =
            MaterialTheme.colorScheme.onBackground
        )

        Button(
            onClick = { cameraPermissionState
                .launchMultiplePermissionRequest()
                },
            colors = ButtonDefaults.buttonColors(
                containerColor =
                MaterialTheme.colorScheme.primary,
                contentColor =
                MaterialTheme.colorScheme.onPrimary
            ),
            contentPadding = PaddingValues(12.dp)
        ) {
            Text("Request Permission",
                fontSize = 14.sp,
                    fontWeight = FontWeight.Bold)
        }
        }
        }
        }
    }
}
```

In the previous code block, we're displaying a message explaining the need for the permission and providing a Button component to initiate the permission request process. The onClick handler of the button triggers the launchPermissionRequest() method of the cameraPermissionState object, which prompts the user to grant the permission.

The launchPermissionRequest() method opens a system dialogue requesting the user to grant the CAMERA permission. The dialogue provides clear instructions and explains the reasons why the permission is required.

If we run this code now, we should see the two screens. First, we will see our screen with the message to request the permissions (left). Once we click **Request permission**, we will see the system prompt to accept the permission (right):

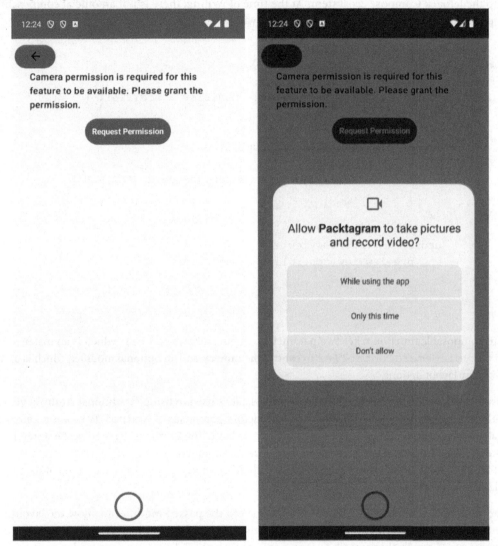

Figure 5.1: Camera permission requested in our app (left) and system
prompt to grant capture and record permissions (right)

Once the permissions have been granted, `CameraPreview` can start working. We will use the `onPermissionGranted` callback to show it.

Creating our own CameraPreview

The following `CameraPreview` composable function is designed to elegantly integrate CameraX into the Jetpack Compose ecosystem. At the time of writing, there is not an official composable implementation for the CameraX preview, so we will use `AndroidView`:

```
@Composable
@Composable
fun CameraPreview(cameraController:
LifecycleCameraController, modifier: Modifier = Modifier) {
    AndroidView(
        factory = { context ->
            PreviewView(context).apply {
                implementationMode =
                    PreviewView.ImplementationMode.COMPATIBLE
            }
        },
        modifier = modifier,
        update = { previewView ->
            previewView.controller = cameraController
        }
    )
}
```

This composable function takes two parameters: `cameraController`, which is an instance of `LifecycleCameraController` to control the camera, and an optional modifier, which is used to specify layout options.

Inside the function, an `AndroidView` composable is used to bridge traditional Android views with the Jetpack Compose UI framework. The factory parameter of `AndroidView` is a Lambda that provides context and returns a `PreviewView` object. The `PreviewView` object is a standard Android view that's used to display the camera feed. It is configured with `implementationMode` set to COMPATIBLE to ensure compatibility with different devices and scenarios (one of the most relevant CameraX features).

The modifier parameter of `AndroidView` is set to the passed modifier to allow the layout to be customized. The `update` parameter is another Lambda that's called to perform updates on `PreviewView`. In this case, it assigns `cameraController` to the controller property of `PreviewView`, linking the camera preview to `LifecycleCameraController`.

Now, let's integrate the preview into our existing code. In the `StoryContent` composable, we will include the following code, where we expect to have the camera image:

```
CameraPermissionRequester {
    Box(contentAlignment = Alignment.BottomCenter,
    modifier = Modifier.fillMaxSize()) {
        CameraPreview(
            cameraController = cameraController,
            modifier = Modifier.fillMaxSize()
        )
    }
}
```

With that, we should be ready to use the camera! At this point, we've learned how to integrate `CameraPreview`, check the permissions, and show the camera image stream. Now, let's add the possibility of saving the photos!

Adding photo-saving functionality

The capture functionality is a staple for every app using the camera. We will need to add some logic to our existing code to handle the capture storage. Let's start with a use case (where we are going to put our domain logic) to store the captured image.

Creating the SaveCaptureUseCase

The primary responsibility of `SaveCaptureUseCase` will be to take a bitmap object (the format we will use for our photos) and save it as an image file in the device's gallery. Additionally, it will handle the different approaches based on the Android version as how media storage is accessed is different, depending on the version.

For example, we will need to obtain the URI (the route in the storage of the device) where we are going to store the image. If the user has a version of Android more recent than 9.0, the location will be different than in the previous versions. The following code block shows what the check to obtain the corresponding route will look like:

```
if (Build.VERSION.SDK_INT >= Build.VERSION_CODES.Q) {
        MediaStore.Images.Media.getContentUri(
            MediaStore.VOLUME_EXTERNAL_PRIMARY)
    } else {
        MediaStore.Images.Media.EXTERNAL_CONTENT_URI
    }
}
```

Here, we are evaluating if the version is major or equal to Android 9.0 and obtaining the URI using `MediaStore.Images.Media.getContentUri(MediaStore.VOLUME_EXTERNAL_ PRIMARY)`. If the version doesn't meet those requirements, we obtain the URI from `MediaStore. Images.Media.EXTERNAL_CONTENT_URI`. We should take all these different cases into account so that our use case handles the different Android versions properly.

Now, let's create the `SaveCaptureUse` class:

```
class SaveCaptureUseCase(private val context: Context) {


}
```

Then, we can create the main function of this use case, `save()`, which will take care of saving the capture:

```
suspend fun save(capturePhotoBitmap: Bitmap):
Result<Uri> = withContext(Dispatchers.IO) {
    val resolver: ContentResolver =
        context.applicationContext.contentResolver
    val imageCollection = getImageCollectionUri()
    val nowTimestamp = System.currentTimeMillis()
    val imageContentValues =
        createContentValues(nowTimestamp)

    val imageMediaStoreUri: Uri? =
        resolver.insert(imageCollection,
            imageContentValues)

    return@withContext imageMediaStoreUri?.let { uri ->
        saveBitmapToUri(resolver, uri,
            capturePhotoBitmap, imageContentValues)
    } ?: Result.failure(Exception("Couldn't create file
                            for gallery"))
}
```

In this code block, we are starting to create the save function. As it is marked as a `suspend` function, the save function is designed to be called within a coroutine context. It uses `withContext(Dispatchers. IO)` to ensure that all I/O operations are performed on a background thread. This is crucial for maintaining UI responsiveness as I/O operations can be time-consuming.

Next, we are declaring `ContextResolver`. This resolver is used to interact with `MediaStore`, which is Android's central repository for media files.

Then, the function will call `getImageCollectionUri()`, a helper function that provides the appropriate URI for `MediaStore` based on the Android version. This URI is where the image will be saved. We will implement this function next.

After, the current system time (`nowTimestamp`) is captured, and `createContentValues(nowTimestamp)` is invoked to prepare the metadata for the image. This metadata, which is stored in a `ContentValues` object, includes details such as the image's display name, `MIME` type, and timestamps.

The function then attempts to insert a new record into `MediaStore` using the resolved URI and the prepared metadata. The `insert` method returns a URI that points to the newly created record. If this operation is successful, a non-null URI is returned, representing the location of the new image record in `MediaStore`.

Finally, if the URI is not null, the `saveBitmapToUri` function is called with the resolver, the URI, the bitmap to be saved, and the image metadata. This function handles the actual process of writing the bitmap data to the location pointed to by the URI. We will implement it soon.

Regarding error handling, our `save` function uses Kotlin's `Result` class for structured error handling. If the insertion into the MediaStore is successful and the bitmap is saved correctly, the function returns `Result.success(Unit)`. If there is a failure at any point (for example, the URI is null, indicating that the insertion failed), the function returns `Result.failure`, encapsulating an exception with an appropriate error message.

Now, let's implement the `getImageCollectionUri()` function, which will return the correct URI based on the Android version:

```
private fun getImageCollectionUri(): Uri =
    if (Build.VERSION.SDK_INT >= Build.VERSION_CODES.Q)
    {
        MediaStore.Images.Media.getContentUri(
            MediaStore.VOLUME_EXTERNAL_PRIMARY)
    } else {
        MediaStore.Images.Media.EXTERNAL_CONTENT_URI
    }
```

Then, we can create the `createContentValues` function:

```
private fun createContentValues(timestamp: Long):
ContentValues = ContentValues().apply {
    put(MediaStore.Images.Media.DISPLAY_NAME,
        "$FILE_NAME_PREFIX${System.currentTimeMillis()}
            .jpg")
    put(MediaStore.Images.Media.MIME_TYPE, "image/jpg")
    if (Build.VERSION.SDK_INT >= Build.VERSION_CODES.Q)
    {
```

```
        put(MediaStore.MediaColumns.DATE_TAKEN,
            timestamp)
        put(MediaStore.MediaColumns.RELATIVE_PATH,
            "${Environment.DIRECTORY_DCIM}/Packtagram")
        put(MediaStore.MediaColumns.IS_PENDING, 1)
    }
    if (Build.VERSION.SDK_INT >= Build.VERSION_CODES.R)
    {
        put(MediaStore.Images.Media.DATE_ADDED,
            timestamp)
        put(MediaStore.Images.Media.DATE_MODIFIED,
            timestamp)
        put(MediaStore.Images.Media.AUTHOR,
            AUTHOR_NAME)
        put(MediaStore.Images.Media.DESCRIPTION,
            DESCRIPTION)
    }
}
```

The `createContentValues` function is designed to prepare the metadata for an image file before it is saved to the device's gallery via `MediaStore`. This method is pivotal in ensuring that the saved image has the correct and necessary information associated with it. So, let's break down its functionality:

- First, the function initiates a `ContentValues` object. Here, `ContentValues` is a key-value pair that's used in Android to store a set of values that `ContentResolver` can process. It is commonly used for passing data to Android's content providers

- Next, the display name of the image in `MediaStore` is set. We will use a predefined `FILE_NAME_PREFIX` constant and append the current timestamp to it, followed by the `.jpg` extension, ensuring each saved image has a unique name.

- Then, the `MIME` type of the image is set to `image/jpg`. This information is used by `MediaStore` and other apps to understand the file format of the image.

- We have to store it differently, depending on the Android version of the device:

  - For Android Q (API Level 29) and above, we must do the following:

    - We need to add the timestamp of when the image is being stored and use the `MediaStore.MediaColumns.DATE_TAKEN` key.

    - We must use the `createContentValues` function to specify a relative path for the image file, pointing to a directory within the **Digital Camera Images (DCIM)** folder using `put(MediaStore.MediaColumns.RELATIVE_PATH, "${Environment.DIRECTORY_DCIM}/Packtagram")`. This helps in organizing the saved images in a specific subdirectory, making them easier to locate.

- We need to update the `ContentValues` instance and set `IS_PENDING` to 1 (true), indicating that file creation is in progress. This is a way to inform the system and other apps that the file is not yet fully written and should not be accessed until the status is reverted.

- For Android R (API Level 30) and above, our function should add more metadata, including the date added, date modified, author name, and a description. This is part of the enhanced metadata management in newer Android versions, allowing for more detailed information to be stored with media files.

Now that we are handling the URI that's needed to store the file, as well as the values and metadata needed to create the file, let's proceed to do the saving itself. To do so, we will create a new private function called `saveBitmapToUri`, as follows:

```
private fun saveBitmapToUri(
    resolver: ContentResolver,
    uri: Uri,
    bitmap: Bitmap,
    contentValues: ContentValues
): Result<Uri> = kotlin.runCatching {
    resolver.openOutputStream(uri).use { outputStream ->
        checkNotNull(outputStream) { "Couldn't create
            file for gallery, MediaStore output stream
                is null»}`
        bitmap.compress(Bitmap.CompressFormat.JPEG,
            IMAGE_QUALITY, outputStream)
    }
```

The function starts by attempting to open `OutputStream` for the given URI. This stream is where the bitmap data will be written. Here, `Resolver.openOutputStream(uri)` is used to obtain the stream, and the `use` block ensures that this stream is closed properly after its operations, following the best practices in resource management.

Inside the `use` block, the function checks if `outputStream` is not `null`, throwing an exception with a descriptive message if it is. If the stream is valid, the bitmap is compressed and written to this stream. The compression format is set to JPEG, and the quality is determined by the `IMAGE_QUALITY` constant.

Now, if the image is saved successfully, we have to update and return the result. If something has failed, we have to return an error:

```
if (Build.VERSION.SDK_INT >= Build.VERSION_CODES.Q)
{
    contentValues.clear()
    contentValues.put(
        MediaStore.MediaColumns.IS_PENDING, 0)
    resolver.update(uri, contentValues, null, null)
```

```
        }

        return Result.success(Unit)
    }.getOrElse { exception ->
        exception.message?.let(::println)
        resolver.delete(uri, null, null)
        return Result.failure(exception)
    }
}
```

For devices running Android Q (API level 29) or higher, after the image is saved, the function updates the MediaStore entry to indicate that the image is no longer pending. This is done by clearing the existing contentValues, setting IS_PENDING to 0 (false), and then updating the MediaStore entry with these new values. This step is crucial for making the image available to the user and other applications.

The entire operation is wrapped in a runCatching block, which is a Kotlin construct that's used for simplified exception handling. This block captures any exceptions that occur during the OutputStream operation or MediaStore update. If an exception occurs, it is logged, and the function attempts to delete the possibly corrupted or incomplete file from MediaStore. This cleanup is essential to prevent cluttering the storage with unusable files.

The function returns Result<Uri>, indicating the success or failure of the operation. In case of success, Result.success(uri) is returned. In case of an exception, Result.failure(exception) is returned, encapsulating the exception details.

The only thing left will be to add the parameters that will be used during the development of these classes. For simplicity, we will add them as constants, but they could also be provided to the class:

```
companion object {
    private const val IMAGE_QUALITY = 100
    private const val FILE_NAME_PREFIX = "YourImageName"
    private const val AUTHOR_NAME = "Your Name"
    private const val DESCRIPTION = "Your description"
}
```

The next step is to integrate this use case in StoryEditorViewModel.

Integrating SaveCaptureUseCase in StoryEditorViewModel

Here, we need to create a new property and function in `StoryEditorViewModel` to store the captured image:

```
class StoryEditorViewModel(
    private val saveCaptureUseCase: SaveCaptureUseCase
): ViewModel() {

    private val _isEditing = MutableStateFlow(false)
    val isEditing: StateFlow<Boolean> = _isEditing

    private val _imageCaptured: MutableStateFlow<Uri> =
        MutableStateFlow(Uri.EMPTY)
    val imageCaptured: StateFlow<Uri> = _imageCaptured

    fun storePhotoInGallery(bitmap: Bitmap) {
        viewModelScope.launch {
            val imageUri =
                saveCaptureUseCase.save(bitmap).getOrNull()
            if (imageUri != null) {
                _imageCaptured.value = imageUri
                _isEditing.value = true
            }
        }
    }
}
```

In this `storePhotoInGallery` function, we are just launching a coroutine to call the `saveCaptureUseCase.save` method. Then, once we've obtained the URI, we check if it is not `null` and update the `imageCaptured` property.

Finally, we are ready to add this functionality to the UI.

Adding the capture functionality to StoryContent

To add the capture functionality to `StoryContent`, we need to add a Lambda to the `StoryContent` composable so that whenever we use `StoryContent`, capture handling will be delegated. For example, in our case, we will call the already implemented `storePhotoInGallery` function from `StoryEditorViewModel`:

```
@Composable
fun StoryContent(
    isEditing: Boolean = false,
    onImageCaptured: (Bitmap) -> Any,
```

```
        modifier: Modifier = Modifier,
) { ... }
```

Next, let's integrate the code that's needed to take the capture from our camera:

```
fun capturePhoto(
        context: Context,
        cameraController: LifecycleCameraController,
        onPhotoCaptured: (Bitmap) -> Unit,
        onError: (Exception) -> Unit
    ) {
```

The parameters we are using in the previous code block are as follows:

- `context`: The Android context that we will use to obtain `MainExecutor`.
- `cameraController`: A `LifecycleCameraController` object from `CameraX`, which controls the camera's life cycle and operations.
- `onPhotoCaptured`: The callback function that will be invoked when a photo is successfully captured and processed. It accepts a `Bitmap` as its parameter.
- `onError`: A callback function to handle any errors that occur during the photo capture process.

Let's continue by defining the necessary properties:

```
val mainExecutor: Executor =
ContextCompat.getMainExecutor(context)
```

Here, we will retrieve `MainExecutor`. This executor is used to run tasks on the Android main thread, which is essential for UI updates and certain CameraX operations. It is needed for `CameraController`.

Next, we will execute the take picture action:

```
        cameraController.takePicture(mainExecutor,
        @ExperimentalGetImage object :
        ImageCapture.OnImageCapturedCallback() {
            override fun onCaptureSuccess(image:
            ImageProxy) {
                try {
                    CoroutineScope(Dispatchers.IO).launch {
                        val correctedBitmap: Bitmap? =
                            image
                                ?.image
                                ?.toBitmap()
                                ?.rotateBitmap(image
                                    .imageInfo
```

```
                            .rotationDegrees)

                    correctedBitmap?.let {
                        withContext(Dispatchers.Main) {
                            onPhotoCaptured(
                                correctedBitmap)
                        }
                    }

                    image.close()
                }
            } catch (e: Exception) {
                onError(e)
            } finally {
                image.close()
            }
        }

        override fun onError(exception:
        ImageCaptureException) {
            Log.e("CameraContent", "Error capturing
                image", exception)
            onError(exception)
        }
    })
}
```

Here, we call the `cameraController.takePicture` method. We will need to provide it with the executor and an `ImageCapture.OnImageCapturedCallback` class. This class provides callback methods for when an image is successfully captured or when an error occurs.

In the case of success, we will switch to the **I/O dispatcher** so that we can process the ImageProxy transformation into a bitmap in the background. Once it's been transformed, we call the onPhotoCaptured Lambda from the main dispatcher. Alternatively, if there is any error, we will receive them via the `onError(exception: ImageCaptureException)` callback. Then, we will pass the error to the `onError` callback function, which we received as the parameter of the `capturePhoto()` function.

Now, let's link the capture functionality with our UI. We already have a button for doing the capture in our `StoryContent` composable, `OutlinedButton`, so let's see how we can call this capture function from it:

```
OutlinedButton(
            onClick = { capturePhoto(
                context = localContext,
                cameraController =
                    cameraController,
                onPhotoCaptured = {
                    onImageCaptured(it) },
                onError = { /* Show error */ }
                )
            },
            modifier = Modifier.size(50.dp),
            shape = CircleShape,
            border = BorderStroke(4.dp,
                MaterialTheme.colorScheme.primary),
            contentPadding = PaddingValues(0.dp),
            colors =
                ButtonDefaults.outlinedButtonColors
                    (contentColor =
                        MaterialTheme.colorScheme
                            .primary)
    ) {
    }
```

As we can see, we are calling the `capturePhoto` function from the `onClick` button.

With this, we are ready to capture our photos:

Figure 5.2: Image preview with the capture button

With that, we have created a use case so that we can store our photos and link the functionality with our already existing UI. Our users can also capture and store their photos. Next, let's see if we can enable them so that we can edit some aspects of them.

Adding photo-editing functionalities

There are multiple operations that we can enable for the user to edit and modify their images: we can allow them to crop, resize, and rotate the image, as well as adjust the brightness and contrast, apply filters, or add text overlays.

As part of this chapter, we are going to implement two operations: a black-and-white filter and a text overlay.

Adding filters

Creating filters over an existing image is as easy as modifying the values of the bitmap that contains the image. There are several well-known filters, such as sepia, vintage, and black and white. As an example, we are going to implement the black and white filter, like so:

```
@Composable
fun BlackAndWhiteFilter(
    imageUri: Uri,
    modifier: Modifier = Modifier
) {
    var isBlackAndWhiteEnabled by remember {
    mutableStateOf(false) }
    val localContext = LocalContext.current

    Box(modifier = modifier.fillMaxSize()) {
        Canvas(modifier = Modifier.fillMaxSize()) {
            getBitmapFromUri(localContext, imageUri)?.let {
                val imageBitMap = it.asImageBitmap()

                val colorFilter = if
                (isBlackAndWhiteEnabled) {
                    val colorMatrix = ColorMatrix().apply {
                        setToSaturation(0f) }
                    ColorFilter.colorMatrix(colorMatrix)
                } else {
                    null
                }
                val (offsetX, offsetY) =
                    getCanvasImageOffset(imageBitMap)
                val scaleFactor =
                    getCanvasImageScale(imageBitMap)

                with(drawContext.canvas) {
                    save()
                    translate(offsetX, offsetY)
                    scale(scaleFactor, scaleFactor)
                    drawImage(
                        image = imageBitMap,
                        topLeft =
```

```
                        androidx.compose.ui.geometry
                            .Offset.Zero,
                    colorFilter = colorFilter
                )
                restore()
            }
        }
    }

    Button(
        onClick = { isBlackAndWhiteEnabled =
            !isBlackAndWhiteEnabled },
        modifier = Modifier.padding(16.dp)
    ) {
        Text("Apply Black and White Filter")
    }
    }
}
```

This function starts by accepting imageUri, which is the URI representing the image to be displayed, and an optional modifier parameter to customize the layout.

Within the function, a state variable called isBlackAndWhiteEnabled is declared using remember and mutableStateOf, which tracks whether the black-and-white filter is applied. Here, LocalContext.current provides the context needed to load the image from the URI.

A Box composable is used to contain the entire layout, ensuring that the content fills the available space. Inside Box, a Canvas composable is used to draw the image. The Canvas modifier is set to fill the available size.

The Canvas composable uses the getBitmapFromUri function to load the image as a Bitmap, which is then converted into ImageBitmap using the asImageBitmap extension function. If the isBlackAndWhiteEnabled state is true, a ColorMatrix value with zero saturation is applied to create a black-and-white ColorFilter. Otherwise, no color filter is applied.

The getCanvasImageOffset and getCanvasImageScale functions are used to calculate the offset and scale factor needed to center and scale the image within the canvas. The with(drawContext. canvas) block is used to draw the image. Within this block, save and restore are called to save and restore the canvas state, ensuring that transformations do not affect subsequent drawing operations. The translate function applies the calculated offsets, and the scale function applies the scale factor, to fill the entire Canvas with the image. Finally, the drawImage function draws the image on the canvas with the optional color filter.

Below `Canvas`, a `Button` composable is placed within `Box`. This button is used to toggle the `isBlackAndWhiteEnabled` state when clicked. The button's `onClick` Lambda updates the state variable, and the button's text is set to **Apply Black and White Filter**. The modifier parameter for the button includes padding to ensure it is not placed at the edge of the screen.

Now that we have built our first filter, let's learn how to implement text overlays.

Adding a text overlay

Adding a text overlay is a typical image editing functionality that allows us to tag other people, add a hashtag to an image, or add an accompanying written message. Let's see how we can offer our users this functionality.

First, we are going to create a composable that contains the state of the `Text` and `Image` components. This state will update as the user updates the text. Here's the code:

```
@Composable
fun ImageWithTextOverlay(capturedBitmap: Bitmap) {
    var textOverlay = remember { mutableStateOf("Add your
        text here") }
    var showTextField = remember { mutableStateOf(false) }

    Box(modifier = Modifier.fillMaxSize()) {
        Image(
            bitmap = capturedBitmap.asImageBitmap(),
            contentDescription = "Captured Image",
            modifier = Modifier.matchParentSize()
        )

        if (showTextField) {
            TextField(
                value = textOverlay,
                onValueChange = { textOverlay = it },
                modifier = Modifier
                    .align(Alignment.Center)
                    .padding(16.dp)
            )
        }

        Text(
            text = textOverlay,
            color = Color.White,
            fontSize = 24.sp,
            modifier = Modifier.align(Alignment.Center)
```

```
        )

        FloatingActionButton(
            onClick = { showTextField = !showTextField },
            modifier = Modifier
                .align(Alignment.BottomEnd)
                .padding(16.dp)
        ) {
            Icon(Icons.Default.Edit, contentDescription =
                "Edit Text")
        }
    }
}
```

This example defines a composable function called `ImageWithTextOverlay`. It accepts a bitmap object named `capturedBitmap`, which represents the captured image that will be displayed with a text overlay.

The function starts by defining two pieces of state:

- First, we have `textOverlay`, which holds the text that will be displayed over the image. It's initially set to a default value of **Add your text here**.

- Then, we have a `showTextField` Boolean, which determines whether the text editing field (`TextField`) is visible or not. It's initially set to `false`.

Within the function, we use a `Box` composable as a container. The `Box` composable allows us to layer its child components, and we set its size to fill the maximum available space. This creates an area where we can overlay text on top of an image.

The first child of the `Box` composable is an `Image` composable, which is responsible for displaying the captured photo. The photo is passed to this function as a bitmap, and we ensure that it fills the entire parent container, ensuring that the image takes up the whole screen space available.

Next, we check the state of `showTextField`. If it's `true`, we display `TextField` in the center of the screen. This `TextField` allows the user to input or edit the text that will be overlaid on the image. As the user types, the text in `textOverlay` is updated in real time thanks to the two-way binding provided by Jetpack Compose.

Regardless of the state of `showTextField`, we always display a `Text` composable. This component is responsible for rendering the overlay text on top of the image. We style this text to be white and of a reasonable font size, ensuring it's visible against a variety of backgrounds.

Finally, at the bottom corner of the `Box` composable, we place `FloatingActionButton`. This button, when clicked, toggles the visibility of `TextField`, allowing the user to switch between viewing the overlaid text and editing it. The button is intuitively designed with an edit icon, signaling its purpose to the user.

Now, imagine that we want to allow the user to move the text whenever they want in the image. Let's implement some drag-and-drop magic. We will start by updating the `ImageWithTextOverlay` composable function:

```
@Composable
fun ImageWithTextOverlay(capturedBitmap: Bitmap) {
    var textOverlay = remember { mutableStateOf("Your text
        here") }
    var showTextField = remember { mutableStateOf(false) }
    var textPosition by remember {
        mutableStateOf(Offset.Zero) }
```

In this updated version of the `ImageWithTextOverlay` composable function, we've introduced an interactive feature that allows users to drag and position the text overlay anywhere on the image. To achieve this, we added a new state variable, `textPosition`, initialized to `Offset.Zero`. This state holds the current position of the text overlay on the screen. Now, we must create a new composable function, `DraggableText`, to handle the text display and its draggable functionality.

Let's add this `DraggableText` to our existing code:

```
val imageModifier = Modifier.fillMaxSize()

Box(modifier = Modifier.fillMaxSize()) {
    Image(
        bitmap = capturedBitmap.asImageBitmap(),
        contentDescription = "Captured Image",
        modifier = imageModifier
    )

    if (showTextField) {
        TextField(
            value = textOverlay,
            onValueChange = { textOverlay = it },
            modifier = Modifier
                .align(Alignment.Center)
                .padding(16.dp)
        )
    }
```

```
DraggableText(
    text = textOverlay,
    position = textPosition,
    onPositionChange = { newPosition ->
        textPosition = newPosition },
    modifier = Modifier
        .offset { IntOffset(textPosition.x.toInt(),
            textPosition.y.toInt()) }
        .align(Alignment.Center)
)

FloatingActionButton(
    onClick = { showTextField = !showTextField },
    modifier = Modifier
        .align(Alignment.BottomEnd)
        .padding(16.dp)
) {
    Icon(Icons.Default.Edit, contentDescription =
        "Edit Text")
}
}
}
```

Here, the existing functionality for editing the text through `TextField` is the same. The `TextField` field appears when the user wishes to edit the text, facilitated by a floating action button. This button toggles the visibility of `TextField`, allowing users to switch seamlessly between editing the text and adjusting its position.

Now, we are ready to create the `DraggableText` composable:

```
@Composable
fun DraggableText(
    text: String,
    position: Offset,
    onPositionChange: (Offset) -> Unit,
    modifier: Modifier = Modifier
) {
```

The `DraggableText` composable takes several parameters, including the text to display, its current position, and a callback function, `onPositionChange`, which updates this position. Within `DraggableText`, we utilize the draggable modifier on the `Text` composable. This modifier is pivotal as it allows the text to be moved across the screen. As the user drags the text, the drag offset is updated, which, in turn, updates the `textPosition` state in the main `ImageWithTextOverlay` function.

Finally, define the variables that are needed and the Text composable to show the text:

```
var dragOffset = remember { mutableStateOf(position) }

Text(
    text = text,
    color = Color.White,
    fontSize = 24.sp,
    modifier = modifier
        .offset {
            IntOffset(dragOffset.value.x.roundToInt(),
                dragOffset.value.y.roundToInt()) }
        .pointerInput(Unit) {
            detectDragGestures { change, dragAmount ->
                change.consume()
                dragOffset.value =
                    Offset((dragOffset.value.x +
                        dragAmount.x),
                            (dragOffset.value.y +
                                dragAmount.y))
                onPositionChange(dragOffset.value)
            }
        }
        .background(
            color = Color.Black.copy(alpha = 0.5f),
            shape = RoundedCornerShape(8.dp)
        )
)
```

We begin by initializing a state to hold the current drag offset. This state will track the position of the text as it is dragged.

Next, we define the Text composable to display our draggable text. To control the positioning of the text, we use the offset modifier, which positions the text based on the current drag offset.

The pointerInput modifier allows us to handle drag gestures on the text element. Within the detectDragGestures block, we update the drag offset by adding the drag amount to the current offset each time the user drags the text. The gesture change is consumed to indicate that the drag event has been handled, and we call a function to handle any additional actions that are needed when the position changes.

And with that, here are the two filters we have created:

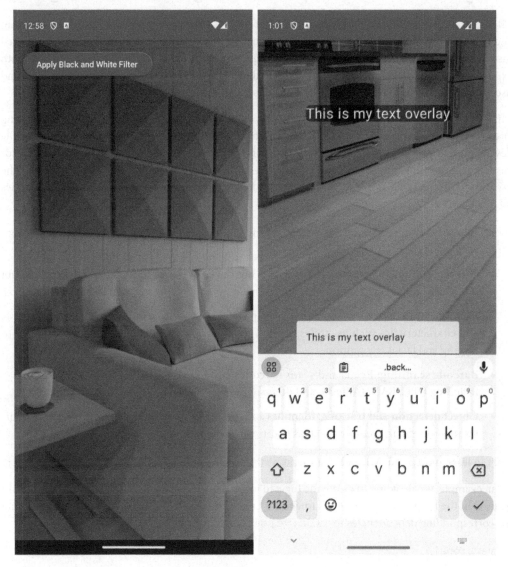

Figure 5.3: The black and white filter composable (left) and text overlay (right)

At this point, we have already implemented some cool features for our users, such as a black-and-white filter and the possibility to add a caption. So, why don't leverage the use of ML to build outstanding features? We'll look at this in the next section.

Using ML to categorize photos and generate hashtags

ML is a branch of **artificial intelligence** (**AI**) that focuses on building systems that can learn from and make decisions based on data. Unlike traditional software, which follows explicitly programmed instructions, ML algorithms use statistical techniques to enable computers to improve at tasks with experience. The fundamental premise of ML is to develop algorithms that can receive input data and use statistical analysis to predict or make decisions about some aspect of the data.

ML is a huge field that is outside the scope of this book, but we still can do interesting things using already-built libraries. For example, **ML Kit** is a powerful ML solution offered by Google for mobile developers that provides a suite of ready-to-use APIs for various ML tasks, both on-device and cloud-based. These functionalities are designed to be easily integrated into mobile applications, facilitating the use of ML without requiring deep expertise in the field. Here's an overview of the key functionalities offered by ML Kit:

- **Image labeling**: Identifies objects, locations, activities, animal species, products, and more within an image.

- **Text recognition**: Extracts text from images. This can be useful for **optical character recognition** (**OCR**) applications, such as scanning documents, business cards, or any printed or handwritten text.

- **Face detection**: Detects faces in an image, including key facial features such as eyes and nose, and characteristics such as smiles or head tilt. This is useful in applications such as photo tagging and facial recognition.

- **Barcode scanning**: Reads and scans barcodes and QR codes. It supports various formats, including UPC, EAN, Code 39, and others.

- **Object detection and tracking**: Identifies and tracks objects in an image or video stream. This feature is useful in scenarios such as real-time video analysis.

You can learn more about ML Kit's features at `https://developers.google.com/ml-kit`.

As an example, we are going to create the logic to identify and label elements in the photo that could be used in the future to categorize the images or create automatic hashtags. We will start by adding the corresponding dependencies to `libs.versions.toml`:

```
[versions]
...
ml-labeling = "17.0.5"

[libraries]
...
mlKitLabeling= { group = "com.google.mlkit", name = "image-labeling",
version.ref="ml-labeling"}
```

Then, we will add these dependencies to the `build.gradle` file of the module. This is where we are creating this functionality (`feature:stories`):

```
implementation(libs.mlKitLabeling)
```

Now, we can create the actual code. We are going to leverage the image analysis feature from CameraX and analyze the preview using MLKitLabeling before using the results to write them in over the image. To do this, we will create a new preview composable just for this feature:

```
@Composable
fun CameraPreviewWithImageLabeler(cameraController:
LifecycleCameraController, modifier: Modifier = Modifier) {
    val context = LocalContext.current

    var labels by remember {
        mutableStateOf<List<String>>(emptyList()) }
    val cameraProviderFuture = remember {
        ProcessCameraProvider.getInstance(context) }

    val previewView = remember { PreviewView(context) }
    val imageAnalysis = remember {
        ImageAnalysis.Builder()
            .setTargetResolution(Size(1280, 720))
            .setBackpressureStrategy(
                ImageAnalysis.STRATEGY_KEEP_ONLY_LATEST)
            .build()
    }

    DisposableEffect(Unit) {
        val cameraProvider = cameraProviderFuture.get()
        val preview = Preview.Builder().build().also {
            it.setSurfaceProvider(
                previewView.surfaceProvider)
        }

        val cameraSelector =
            CameraSelector.DEFAULT_BACK_CAMERA

        cameraProvider.bindToLifecycle(
            context as LifecycleOwner, cameraSelector,
                preview, imageAnalysis)

        onDispose {
            cameraProvider.unbindAll()
```

```
        }
    }

    imageAnalysis.setAnalyzer(ContextCompat.getMainExecutor
    (context)) { imageProxy ->
        processImageProxyForLabeling(imageProxy) {
        detectedLabels ->
            labels = detectedLabels
        }
    }

    Box(modifier = modifier) {
        AndroidView(
            factory = { previewView },
            modifier = modifier
        )
        Canvas(modifier = Modifier.fillMaxSize()) {
            drawIntoCanvas { canvas ->
                val paint = android.graphics.Paint().apply
                {
                    color = android.graphics.Color.RED
                    textSize = 60f
                }
                labels.forEachIndexed { index, label ->
                    canvas.nativeCanvas.drawText(label,
                        10f, 100f + index * 70f, paint)
                }
            }
        }
    }
}
```

The start of this function is pretty similar to our already existing CameraPreview composable. After the camera provider is defined, an ImageAnalysis instance is configured with a target resolution of 1,280x720 pixels and a backpressure strategy set to STRATEGY_KEEP_ONLY_LATEST to process the latest image frame.

The imageAnalysis.setAnalyzer method sets an analyzer to process image frames using ML Kit's Image Labeler. The processImageProxyForLabeling function is called to process each image frame. The detected labels are passed to a Lambda function that updates the labels state variable. We will see how to implement this function shortly.

In the end, the `Box` composable is used to overlay `PreviewView` and a `Canvas` composable. The `Canvas` composable is used to draw the detected labels on top of the camera preview. The `drawIntoCanvas` method accesses the native `canvas` for drawing. A `Paint` object is configured with a red color and a text size of 60 pixels. The `forEachIndexed` method iterates over the labels list, drawing each label at a specified position on the canvas.

Now, let's learn how we can implement the image analyzer:

```
@OptIn(ExperimentalGetImage::class)
private fun processImageProxyForLabeling(imageProxy:
ImageProxy, onLabelsDetected: (List<String>) -> Unit) {
    val mediaImage = imageProxy.image
    if (mediaImage != null) {
        val image = InputImage.fromMediaImage(mediaImage,
            imageProxy.imageInfo.rotationDegrees)
        val labeler =
        ImageLabeling.getClient(
            ImageLabelerOptions.DEFAULT_OPTIONS)

        labeler.process(image)
            .addOnSuccessListener { labels ->
                val labelNames = labels.map { it.text }
                onLabelsDetected(labelNames)
            }
            .addOnFailureListener { e ->
                e.printStackTrace()
            }
            .addOnCompleteListener {
                imageProxy.close()
            }
    }
}
```

This function takes the `ImageProxy` object and a callback function, `onLabelsDetected`, as parameters, where the callback function is invoked with a list of detected labels.

Within the function, `mediaImage` is extracted from the `ImageProxy` object. If `mediaImage` is not `null`, it is converted into `InputImage` using the `InputImage.fromMediaImage` method, which requires the media image and the rotation degrees from `imageProxy`.

An instance of the image labeler is obtained by calling `ImageLabeling.getClient` with `ImageLabelerOptions.DEFAULT_OPTIONS`. This sets up the labeler with default configuration options suitable for general-purpose image labeling.

The `labeler.process` method processes `InputImage` asynchronously. After, the processing outcome is handled by two listeners:

- In `addOnSuccessListener`, the function receives a list of labels if the processing is successful. Each label in this list represents an element identified in the image, accompanied by a confidence score. The function iterates through these labels, logging the identified element (`label.text`) and its confidence score (`label.confidence`). In future iterations, we could use this information to auto-create automatic overlays over the image or to inform the user of which could be the best hashtags for the image.

- In case of any failure during image processing, `addOnFailureListener` is invoked, which logs the error. This error handling is crucial for diagnosing issues that might occur during the ML process, such as problems with the input image or internal errors in the ML Kit processing pipeline.

Now, if we replace our `CameraPreview` composable with the `CameraPreviewImageLabeler` composable, we should see the results of the image analysis taking place:

Figure 5.4: ML labeling taking place in the live preview

If you want to know more about what can be done with the ML Kit library, check out `https://developer.android.com/ml`.

Summary

In this chapter, we started by familiarizing ourselves with CameraX, a key component of the Android Jetpack suite. We learned how to set up CameraX in our applications while enabling features such as live camera preview and image capture.

Moving on, we delved into the practical implementation of capturing images using CameraX. Additionally, we introduced basic image editing functionalities, guiding you through the process of creating a filter and adding a text overlay. These skills are pivotal in enhancing the interactivity and user experience of photography apps.

Finally, we unveiled the integration of Google's ML Kit, demonstrating how to add advanced ML capabilities to the app. We explored how to use ML Kit to identify elements in images, such as objects. This experience highlighted the practical application of these technologies in enhancing the functionality of photography apps.

At this point, you should have gained valuable insights and practical skills in building feature-rich photography apps using CameraX and ML Kit.

In the next chapter, we will give life to those images by learning how to capture and edit video for our Packtagram app.

6

Adding Video and Editing Functionality to Packtagram

Having already mastered the art of capturing stunning photographs and applying mesmerizing filters with CameraX, it's time to elevate our Packtagram app to new heights. Now, we will embark on an exciting new venture: diving into the world of video.

Videos are not just moving pictures; they are powerful storytelling tools that breathe life into our apps. They create dynamic interactions, keeping users engaged and offering them a canvas to express creativity. In this chapter, we'll guide you through the process of integrating video capabilities into your app, akin to adding a new dimension to the Instagram-like experience we have been crafting.

We will start by exploring how to capture high-quality videos using the CameraX library, an extension of the skills you've already honed for photo capture. Then, we'll delve into the world of **Fast Forward Moving Picture Expert Group (Ffmpeg)**, a robust library for video processing, to add layers of creativity to your videos – from simple captions that convey messages to sophisticated filters that transform the visual mood.

You'll learn to not only capture and edit videos but also to efficiently upload them to Firebase Storage, ensuring that your app can handle large files seamlessly and provide a smooth user experience.

By the end of this chapter, you will have added a significant feature to your app, making it not just a photo-sharing platform but a comprehensive multimedia experience.

To accomplish that, in this chapter, we will cover the following topics:

- Adding video functionality to our app
- Getting to know FFmpeg
- Adding a caption to a video with FFmpeg
- Adding a filter to a video with FFmpeg
- Uploading the video

Technical requirements

As in the previous chapter, you will need to have installed Android Studio (or another editor of your preference).

You can find the complete code that we will be using in this chapter in this book's GitHub repository: https://github.com/PacktPublishing/Thriving-in-Android-Development-using-Kotlin/tree/main/Chapter-6.

Adding video functionality to our app

In this section, we will extend the functionality of our Android app so that it includes video-capturing capabilities through CameraX. This powerful library not only simplifies the process of capturing photos but also provides an efficient way to record videos. We'll start by adapting our existing CameraX setup, which is designed for capturing photos, to also handle video recording. The aim is to provide a seamless integration, maintaining the simplicity and robustness of CameraX.

First, we need to set up the preview for the video recording. In the previous chapter, we created a CameraPreview composable. We'll reuse the same composable here:

```
@Composable
fun CameraPreview(cameraController:
LifecycleCameraController, modifier: Modifier = Modifier) {
    AndroidView(
        factory = { context ->
            PreviewView(context).apply {
                implementationMode =
                    PreviewView.ImplementationMode.COMPATIBLE
            }
        },
        modifier = modifier,
        update = { previewView ->
            previewView.controller = cameraController
        }
    )
}
```

Now, we need to create a new button composable to record images and sound from the preview (instead of just capturing the image):

```kotlin
@Composable
fun CaptureVideoButton(
    cameraController: LifecycleCameraController,
    onRecordingFinished: (String) -> Unit,
) {

    val context = LocalContext.current
    val recording = remember {
        mutableStateOf<Recording?>(null) }

    IconButton(
        onClick = {
            cameraController.setEnabledUseCases(
                LifecycleCameraController.VIDEO_CAPTURE)
            if (recording.value == null) {
                recording.value =
                    startRecording(cameraController,
                        context, onRecordingFinished)
            } else {
                stopRecording(recording.value)
                recording.value = null
            }
        },
        modifier = Modifier
            .size(60.dp)
            .padding(8.dp),
    ) {
        Icon(
            painter = if (recording.value == null)
                painterResource(id =
                    R.drawable.ic_videocam) else
                        painterResource(id =
                            R.drawable.ic_stop),
            contentDescription = "Capture video",
            tint = MaterialTheme.colorScheme.onPrimary
        )
    }
}
```

Here, we are creating a new composable called `CaptureVideoButton`. It is similar to the `CaptureButton` composable but with some modifications. For example, now, we'll need to create a variable recording. The `Recording` class in CameraX is responsible for managing an active video recording session. It encapsulates the state and operations needed to start, pause, resume, and stop the recording. In our code, the `recording` variable will be used to manage the current recording session.

Once the user clicks the button, we'll configure the video capture use case, `cameraController.setEnabledUseCases(LifecycleCameraController.VIDEO_CAPTURE)`, so that `cameraController` can start and manage the video recording process, ensuring that the camera is correctly set up for capturing high-quality video and enabling the necessary configurations and resources for the recording session to proceed smoothly. Then, if a recording hasn't been already initiated, we'll start a new recording. If it has already been initiated, we'll stop it.

The icon of the button will show a camera prior to the recording being initiated and a stop button if the recording is already in progress, to indicate to the user that they should click it to stop the recording.

To finish this recording functionality, we need to implement the `startRecording` function:

```
@SuppressLint("MissingPermission")
private fun startRecording(
    cameraController: LifecycleCameraController,
    context: Context,
    onRecordingFinished: (String) -> Unit
): Recording {
    val videoFile = File(context.filesDir,
        "video_${System.currentTimeMillis()}.mp4")
    val outputOptions =
        FileOutputOptions.Builder(videoFile).build()
    val audioConfig = AudioConfig.create(true)
    val executor = Executors.newSingleThreadExecutor()

    return cameraController.startRecording(
        outputOptions,
        audioConfig,
        executor
    ) { recordEvent ->
        when (recordEvent) {
            is VideoRecordEvent.Finalize -> {
                if (recordEvent.hasError()) {
                    Log.e("CaptureVideoButton",
                        "Video recording error:
                            ${recordEvent.error}")
                } else {
                    onRecordingFinished(
```

```
                            videoFile.absolutePath)
            }
        }
    }
    }
}
```

This function is marked with the @SuppressLint("MissingPermission") annotation, indicating an assumption that the necessary runtime permissions, such as access to the camera and microphone, have already been granted. We will handle these permissions the same way we did with the photo capture, so the annotation is safe to use here as the permissions would have already been granted.

The function begins by defining the location and filename for the video recording. It uses the File class to create a reference to a video_${System.currentTimeMillis()}.mp4 file, which is stored in the app-specific directory on the external storage. This approach to file storage is advantageous as it does not require additional permissions and ensures that the stored data is private to the application.

Next, the code sets up FileOutputOptions using the previously defined file. This step is crucial as it configures how the recorded video data will be written to the filesystem. The FileOutputOptions class, part of the CameraX library, offers an intuitive API to set these parameters efficiently – for example, it allows us to specify the video location using ContentResolver (you can find additional information about FileOutputOptions here: https://developer.android.com/reference/androidx/camera/video/FileOutputOptions). Next, the audio configuration is created, in this case to allow audio using AudioConfig.create(true).

Then, an executor is created using Executors.newSingleThreadExecutor(), which facilitates the execution of tasks in a background thread, thereby keeping the UI thread unblocked and responsive. With these parameters defined (fileOutputOptions, AudioConfig, and Executor), we can execute the cameraController.startRecording function, which will initiate the recording.

Additionally, an event listener is defined using the Consumer<VideoRecordEvent> interface. This listener uses a when statement to handle different types of VideoRecordEvent, such as VideoRecordEvent.Finalize, which indicates the completion of the recording. The event listener also checks for errors during the recording process, ensuring robust error handling.

Then, a Recording object is returned, representing the ongoing recording session. This recording object is crucial for the next step.

Now, let's implement the stopRecording function:

```
fun stopRecording(recording: Recording?) {
    recording?.stop()
}
```

In this concise and straightforward function, we only have one line of code, but it does something essential. The function takes a single parameter, `recording`, which is our instance of the `Recording` class from the CameraX library.

The core action in this function is to invoke `stop()` on the `recording` object. When this method is called, it tells the `recording` instance to terminate the current video recording session. This involves stopping video frames from being captured and finalizing the video file that's being recorded. The video file is then saved to the location that's specified when the recording has finished.

Now, we will include the new button in `CaptureModeContent`, which we built previously for the capture feature:

```
@Composable
private fun CaptureModeContent(
    cameraController: LifecycleCameraController,
    onImageCaptured: (Bitmap) -> Any,
    onVideoCaptured: (String) -> Any
) {
    Box(modifier = Modifier.fillMaxSize()) {
        CameraPermissionRequester {
            Box(
                contentAlignment = Alignment.BottomCenter,
                modifier = Modifier.fillMaxSize()
            ) {
                CameraPreview(...)
                Row {
                    CaptureButton(...)
                    CaptureVideoButton(
                        cameraController =
                            cameraController,
                        onRecordingFinished = { videoPath ->
                            onVideoCaptured(videoPath)
                        }
                    )
                }
            }
        }
    }
}
```

Here, we have added a Row composable to show both buttons horizontally side by side. We have also added a new Lambda (`onVideoCaptured`) that we will use to pass the video file path when the recording has finished.

With these changes, we should be able to see the newly implemented button:

Figure 6.1: The video capture button already integrated into the
StoryContent screen when the video is not being recorded

When we click the video capture button, we should see its icon change to the stop symbol:

Figure 6.2: Video recording in progress

And with this, we are ready to record our videos using CameraX! Now, it is time for us to learn how to modify or edit the recorded videos. With these aspects in mind, let me introduce you to the FFmpeg library.

Getting to know FFmpeg

FFmpeg is an open-source multimedia framework that has become a cornerstone in the world of audio and video processing. Renowned for its versatility and power, FFmpeg offers a comprehensive suite of libraries and tools to handle video, audio, and other multimedia files and streams. At its core, FFmpeg is a command-line tool, enabling users to convert media files from one format into another, manipulate video and audio recordings, and perform a wide array of other multimedia processing tasks.

> **Note**
> You can find the official FFmpeg documentation here: `https://ffmpeg.org/`.

Through the following subsections, we will learn what components are part of FFmpeg, its key features, and how to integrate this powerful library in our Android apps.

The components of FFmpeg

The FFmpeg project is composed of several components, each serving a specific role in multimedia processing:

- `libavcodec`: A library containing decoders and encoders for audio/video codecs
- `libavformat`: This library deals with the container formats, managing the multiplexing and demultiplexing aspects of multimedia streams
- `libavutil`: A utility library that provides a range of helper functions and data structures
- `libavfilter`: Used for applying various audio and video filters
- `libswscale`: Dedicated to handling image scaling and color format conversions

Together, these components provide a robust foundation for handling a wide array of multimedia processing tasks.

Key features of FFmpeg

FFmpeg stands out for its extensive range of capabilities. Some of its key features include the following:

- **Format support**: FFmpeg supports a vast number of audio and video formats, both in terms of encoding and decoding, making it incredibly versatile for multimedia processing
- **Conversion**: It can convert media files between various formats with high efficiency, a feature that's widely used in various applications and services

- **Streaming**: FFmpeg excels in streaming capabilities, allowing for audio and video to be captured, encoded, and streamed in real time

- **Filtering**: With its powerful filtering capabilities, users can apply various transformations, overlays, and effects to their media

Integrating mobile-ffmpeg into our project

In the context of Android development, FFmpeg can be used as a powerful tool for video editing functionalities, such as applying filters, transcoding, or even adding subtitles. However, integrating FFmpeg into Android applications while using C++ code requires using **Java Native Interface (JNI)**. Luckily, there is an easier option, which is leveraging an Android-compatible wrapper of FFmpeg, such as mobile-ffmpeg.

mobile-ffmpeg is a specialized port of Ffmpeg that's designed for mobile platforms such as Android and iOS. It provides pre-built binaries, mobile-specific APIs, and optimizations tailored to the constraints of mobile hardware. This makes it easier to integrate FFmpeg's powerful capabilities into mobile applications, allowing developers to leverage advanced multimedia processing features with less complexity.

To integrate the mobile-ffmpeg library into our project, we will start by opening our libs. versions.toml file. There, we will add the version and the library group and name:

```
[versions]
...
mobileffmpeg = "4.4"

[libraries]
...
mobileffmpeg = { group = "com.arthenica", name = "mobile-ffmpeg-full",
version.ref = "mobileffmpeg" }
```

Here, we have just added the latest mobile-ffmpeg version and the library reference to our version catalog.

As always, to use it in any of our modules, we will have to add the dependency in the build. gradle.kts file:

```
dependencies {
    ....
    implementation(libs.mobileffmpeg)
}
```

Once it's added to our dependencies, we will have to sync our Gradle files so that it's ready to be used in our code. But first, let's learn how FFmpeg works and can be used.

Understanding the FFmpeg command-line syntax

As we have seen, FFmpeg is a powerful multimedia framework that's capable of decoding, encoding, transcoding, multiplexing (joining, for example, audio and video in a single file), demultiplexing (separating audio and video in different files), streaming, filtering, and playing almost any type of media file. Understanding its command-line syntax is crucial for effective video processing, especially in Android environments.

Keep in mind that we will not be executing these commands in a terminal, but the `mobile-ffmpeg` library uses the same syntax to allow us to execute them using a function called `FFmpeg.execute()`, as we will see now.

At its core, an FFmpeg command follows a basic structure:

```
FFmpeg.execute("[global_options] {[input_file_options] [flags] input_
url} ... {[output_file_options] output_url} ...")
```

Let's take a closer look at the components of this syntax:

- `global_options`: These are settings that can be applied throughout the command, such as configuring logging levels or overriding default configurations.

- `input_file_options`: These are options that specifically affect the input file, such as the format, codec, or frame rate.

- `input_url`: The path to the input file.

- `output_file_options`: These are similar to input file options but they affect the output file, such as the format, codec, or bitrate.

- `output_url`: The path for the output file.

- `options/flags`: These start with a dash (-) and modify how FFmpeg processes files. The most used options and flags are as follows:

    - `-i`: Specifies the input file

    - `-c`: Indicates the codec; use `-c:v` for video and `-c:a` for audio

    - `-b`: Sets the bitrate; `-b:v` for video and `-b:a` for audio

    - `-s`: Defines the frame size (resolution)

    - `-r`: Sets the frame rate

    - `-f`: Indicates the format

Let's see how we can use this syntax to complete some basic operations.

Basic conversion

Converting a video file from one format into another is a fundamental task in video editing. For example, converting an MP4 file into an AVI file can be done like so:

```
FFmpeg.execute("-i input.mp4 output.avi")
```

This command tells FFmpeg to take `input.mp4` and convert it into `output.avi` using the default settings for codecs and quality (the default values are used here because we didn't specify any settings).

Specifying codecs

Codecs are algorithms that are used for encoding (compressing) or decoding (decompressing) video and audio streams. In FFmpeg, you can specify different codecs for the video and audio components of a file:

- **Video codec**: A video codec processes the visual data in the file. Choosing the right video codec affects the video's quality, size, and compatibility with different players and devices.
- **Audio codec**: An audio codec deals with the sound component. It determines the audio quality, file size, and compatibility with audio playback systems.

To specify codecs in FFmpeg, use the `-c` flag followed by a colon, then either `v` for video or `a` for audio, and then specify the codec's name:

```
ffmpeg -i input.file -c:v [video_codec] -c:a [audio_codec] output.file
```

So, for example, to specify the H.264 and AAC codecs, you can run the following command:

```
ffmpeg -i input.mp4 -c:v libx264 -c:a aac output.mp4
```

Let's understand what the values of this command mean:

- `-i`: This indicates that the next parameter is going to be the input file.
- `input.mp4`: This is the route to the input file.
- `-c:v libx264`: This value sets the video codec to `libx264`, a popular codec for H.264 video encoding. It's known for its efficiency and compatibility with most video platforms.
- `-c:a aac`: This value sets the audio codec to `aac` (which stands for Advanced Audio Coded), known for good quality audio at lower bitrates, making it ideal for web videos.
- `output.mp4`: This indicates the route to the output file.

Note that higher-quality codecs often result in larger file sizes – the balance between quality and file size can be key, depending on the use case.

Also, it is important to know that some codecs require licensing for commercial use (for example, H.264), whereas others are open source and free (for example, VP9 and Opus).

Adjusting video quality

In video processing, one of the most crucial aspects to manage is the quality of the output video. The quality is often directly influenced by the bitrate. The **bitrate** is measured in **bits per second (bps)** and represents the amount of video or audio data that's encoded for 1 second of playback. Higher bitrates generally mean better quality but also larger file sizes.

There are two types of bitrate:

- **Constant bitrate** (**CBR**): This encodes the file at a consistent bitrate throughout, leading to predictable file sizes but potentially varying quality
- **Variable bitrate** (**VBR**): This adjusts the bitrate according to the complexity of each part of the video, balancing quality and file size more effectively

To adjust the bitrate in FFmpeg, we can use the -b:v flag for video bitrate and -b:a for audio bitrate:

```
ffmpeg -i input.file -b:v [video_bitrate] -b:a [audio_bitrate] output.
file
```

For example, to set standard definition video with moderate quality, we can run the following command:

```
ffmpeg -i input.mp4 -b:v 1500k -b:a 128k output.mp4
```

Let's see what the values of this command mean:

- -i: This indicates that the next parameter is going to be the input file
- input.mp4: This is the route to the input file
- -b:v 1500k: Sets the video bitrate to 1,500 kbps, which is suitable for standard-definition content
- -b:a 128k: Sets the audio bitrate to 128 kbps, providing decent audio quality without excessive file size
- output.mp4: Indicates the route to the output file

It's worth noting that lower bitrates may lead to noticeable compression artifacts, especially in fast-moving or complex scenes. On the other hand, higher bitrates offer better quality but at the expense of larger file sizes, which might be an issue for online streaming or limited storage.

Resizing video

Resizing or scaling videos is a common task in video editing, whether it's to fit different screen sizes, reduce file size, or conform to specific resolution requirements. FFmpeg offers powerful tools to resize videos with ease, but understanding the impact of these changes is crucial for maintaining quality.

But what are video resolution and aspect ratio?

- **Resolution**: The resolution of a video is the dimension in pixels, given as width x height. Standard resolutions include 480p (SD), 720p (HD), 1080p (Full HD), and 4K (Ultra HD).

- **Aspect ratio**: This is the ratio of the width to the height of the video. Common aspect ratios are 16:9 (widescreen) and 4:3 (traditional).

To resize videos in FFmpeg, the -s (size) flag is used. It sets the resolution:

```
ffmpeg -i input.file -s [width]x[height] output.file
```

For example, to resize to 1080p, the command will be as follows:

```
ffmpeg -i input.mp4 -s 1920x1080 output.mp4
```

Let's see what the values of this command mean:

- -i: Indicates that the next parameter is going to be the input file

- input.mp4: The route to the input file

- -s 1920x1080: Resizes the video to full HD (1080p), which is suitable for high-quality presentations and large displays

- output.mp4: Indicates the route to the output file

There are some things to consider when resizing videos:

- Choose the resolution based on where and how the video will be viewed. For instance, you should choose a high resolution for TV broadcasts and something lower for web or mobile use.

- Higher resolutions lead to larger files, which can be a concern for storage and streaming.

- Always consider the quality of the source video. Upscaling low-quality footage might not yield desirable results.

Now that we are familiar with the basic features of FFmpeg, we will learn about the advanced ones.

Advanced syntax and options in FFmpeg

FFmpeg's true power lies in its advanced options, allowing for sophisticated manipulation and processing of audio and video files. This section delves deeper into these advanced features, providing insights into how they can be leveraged for complex tasks.

Using filters for enhanced video and audio manipulation

FFmpeg comes equipped with an extensive range of filters for both video and audio. These can be applied to tasks such as cropping, rotating, adding watermarks, and adjusting brightness or contrast.

To apply filters, you can use the `-vf` (video filters) or `-af` (audio filters) option. Here is the schema of how the filter syntax would work:

```
ffmpeg -i input.file -vf "[filter1],[filter2]" output.file
```

For example, imagine a scenario where you need to crop a video and adjust its color properties. You can do this by running the following command:

```
ffmpeg -i input.mp4 -vf "crop=640:480:0:0, hue=h=60:s=1" -c:a copy
output.mp4
```

Let's take a closer look at the values of this command:

- `-i`: Indicates that the next parameter is going to be the input file.
- `input.mp4`: This is the route to the input file.
- `-vf`: This stands for video filters, and allows you to apply one or more filters to the video stream.
- `crop=640:480:0:0`: This is the crop filter. It crops the video to a width of 640 pixels and a height of 480 pixels. The 0:0 value at the end specifies the *x* and *y* coordinates of the top-left corner of the crop area. In this case, it's set to the top-left corner of the original video. So, this filter effectively crops the video to a 640x480 rectangle starting from the top-left corner.
- `hue=h=60:s=1`: There are two parts to this code:
  - `h=60` adjusts the hue of the video. Hue is a color component that allows us to shift colors on a 360-degree color wheel. A value of 60 shifts the colors by 60 degrees. For example, blue might become green, red might become yellow, and so on.
  - `s=1` sets the saturation level. A saturation of 1 means that the colors are left as-is in terms of intensity. Decreasing this value would desaturate the colors, leading to a more grayscale image.
- `-c:a`: Resizes the video to full HD (1080p).
- `output.mp4`: Indicates the route to the output file.

In summary, this FFmpeg command reads `input.mp4`, crops the video to a 640x480 resolution starting from the top-left corner, shifts the hue of the video colors by 60 degrees on the color wheel, maintains the original saturation, copies the audio without re-encoding, and saves all these changes in `output.mp4`.

Using an overlay video filter

The overlay filter in FFmpeg is a versatile feature that allows users to superimpose one video or image over another. This is particularly useful for adding logos, watermarks, subtitles, picture-in-picture effects, or any additional visual elements to a video.

The overlay filter can be applied with the `-filter_complex` option in FFmpeg, which is used for more complex filtering that involves multiple input streams (such as combining two videos or adding an image to a video).

The basic syntax for the overlay filter is as follows:

```
ffmpeg -i main_video.mp4 -i overlay.mp4 -filter_complex "overlay=x:y"
output.mp4
```

Here, `main_video.mp4` is our primary video, and `overlay.mp4` is the video or image we want to overlay. The x and y values in the overlay filter specify the position of the overlay image/video on the main video.

As an example, let's say we want to add a company logo to the bottom-right corner of a video. First, we must prepare the files. In this case, we have the following:

- The main video file will be `video.mp4`
- The logo image will be `logo.png` (preferably with a transparent background)

Then, we will determine the logo's position. The logo's position will depend on the resolution of the main video. For example, if the video is 1920x1080 (full HD), and you want to place the logo 10 pixels from the bottom and right edges, the coordinates would be (x=1900, y=1060).

With this in mind, we will have to execute the following command:

```
ffmpeg -i video.mp4 -i logo.png -filter_complex "overlay=1900:1060"
-codec:a copy output.mp4
```

In this command, we have the following:

- `-i video.mp4`: Specifies the main video file.
- `-i logo.png`: Specifies the overlay file (logo).
- `-filter_complex "overlay=1900:1060"`: Applies the overlay filter. The logo is positioned at (1900,1060), which is near the bottom-right corner.
- `-codec:a copy`: Copies the audio from the main video without re-encoding.
- `output.mp4`: The output file with the logo overlaid on the video.

Is this all we can do with the overlay filter? No, there's much more! For example, we can move this overlay dynamically.

Dynamic positioning with the overlay filter in FFmpeg

The overlay filter in FFmpeg not only allows static placement of images or videos over a main video but also offers dynamic positioning capabilities. This advanced feature enables the overlay to move across the screen or change its appearance over time, adding a dynamic element to your videos.

First, let's explore how to create the effect of moving an overlay across the screen. This technique is particularly effective for adding motion to logos, text, or other graphical elements.

Before we dive into the command, it's important to understand how FFmpeg processes expressions for movement. These expressions allow the position of the overlay to change frame by frame, creating the illusion of motion.

The command for moving an overlay is as follows:

```
ffmpeg -i main_video.mp4 -i logo.png -filter_complex
"overlay=x='t*100':y=50" output.mp4
```

In this command, we have the following:

- `x='t*100'`: The horizontal position (x) of the overlay starts at 0 and increases by 100 pixels every second. The `t` variable represents the current time in seconds.

- `y=50`: The vertical position (y) is fixed at 50 pixels from the top of the frame.

We can play with these values to introduce different effects in our video overlay. For example, if we create a complete video editor, we could allow the users to move an element over the video and change its position during the video playback. Then, we could map those different positions to the seconds where we want it to be moved using FFmpeg. However, we won't be doing this as it would take another book entirely!

If you are curious about this, here is the documentation for the `overlay` parameter: `https://ffmpeg.org/ffmpeg-filters.html#overlay-1`.

Another feature we can use is fade-in and fade-out effects, which we can apply to our overlay. Let's see how it works.

Introducing the fade-in/out command

To achieve a fade-in/out effect, we combine the overlay filter with the fade filter. Let's break down the command to understand how it's structured:

```
ffmpeg -i main_video.mp4 -i logo.png -filter_complex "[1:v]
fade=t=in:st=0:d=1,fade=t=out:st=3:d=1[logo];[0:v][logo]overlay=10:10"
output.mp4
```

Let's understand how this command is configured:

- `[1:v]fade=t=in:st=0:d=1`: Applies a fade-in effect to the overlay, starting at 0 seconds and lasting for 1 second

- `fade=t=out:st=3:d=1[logo]`: Subsequently, a fade-out effect starts at 3 seconds and also lasts for 1 second

- `overlay=10:10`: The overlay is placed at the coordinates (10,10) on the main video

But there is more that we can do with FFmpeg, apart from using exposed filters. Let's see how we can use the mobile-ffmpeg library that we've already integrated into our project to improve the videos we are already recording.

Using mobile-ffmpeg to execute FFmpeg commands

With mobile-ffmpeg integrated, executing FFmpeg commands in Android becomes a streamlined process.

The library's FFmpeg.execute() method is the gateway to running FFmpeg commands. For instance, a command such as -i input.mp4 -c:v libx264 output.mp4, which converts an input video so that it uses the H.264 codec, is seamlessly executed within the Android environment. This function mirrors the command-line syntax of FFmpeg, maintaining familiarity for those accustomed to FFmpeg's command-line interface.

Here's how it would work:

```
val command = "-i input.mp4 -c:v libx264 output.mp4"
val returnCode = FFmpeg.execute(command)
```

In the previous code block, we are building a string with the command instruction and storing it in the command variable. Then, we are using the FFmpeg.execute() method to execute the command. Note that this execution will happen in the current thread, which could be undesirable performance-wise.

Managing performance and user experience is crucial in Android, especially for resource-intensive tasks such as video processing. mobile-ffmpeg accommodates this by offering asynchronous execution of commands. Utilizing FFmpeg.executeAsync() ensures that longer operations do not block the main thread, thus maintaining the application's responsiveness. This method becomes instrumental when handling complex transformations or filters, such as scaling a video.

Here's how we can use the executeAsync function:

```
FFmpeg.executeAsync(command) { executionId, returnCode ->
    when (returnCode) {
        Config.RETURN_CODE_SUCCESS -> {
            // Processing was successful
        }
        Config.RETURN_CODE_CANCEL -> {
            // Command execution was cancelled
        }
        else -> {
            // Command execution failed
        }
    }
}
```

In this example, the `executeAsync()` method is called with the FFmpeg command in string format. This command is what we intend FFmpeg to execute, such as converting a video file, applying filters, or any other media processing task supported by FFmpeg. The execution of this command occurs in a separate thread, preventing any blocking of the main UI thread of the application.

When the command has finished executing, a Lambda function is triggered. This function is structured to receive two parameters: `executionId` and `returnCode`. The `executionId` parameter is a unique identifier for this particular execution instance of the FFmpeg command and can be useful for tracking or managing this specific operation, especially if our application handles multiple FFmpeg processes concurrently.

The `returnCode` parameter is crucial as it indicates the outcome of the executed FFmpeg command. The different return codes and their implications are as follows:

- `Config.RETURN_CODE_SUCCESS`: This code signifies that the FFmpeg command was executed successfully without any errors. In the corresponding block of the when statement, you might want to implement functionality that deals with the successful completion of the media processing task. This could include updating the user interface, processing or displaying the output file, or triggering subsequent application logic.

- `Config.RETURN_CODE_CANCEL`: This return code indicates that the execution of the FFmpeg command was canceled. This can occur if the execution is programmatically aborted or if certain external conditions pre-emptively stop the command. The handling code block for this return code could involve notifying the user of the cancellation, cleaning up resources, or setting the stage for a potential retry of the operation.

- `else`: This block catches all other cases, which generally suggests that an error occurred during the execution of the FFmpeg command. Here, error-handling strategies come into play, such as logging the error for diagnostic purposes, informing the user of the failure, or attempting to retry the operation under certain conditions.

To further refine the integration, `mobile-ffmpeg` allows us to handle progress and log outputs. This is essential for debugging and enhancing the user experience. Here's how it works:

```
FFmpeg.executeAsync(command, ExecuteCallback { executionId,
returnCode ->
    // Handle execution result
}, LogCallback { logMessage ->
    // Handle log message
}, StatisticsCallback { statistics ->
    // Handle progress updates
})
```

Here, `LogCallback` complements the execution callback that we described before. FFmpeg is known for its verbose logging, providing a wealth of information about the ongoing operation. The `logMessage` parameter in this callback gives you access to these logs, enabling you to handle them as per your application's needs. Whether it's displaying these logs for debugging purposes, analyzing them for detailed error reporting, or simply directing them to a file for record-keeping, this callback plays a pivotal role in understanding and managing the intricacies of FFmpeg's operations.

Last but not least, `StatisticsCallback` opens the door to real-time monitoring of the FFmpeg process. This callback, through the `statistics` parameter, provides live data, such as the frame currently being processed, elapsed time, and bitrate, among others. Utilizing this data can significantly enhance the user experience, enabling you to implement dynamic features such as progress bars, estimated-time-to-completion indicators, or even detailed reports of the ongoing operation's status.

Now that we know how to execute our FFmpeg commands in Android, let's build something. We will start by adding a caption to the video.

Adding a caption to the video with FFmpeg

In this section, we will create all the components we'll need to add a caption to a video using FFmpeg. We'll start this new feature by creating a use case where the business logic of adding the caption to the video will be defined. We will call it `AddCaptionToVideoUseCase`, and its responsibility will be to add the caption to the video and return the new video file once it has been added.

This is how we can build `AddCaptionToVideoUseCase`:

```
class AddCaptionToVideoUseCase() {

    suspend fun addCaption(videoFile: File, captionText:
    String): Result<File> = withContext(Dispatchers.IO) {
        val outputFile = File(
            videoFile.parent,
                "${videoFile.nameWithoutExtension}
                    _captioned.mp4")
        val fontFilePath =
            "/system/fonts/Roboto-Regular.ttf"
        val ffmpegCommand = arrayOf(
            "-i", videoFile.absolutePath,
            "-vf", "drawtext=fontfile=$fontFilePath:
                text='$captionText':
                    fontcolor=white:
                        fontsize=24:x=(w-text_w)/2:
                            y=(h-text_h)-10",
            "-c:a", "aac",
            "-b:a", "192k",
```

```
                    outputFile.absolutePath
            )

        try {
            val executionId =
            FFmpeg.executeAsync(ffmpegCommand)
            { _, returnCode ->
                if (returnCode !=
                Config.RETURN_CODE_SUCCESS) {
                    Result.failure<AddCaptionToVideoError>(
                        AddCaptionToVideoError)
                }
            }
            // Optionally handle the executionId, e.g., for
                cancellation
            Result.success(outputFile)
        } catch (e: Exception) {
            Result.failure(e)
        }
    }
}

object AddCaptionToVideoError: Throwable("There was an
error adding the caption to the video") {
    private fun readResolve(): Any = AddCaptionToVideoError
}
```

In the preceding code, we start by creating a suspend function, addCaption, which is specifically designed to facilitate asynchronous execution via coroutines. As the action of adding a caption involves intensive tasks such as video processing, we should avoid executing this kind of logic in the main thread to prevent any lag or unresponsiveness in the application. The function takes two parameters: a File object representing the video file and a String containing the caption text to be added.

Inside the addCaption function, the execution context is switched to the I/O dispatcher. This is done to optimize for I/O operations, ensuring that the file processing workload is handled appropriately without straining the main thread. The function proceeds to create an outputFile object. This object represents the new video file that will be generated post-captioning.

The next segment in the function involves constructing a command string for FFmpeg. This command is carefully crafted to utilize FFmpeg's drawtext filter, enabling the provided caption text to be overlaid on the video. Let's analyze the command that we used in the previous code block:

```
val command = "-i ${videoFile.absolutePath} -vf drawtext=text='$cap
tionText':fontcolor=white:fontsize=24:x=(w-text_w)/2:y=(h-text_h)/2
-codec:a copy ${outputFile.absolutePath}"
```

Let's break this command down:

- `-i ${videoFile.absolutePath}`: This part of the command specifies the input file for FFmpeg to process. The `-i` flag is used for input files in FFmpeg and `${videoFile.absolutePath}` dynamically inserts the absolute path of the video file you're processing.

- `-vf drawtext=text='$captionText':...`: The `-vf` (video filter) flag is used to apply filters to the video. Here, the `drawtext` filter is used to add text to the video.

- `text='$captionText'`: This specifies the text to be drawn. Here, `$captionText` is the variable holding the caption text, which is dynamically inserted into the command.

- `fontcolor=white`: Sets the font color of the text to white.

- `fontsize=24`: Defines the size of the font used for the text.

- `x=(w-text_w)/2`: This sets the horizontal position of the text. Here, w represents the width of the video, and `text_w` is the width of the text. By setting `x to (w-text_w)/2`, the text is horizontally centered.

- `y=(h-text_h)/2`: Similarly, this sets the vertical position of the text. Here, h is the height of the video, and `text_h` is the height of the text. This formula vertically centers the text within the video.

- `-codec:a acc`: This part of the command instructs FFmpeg to use `acc` as the codec for audio streaming.

- `-b:a=192k`: This part of the command sets the bitrate to 192k.

- `${outputFile.absolutePath}`: The last part of the command specifies the output file's path, where the processed video (with the caption added) will be saved.

Executing this FFmpeg command is handled asynchronously with `FFmpeg.executeAsync()`. This method is pivotal for running the command in a non-blocking manner and is accompanied by a Lambda function for handling the execution result. The Lambda function evaluates `returnCode` from the FFmpeg execution. In the case of a non-successful execution (indicated by any return code other than `RETURN_CODE_SUCCESS`), the function constructs `Result.failure`, wrapping a custom `AddCaptionToVideoError` object. This custom error object, defined as a singleton, provides a specific error message indicating an issue with the captioning process.

On the flip side, successful command execution results in `Result.success`, passing along `outputFile`. This bifurcation in handling success and failure scenarios ensures robust error management and clear feedback regarding the outcome of the captioning process.

Now, we can use `AddCaptionToVideoUseCase` in `StoryEditorViewModel`:

```
class StoryEditorViewModel(
    private val saveCaptureUseCase: SaveCaptureUseCase,
    private val addCaptionToVideoUseCase:
    AddCaptionToVideoUseCase
): ViewModel() {

  // Other variables we defined for the photo feature
    var videoFile: File? = null

  // Other code we already added for the photo feature

    fun addCaptionToVideo(captionText: String) {
        videoFile?.let { file ->
            viewModelScope.launch {
                val result =
                    addCaptionToVideoUseCase.addCaption(
                        file, captionText)
                // Handle the result of the captioning
                    process
            }
        }
    }
}
```

We start by injecting `AddCaptionToVideoUseCase` into `StoryEditorViewModel` using its constructor. Then, we declare a `videoFile` variable in `ViewModel`, which holds the video we're working with – it's nullable because there might be times when we don't have a video to display or edit. In `videoFile`, we should have stored the view we have already recorded.

Next, the core function in this `ViewModel` is `addCaptionToVideo`. This function takes the caption text as input and uses the video file we have. First, it checks if `videoFile` isn't `null`. If we have a video, it proceeds; if not, nothing happens.

Inside `addCaptionToVideo`, by launching a coroutine within `viewModelScope`, we ensure that our caption-adding process doesn't freeze the UI. This is crucial for maintaining a smooth user experience.

The `addCaption` method of our use case is then called with the video file and caption text. Whatever comes back from this operation – success or failure – is stored in the result.

The `// Handle the result of the captioning process` comment is where you'd put our code to update the UI based on the result. This could mean displaying the captioned video, showing an error message, or whatever else makes sense for our app. For simplicity, we won't be adding it here just yet, but we will learn more about video playback in the last three chapters of this book when we create a Netflix-esque app.

But we can still test the effect in our video. We just have to look at the internal app files using Device Explorer in Android Studio. There, we'll see two files – one of the original video, and the other a modified one with the `_captioned` suffix:

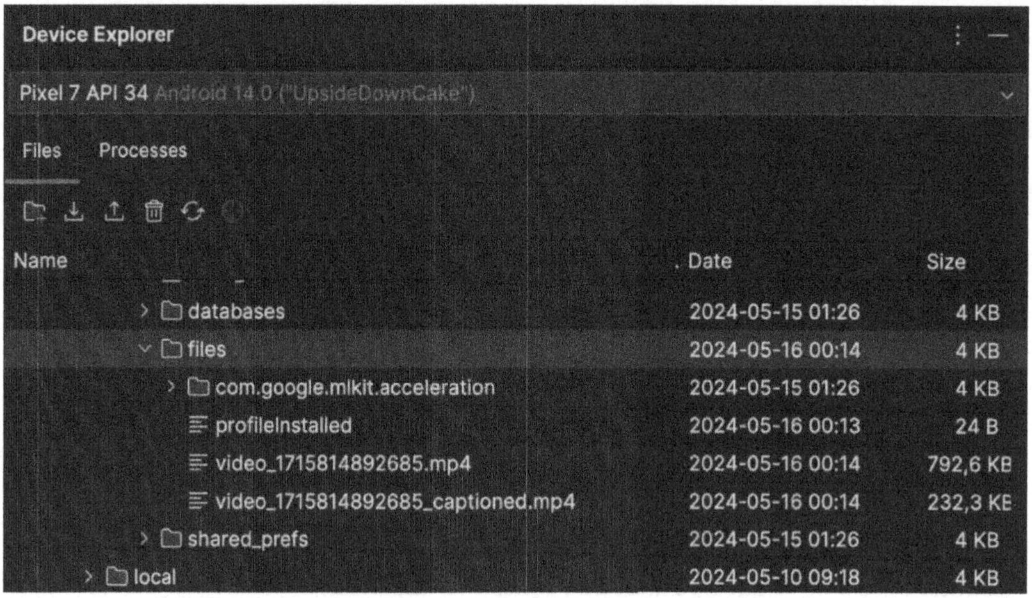

Figure 6.3: Device Explorer with video files in Android Studio

If we download the captioned file video and play it, we should see that a caption has been added to the video:

Figure 6.4: A video with caption text stating, "This is the caption text"

Now that we know how to apply a caption to our video, let's see how we can apply a filter.

Adding a filter to a video with FFmpeg

In this section, we will learn how to add a filter to our video. A popular filter that is visually impactful is the "vignette" effect – this effect typically darkens the edges of the frame, drawing the viewer's attention toward the center of the image or video, and can add a dramatic or cinematic quality to the footage. FFmpeg has the capability to apply this artistic filter to videos, so let's try it out!

As we did with the caption, we will start by creating the use case: `AddVignetteEffectUseCase`. The primary role of `AddVignetteEffectUseCase` is to execute the business logic for applying the vignette effect to a given video file by using `mobile-ffmpeg`. We will use a specific `FFmpeg` command, as follows:

```
class AddVignetteEffectUseCase() {

    suspend fun addVignetteEffect(videoFile: File):
    Result<File> = withContext(Dispatchers.IO) {
        val outputFile = File(videoFile.parent,
            "${videoFile.nameWithoutExtension}
                _vignetted.mp4")
        val command = "-i ${videoFile.absolutePath} -vf
            vignette=angle=PI/4 ${outputFile.absolutePath}"

        try {
            val executionId = FFmpeg.executeAsync(command)
            { _, returnCode ->
                if (returnCode !=
                Config.RETURN_CODE_SUCCESS) {
                    Result.failure<AddVignetteEffectError>(
                        AddVignetteEffectError)
                }
            }
            // Optionally handle the executionId, e.g., for
                cancellation
            Result.success(outputFile)
        } catch (e: Exception) {
            Result.failure(e)
        }
    }
}

object AddVignetteEffectError : Throwable("There was an
error adding the vignette effect to the video") {
    private fun readResolve(): Any = AddVignetteEffectError
}
```

Let's walk through the code in `AddVignetteEffectUseCase`. Here, `addVignetteEffect` is a suspend function, meaning it's designed to run asynchronously with Kotlin's coroutines. In this function, we take the video file that needs the vignette effect and start by defining where to save the processed video. We keep the original video intact and create a new file for the output. The output's filename keeps the original name but with `_vignetted` added to it so that it's easy to track.

Next up, we build our FFmpeg command. This command tells FFmpeg to apply the vignette effect. Let's see how this command (already present in the previous code block) works in detail:

```
val command = "-i ${videoFile.absolutePath} -vf vignette=angle=PI/4
${outputFile.absolutePath}"
```

This command is composed of the following segments:

- `-i ${videoFile.absolutePath}`: This part of the command specifies the input file for FFmpeg to process. The `-i` flag is used for input files in FFmpeg and `${videoFile.absolutePath}` dynamically inserts the absolute path of the video file you want to process. In simple terms, it tells FFmpeg, "Here's the video I want you to work on."

- `-vf vignette=angle=PI/4`: This segment is where the vignette effect is applied.

- `-vf` stands for video filters and is a powerful feature in FFmpeg that allows you to apply various transformations or effects to your video.

- `vignette=angle=PI/4`: This is the specific filter and setting for the vignette effect. The vignette filter in FFmpeg is used to apply the vignette effect, which typically darkens the edges of the video to focus attention on the center. The `angle=PI/4` part is a parameter of the vignette filter that controls the angle of the effect. This specific setting, `PI/4`, is chosen to give a visually pleasing vignette. It's a bit of a creative choice, balancing subtlety and impact.

- `${outputFile.absolutePath}`: The last part of the command specifies where to save the processed video. It takes the path where you want the new video (with the vignette effect applied) to be saved. By placing it here in the command, you're telling FFmpeg, "Once you're done adding the effect, save the new video here."

When it comes to running this command, we use `FFmpeg.executeAsync`. This method is great because it runs our command without blocking the app. The method also has a way to check if everything went as planned. If the command runs successfully, we return the path of our new vignette video. But if something goes wrong, we catch it and return an error. Here, `AddVignetteEffectError` is a custom error message we throw if the FFmpeg command doesn't execute properly. It's a simple way to know exactly what went wrong when we add our vignette effect. And with this, `AddVignetteUseCase` is ready.

Now, we can integrate this use case into `StoryEditorViewModel`:

```
class StoryEditorViewModel(
    private val saveCaptureUseCase: SaveCaptureUseCase,
    private val addCaptionToVideoUseCase:
        AddCaptionToVideoUseCase,
    private val addVignetteEffectUseCase:
        AddVignetteEffectUseCase
): ViewModel() {
```

```
...

    var videoFile: File? = null

...

    fun addVignetteFilterToVideo() {
        videoFile?.let { file ->
            viewModelScope.launch {
                val result =
                    addVignetteEffectUseCase
                        .addVignetteEffect(file)
                // Handle the result of the filter process
            }
        }
    }
}
```

Here, `StoryEditorViewModel` is structured to receive `AddVignetteEffectUseCase` as a dependency.

Within this ViewModel, we maintain a `videoFile` property, which holds a reference to the video file that the vignette effect will be applied to. The nullable nature of this property allows for scenarios where a video file may not be immediately available.

The function to execute this functionality is `addVignetteEffectToVideo`. When invoked, this function checks whether `videoFile` is not null, ensuring that there is a valid file to process. If a video file is available, the function proceeds to launch a coroutine within `viewModelScope`.

Inside the coroutine, the `addVignetteEffectUseCase.addVignetteEffect` method is called with the video file as its argument. This is where the vignette effect is applied to the video. The result of this operation is captured in a variable named `result`. This result could indicate either a successful application of the effect or a failure due to some error.

The commented section within the function, `// Handle the result of the vignette effect process`, is where we would typically handle the outcome of the operation. Depending on whether the vignette effect was successfully applied or not, this section could include code for updating the UI to display the processed video or handling any errors that might have occurred during the process.

As we mentioned when we discussed adding captions, we haven't implemented video playback yet, but we can still test the effect in our video. Just like back in *Figure 6.3*, we can see two files, but this time one of them has a `_vignetted` suffix to indicate it has been modified:

Device Explorer

Pixel 7 API 34 Android 14.0 ("UpsideDownCake")

Files   Processes

Name	Date	Size
⌄ ▢ com.packt.packtagram	2024-05-10 09:18	4 KB
> ▢ cache	2024-05-14 00:09	4 KB
> ▢ code_cache	2024-05-15 12:47	4 KB
> ▢ databases	2024-05-15 01:26	4 KB
⌄ ▢ files	2024-05-15 23:16	4 KB
> ▢ com.google.mlkit.acceleration	2024-05-15 01:26	4 KB
≡ profileInstalled	2024-05-15 23:16	24 B
≡ video_1715811379143.mp4	2024-05-15 23:16	147,5 KB
≡ video_1715811379143_vignetted.mp4	2024-05-15 23:16	168,5 KB

Figure 6.5: Device Explorer in Android Studio

We can download and reproduce both videos to check and test the filter:

Figure 6.6: Video without (left) and with (right) the vignette filter effect applied

Now that we know how to integrate FFmpeg and use its commands to edit the user's videos, it is time to upload those videos so that they can be shared between their contacts.

Uploading the video

Now that our video is ready, it's time to upload it to any service, from where it can be shared with the user contacts. We're going to use Firebase Storage for this (to learn how to set up Firebase Storage, please refer to *Chapter 3*).

We'll start by creating a data source that will be responsible for uploading the video to Firebase Storage. We will call it `VideoStorageDataSource`:

```
class VideoStorageDataSource {
    fun uploadVideo(videoFile: File, onSuccess: (String) ->
    Unit, onError: (Exception) -> Unit) {
        val storageReference =
            FirebaseStorage.getInstance().reference
        val videoRef = storageReference.child(
            "videos/${videoFile.name}")

        val uploadTask =
            videoRef.putFile(Uri.fromFile(videoFile))
        uploadTask.addOnSuccessListener {
        videoRef.downloadUrl.addOnSuccessListener { uri ->
            onSuccess(uri.toString())
        }
        }.addOnFailureListener { exception ->
            onError(exception)
        }
    }
}
```

Inside the `uploadVideo` function, we start indicating that we'll execute the logic in the I/O dispatcher.

Then, the heart of the function is where we use Firebase Storage. First, we obtain the reference of the storage using `FirebaseStorage.getInstance().reference`, after which we set up a reference to where we want our video to be stored in Firebase using `storageReference.child("videos/${videoFile.name}")`.

Next, we start the upload itself. The `putFile` method is used to upload the video file. This is where `await()` comes into play. This `await()` is a suspending function that patiently waits for the upload to complete without blocking the thread. It's part of Kotlin's coroutines magic and is a game-changer for async operations.

Once the upload is done, we need to grab the URL of our video. So, we call `downloadUrl.await()`. Just like with the upload, `await()` suspends the operation until Firebase gives us the video's URL.

We've also got our error handling covered. The upload and URL retrieval process is wrapped in a `try-catch` block. If anything goes sideways during the upload or while fetching the URL, we catch the exception and wrap it up in `Result.failure(e)`. On the other hand, if all goes well, we return `Result.success(downloadUrl.toString())`, handing over the URL of the newly uploaded video.

Next, we will implement the repository that will be responsible for managing and connecting the data sources to the domain layer. We will call its interface `VideoRepository` and the implementation `VideoRepositoryImpl`:

```
interface VideoRepository {
    suspend fun uploadVideo(videoFile: File):
        Result<String>
}


class VideoRepositoryImpl(private val
videoStorageDataSource: VideoStorageDataSource) :
VideoRepository {
    override suspend fun uploadVideo(videoFile: File):
    Result<String> {
        return try {
            var uploadResult: Result<String> =
                Result.failure(RuntimeException("Upload
                    failed"))

            firebaseStorageDataSource.uploadVideo(
            videoFile, { url ->
                uploadResult = Result.success(url)
            }, { exception ->
                uploadResult = Result.failure(exception)
            })

            uploadResult
        } catch (e: Exception) {
            Result.failure(e)
        }
    }
}
```

First up, we have our `VideoRepository` interface. This is a straightforward Kotlin interface with one key function: `uploadVideo`.

Next, we have the `VideoRepositoryImpl` class, which implements the `VideoRepository` interface. This class is where the action happens. It's initialized with an instance of `VideoStorageDataSource`.

Then, the uploadVideo function follows a try-catch pattern for robust error handling. Initially, it sets up a default uploadResult as a failure. This is a cautious approach, assuming things might go wrong, and we'll update this only if the upload succeeds.

Then, we call uploadVideo on videoStorageDataSource, passing the video file along with two Lambda functions for handling success and failure. If the upload is successful, the success Lambda updates uploadResult with the URL of the uploaded video. If there's a failure, the failure Lambda updates uploadResult with the encountered exception.

Finally, we return uploadResult. If all goes well, we'll see the URL of the uploaded video. If not, we'll see the error that occurred during the process. The try-catch block ensures that if there's an unexpected exception anywhere in this process, we catch it and return it as a failure.

Now, it's time for us to implement UploadVideoUseCase:

```
class UploadVideoUseCase(private val videoRepository:
VideoRepository) {
    suspend fun uploadVideo(videoFile: File):
    Result<String> {
        return videoRepository.uploadVideo(videoFile)
    }
}
```

Here, we are injecting VideoRepository. In the uploadVideo function, we call videoRepository and pass videoFile as a parameter.

Finally, we will include UploadVideoUseCase in StoryEditorViewModel and use it from there:

```
class StoryEditorViewModel(
private val saveCaptureUseCase: SaveCaptureUseCase,
private val addCaptionToVideoUseCase:
    AddCaptionToVideoUseCase,
private val addVignetteEffectUseCase:
    AddVignetteEffectUseCase,
private val uploadVideoUseCase: UploadVideoUseCase
) : ViewModel() {

...

    fun uploadVideo(videoFile: File) {
        viewModelScope.launch {
            val result =
                uploadVideoUseCase.uploadVideo(videoFile)
            // Handle the result of the upload process
        }
    }
}
```

In `StoryEditorViewModel`, we add a function called `uploadVideo` that takes the video file and uses `uploadVideoUseCase` to upload it. The operation is performed within a coroutine to ensure it doesn't block the UI thread.

The `// Handle the result of the upload process` comment is where we would implement the logic based on the outcome of the upload. If the upload is successful, we might update the UI to show that the video has been uploaded or display the video URL. In case of failure, we would handle the error, perhaps by showing an error message to the user.

And with this change, we are ready to upload the video from our ViewModel. By doing this, we have completed this chapter, as well as our work on Packtagram!

Summary

Wrapping up this chapter, you've significantly leveled up your Packtagram app's video capabilities.

Starting with CameraX, we expanded its use from snapping photos to capturing high-quality videos, but this was just the beginning. Then, we dived into FFmpeg, an incredibly versatile tool for video editing. Here, you learned how to add a creative touch to videos, be it through captions that tell a story or filters that change the entire look and feel.

But what's a great video if it can't be shared? We tackled that too by integrating Firebase Storage for seamless video uploads. This means your app is now adept at handling large files smoothly, ensuring users enjoy a hiccup-free experience.

With this chapter, we have finished our work on Packtagram. Now, it's time to learn about the project that will be implemented in the last three chapters: a video playback app so that you can view your favorite series and films!

Part 3: Creating Packtflix, a Video Media App

In this final part, you will learn to create a video streaming app called Packtflix. You will start by setting up the app's structure, implementing secure user authentication using OAuth2, and building dynamic UI components with Jetpack Compose to browse movie lists and details. Then, you will master video playback by integrating ExoPlayer, creating an intuitive playback UI, managing media controls, and adding subtitles for accessibility. Finally, you will enhance the app with extended video playback functionalities, including **Picture-in-Picture** (**PiP**) mode and media casting, enabling seamless multitasking and streaming to larger screens.

This part includes the following chapters:

- *Chapter 7, Starting a Video Streaming App and Adding Authentication*
- *Chapter 8, Adding Media Playback to Packtflix with ExoPlayer*
- *Chapter 9, Extending Video Playback in Your Packtflix App*

7

Starting a Video Streaming App and Adding Authentication

Having mastered how to create engaging social apps such as WhatsApp and Instagram, it's now time to dive into the world of video streaming services. This chapter marks the beginning of our third project: a Netflix-like app. Let's call it Packtflix. Here, we will explore a different aspect of Android development, focusing on multimedia content delivery and user authentication, while continuing to build captivating user interfaces.

Our journey will begin by laying the groundwork for our streaming app. We'll start from scratch, setting up a new project and introducing you to the app's structure and modules.

Following the setup, we'll dive into one of the most critical aspects of any app: authenticating your users. In today's digital age, security and privacy are more relevant than ever, so you'll learn how to implement robust authentication mechanisms using OAuth2. This will ensure that your app's users can securely access their accounts and personal preferences.

Once our users can log in, we'll focus on presenting them with a rich selection of movies. We'll employ Jetpack Compose to create dynamic and responsive lists, showcasing the available content.

Finally, we'll delve into the details. Each movie or series in your app deserves its spotlight, and you'll create detailed screens for them using Jetpack Compose. This will provide users with all the information they need to decide what to watch next.

So, this chapter will cover the following topics:

- Creating the app's structure and modules
- Building the login screen
- Authenticating the app's users
- Creating your movie list
- Making the movie and series detail screen

Technical requirements

As in the previous chapter, you will need to have installed Android Studio (or another editor of your preference).

We are going to start a new project in this chapter, so it is not necessary to download the changes made in the previous chapter.

You will find the complete code that we are going to build throughout this chapter in this repository: `https://github.com/PacktPublishing/Thriving-in-Android-Development-using-Kotlin/tree/main/Chapter-7`.

Creating the app's structure and modules

In this section, we'll lay the foundation for our Packtflix app by organizing it into feature modules. As we have seen before, by dividing the app into modules such as login, list, and playback, we can work on one feature at a time without affecting the others and speed up the build process for larger projects. Additionally, we'll set up a version catalog for our dependencies as we did before to streamline the management of libraries such as Jetpack Compose, Dagger Hilt, and Kotlin.

Let's start creating the project. In Android Studio, select **File | New | New Project…**, and choose **Empty Compose Activity**. Then, in the **New Project** panel, fill out **Name**, **Package name**, and **Save location**. For the **Minimum SKD** option, we will choose **API 29** again as it guarantees the best percentage of compatibility at the time of writing.

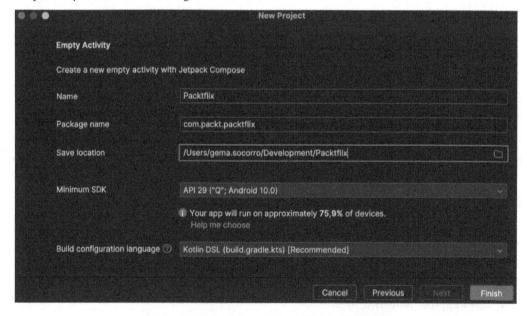

Figure 7.1: New project configuration for Packtflix

The options in *Figure 7.1* are the ones we will see using Android Studio Iguana (version 2023.2.1), though it may have variations depending on the version. For example, in other previous versions of Android Studio, we could also select whether we were going to use the version catalog for our dependencies.

Now, the version catalog is created by default, so we will already get a `libs.versions.toml` file in our project with the following content:

```
[versions]
agp = "8.3.0-alpha18"
kotlin = "1.9.0"
coreKtx = "1.12.0"
junit = "4.13.2"
junitVersion = "1.1.5"
espressoCore = "3.5.1"
lifecycleRuntimeKtx = "2.7.0"
activityCompose = "1.8.2"
composeBom = "2023.08.00"


[libraries]
androidx-core-ktx = { group = "androidx.core", name = "core-ktx",
version.ref = "coreKtx" }
junit = { group = "junit", name = "junit", version.ref = "junit" }
androidx-junit = { group = "androidx.test.ext", name = "junit",
version.ref = "junitVersion" }
androidx-espresso-core = { group = "androidx.test.espresso", name =
"espresso-core", version.ref = "espressoCore" }
androidx-lifecycle-runtime-ktx = { group = "androidx.lifecycle", name
= "lifecycle-runtime-ktx", version.ref = "lifecycleRuntimeKtx" }
androidx-activity-compose = { group = "androidx.activity", name =
"activity-compose", version.ref = "activityCompose" }
androidx-compose-bom = { group = "androidx.compose", name = "compose-
bom", version.ref = "composeBom" }
androidx-ui = { group = "androidx.compose.ui", name = "ui" }
androidx-ui-graphics = { group = "androidx.compose.ui", name = "ui-
graphics" }
androidx-ui-tooling = { group = "androidx.compose.ui", name = "ui-
tooling" }
androidx-ui-tooling-preview = { group = "androidx.compose.ui", name =
"ui-tooling-preview" }
androidx-ui-test-manifest = { group = "androidx.compose.ui", name =
"ui-test-manifest" }
androidx-ui-test-junit4 = { group = "androidx.compose.ui", name = "ui-
test-junit4" }
androidx-material3 = { group = "androidx.compose.material3", name =
"material3" }


[plugins]
```

```
androidApplication = { id = "com.android.application", version.ref =
"agp" }
jetbrainsKotlinAndroid = { id = "org.jetbrains.kotlin.android",
version.ref = "kotlin" }
```

This code adds the basic dependencies to the version catalog to build an app with Kotlin, Android, and Jetpack Compose.

The next step will be to create the modules needed. Here, we will create three feature modules:

- `:feature:login`: We will use this module to include the login feature
- `:feature:list`: In this module, we will include the list screen as well as the detail screen
- `:feature:playback`: In this module, we will host all the playback functionality

We will also create the following common modules:

- `:app`: This module will contain the entry point for our application
- `:common`: This module will contain common functionality needed in more than one module

To create these modules, use the **File | New | New Module...** option, as we have done in the previous projects. The final project structure should look like this:

Figure 7.2: Project module structure

Now that we have created our module structure, it is time to set up the dependency injection framework.

Setting up the dependency injection framework

As we saw in the previous chapters, the need for scalability, performance optimization, and testability has made the use of a dependency injection framework practically a must in Android. In this case, we will use Hilt again (to learn more about it, please refer to *Chapter 1* where we did a complete review of the framework and exposed its main advantages).

Let's start adding the dependency to our version catalog. Open our `libs.versions.toml` file and add the Hilt dependencies in the `versions`, `libraries`, and `plugins` blocks, as follows:

```
[versions]
// ...
hiltVersion = "2.50"
[libraries]
// ...
androidxHilt = { module = "com.google.dagger:hilt-android", name =
"hilt", version.ref = "hiltVersion" }
hiltCompiler = { module = "com.google.dagger:hilt-android-compiler",
name = "hilt-compiler", version.ref = "hiltVersion" }


[plugins]
// ...
hilt = { id = "com.google.dagger.hilt.android", version.ref =
"hiltVersion" }
```

Then, we will add the plugin to the project-level `build.gradle.kts`:

```
plugins {
    ...
    alias(libs.plugins.hilt) apply false
}
```

Next, in the `build.gradle.kts` file of every module, we will have to apply the plugin and add the Hilt dependency:

```
plugins {
//...
    alias(libs.plugins.hilt)
}
dependencies {
//...
    implementation(libs.androidxHilt)
    kapt(libs.hiltCompiler)
}
```

Now, in the : app module, we can create the PacktflixApp class, which will be the entry point for the Hilt configuration:

```
@HiltAndroidApp
class PacktflixApp: Application() {
}
```

With this annotation, we are enabling Hilt to generate the necessary components under the hood that will be used for dependency injection throughout our application.

Finally, we should include PacktflixApp in AndroidManifest.xml, so that our app uses it instead of the default Application class:

```
<?xml version="1.0" encoding="utf-8"?>
<manifest xmlns:android =
"http://schemas.android.com/apk/res/android"
    xmlns:tools = "http://schemas.android.com/tools">

    <application
        android:name = ".PacktflixApp"
        ...>
....
    </application>

</manifest>
```

Now, we are all set to start building our new project. The first step will be to build the login screen as we want our users to authenticate themselves using their credentials. Let's start working on it!

Building the login screen

To build the login screen, we will start creating a LoginScreen composable with Jetpack Compose. We will have to include the app's logo, fields to introduce the email and password, and a **Login** button. We can also include a text to show whether there are any errors when the user tries to log in.

This login screen is going to have four states (Idle, Loading, Success, and Error), so let's start modeling the overall ViewState:

```
sealed class LoginState {
    object Idle : LoginState()
    object Loading : LoginState()
    object Success : LoginState()
    data class Error(val message: String?) : LoginState()
}
```

Now, let's create the `LoginScreen` composable:

```
@Composable
fun LoginScreen() {
    val loginViewModel: LoginViewModel = hiltViewModel()
    val loginState =
        loginViewModel.loginState.collectAsState().value

    var email by remember { mutableStateOf("") }
    var password by remember { mutableStateOf("") }
    var errorMessage by remember { mutableStateOf("") }
//...
}
```

We start the composable function by obtaining `LoginViewModel`, accessed via `hiltViewModel()`. This `ViewModel` component manages the login logic and exposes the current login state through a `StateFlow` stream. The `collectAsState().value` call converts the asynchronous stream of login states into a composable-friendly state that triggers recompositions when the login state changes.

The function uses `remember { mutableStateOf("") }` to maintain the state of user inputs for email and password within the composable's lifecycle. This state is mutable and reactive, meaning any changes to the input fields (handled by `onValueChange`) automatically update the corresponding variables and thus the UI.

Let's continue now with the next part of the composable, which will include the name of the app, the fields for `email` and `password`, and the **Login** button:

```
Surface(color = Color.Black, modifier =
Modifier.fillMaxSize()) {
        Column(
            horizontalAlignment =
                Alignment.CenterHorizontally,
            verticalArrangement = Arrangement.Center,
            modifier = Modifier
                .padding(16.dp)
        ) {
            if (loginState is LoginState.Error) {
                Text(
                    text = loginState.message ?:
                        "Unknown error",
                    color = Color.Red,
                    modifier = Modifier
                        .padding(bottom = 16.dp)
```

```kotlin
        )
    }
    Text(
        text = "PACKTFLIX",
        color = Color.Red,
        fontSize = 36.sp,
        modifier = Modifier.padding(bottom = 32.dp)
    )
    OutlinedTextField(
        value = email,
        onValueChange = { email = it },
        label = { Text("Email") },
        colors = OutlinedTextFieldDefaults.colors(
            focusedContainerColor =
                Color.Transparent,
            focusedTextColor = Color.White,
            focusedBorderColor = Color.Gray,
            unfocusedBorderColor = Color.Gray
        ),
        modifier = Modifier.fillMaxWidth()
    )
    Spacer(modifier = Modifier.height(8.dp))
    OutlinedTextField(
        value = password,
        onValueChange = { password = it },
        label = { Text("Password") },
        visualTransformation =
            PasswordVisualTransformation(),
        colors = OutlinedTextFieldDefaults.colors(
            focusedTextColor = Color.White,
            focusedContainerColor =
                Color.Transparent,
            focusedBorderColor = Color.Gray,
            unfocusedBorderColor = Color.Gray
        ),
        keyboardActions = KeyboardActions(
            onDone = { loginViewModel.login(
                email, password) }
        ),
        modifier = Modifier.fillMaxWidth()
    )
    Spacer(modifier = Modifier.height(24.dp))
```

```
        Button(
            onClick = { loginViewModel.login(email,
                password) },
            colors = ButtonDefaults.buttonColors(
                containerColor = Color.Gray)
        ) {
            Text("Sign In", color = Color.White)
        }
        Spacer(modifier = Modifier.height(24.dp))
        if (loginState is LoginState.Loading) {
            CircularProgressIndicator()
        }
    }
}


LaunchedEffect(loginState) {
    when (loginState) {
        is LoginState.Success -> {
            // Navigate to next screen or show success
                message
        }
        is LoginState.Error -> {
            errorMessage = loginState.message ?:
                "An error occurred"
        }
        else -> Unit // Handle other states if
                        necessary
    }
}
```

The UI dynamically adjusts based on the current login state. For example, if the login state is `LoginState.Error`, the function renders a `Text` composable to display the error message. This conditional rendering is crucial for providing feedback to the user, such as indicating a login failure or showing a loading indicator (`CircularProgressIndicator`) when the login process is underway. This approach to UI development is declarative, with the UI's structure and content directly mapping to the application's state.

The `OutlinedTextField` composables for `email` and `password` capture user inputs, which are then used to initiate the login process (`loginViewModel.login(email, password)`) when the user clicks the **Sign In** button or completes the `password` field (via `KeyboardActions`). This demonstrates how to handle user actions and input in a composable, triggering `ViewModel` actions that ultimately lead to state changes.

Finally, the `LaunchedEffect` block listens for changes in the login state to perform side effects, such as navigation upon successful login or updating the error message state. This pattern separates side effects from the UI logic, ensuring that effects such as navigation or showing toasts only occur in response to state changes, not as a direct result of user actions.

Now, let's start working on `LoginViewModel`:

```
@HiltViewModel
class LoginViewModel @Inject constructor(
    private val loginUseCase: DoLoginUseCase
) : ViewModel() {

    private val _loginState =
        MutableStateFlow<LoginState>(LoginState.Idle)
    val loginState: StateFlow<LoginState> = _loginState

    fun login(email: String, password: String) {
        viewModelScope.launch {
            _loginState.value = LoginState.Loading
            val result = loginUseCase.doLogin(email,
                password)
            _loginState.value = when {
                result.isFailure -> LoginState.Error(
                    result.exceptionOrNull()?.message)
                else -> LoginState.Success
            }
        }
    }
}
```

Here, we start with the dependency injection stuff: the use of `@HiltViewModel` indicates that Hilt will be responsible for the instantiation and provision of `LoginViewModel`. The `@Inject` constructor signifies that Hilt will inject the necessary dependencies into this `ViewModel` instance, in this case, an implementation of a use case called `DoLoginUseCase` (we will implement this use case later).

The `ViewModel` instance manages the login state using `MutableStateFlow<LoginState>`. Here, `_loginState` is a private, mutable state flow that holds the current state of the login process, which can be one of `Idle`, `Loading`, `Success`, or `Error`. The immutable `loginState` property exposes this state to the UI layer as a read-only `StateFlow`, ensuring that state updates are safely and efficiently communicated to the UI.

The login function embodies the core functionality of this `ViewModel` class. It initiates the login process by setting `_loginState` to `Loading`, indicating that the login operation has started. It then proceeds to call the `doLogin` method on the provided `loginUseCase` with the user's email and password.

After attempting to log in, the function evaluates the result. If the login attempt fails (`result.isFailure`), `_loginState` is updated to `Error` with the exception message, providing feedback on why the login failed. If the login succeeds, `_loginState` is set to `Success`, indicating a successful login process. This conditional handling ensures that the UI can react appropriately to different outcomes of the login process.

The login process is launched within `viewModelScope`, a coroutine scope tied to the `ViewModel` lifecycle. This ensures that any ongoing login operation is automatically canceled if the `ViewModel` instance is cleared (typically, when the associated UI component is destroyed), preventing memory leaks and unnecessary work.

With that, we have our login screen ready. The last step is to set up the Hilt modules and set the content of `MainActivity` to show the `LoginScreen` composable:

```
@AndroidEntryPoint
class MainActivity : ComponentActivity() {
    override fun onCreate(savedInstanceState: Bundle?) {
        super.onCreate(savedInstanceState)
        setContent {
            PacktflixTheme {
                LoginScreen()
            }
        }
    }
}
```

If we now execute the app, we should see the following screen:

Figure 7.3: Packtflix login screen

Now that we have finished our UI, the next step will be to authenticate the users. Let's learn how to do it.

Authenticating the app's users

In mobile applications, authentication plays a critical role in protecting user data and personal information from unauthorized access. As mobile devices often serve as personal gateways to a wide array of services and store a significant amount of sensitive data, ensuring that this data is securely managed and accessed is more important than ever. One of the preferred methods for authenticating users is OAuth2.

OAuth2 is an authorization framework that allows third-party services to exchange web resources on behalf of a user. It enables users to grant websites or applications access to their information on other websites without giving them their passwords. This is particularly useful for providing functionalities such as logging in with Google, Facebook, or other social media accounts.

The following is a list of OAuth2's most important features:

- **Security**: It allows the user to authorize an application to access their resources on a different server without sharing their credentials, typically by using access tokens granted through a process involving user consent and secure token exchanges.

  An OAuth **token** is a credential that represents the authorization granted to the application, allowing it to access specific resources on behalf of the user. These tokens can come in various formats, such as opaque tokens or **JSON Web Tokens** (**JWTs**). Opaque tokens are simple strings without any specific structure, while JWTs are structured tokens that consist of three parts – a header, a payload, and a signature – all encoded in Base64.

- **Scalability**: It allows for the delegation of user authentication to the service that hosts the user account, by offloading the technical complexities of secure authentication and infrastructure scalability to dedicated services. These services are usually managed by specific teams in charge of the complex and resource-intensive tasks of securing and scaling authentication processes.

- **Flexibility**: It supports multiple flows (based on grant types, which will determine the flow the authentication process has to follow) for different types of clients, including mobile apps, websites, and server-side applications.

- **User Experience**: It enables a smoother login experience for users, as users can use existing accounts to sign in to new services without creating new credentials.

In essence, OAuth2 provides a secure and efficient way to implement authentication in mobile applications. It leverages existing user accounts, which simplifies the login process for users, and offloads the complexity of managing user credentials and sessions to a third-party service, enhancing both security and user experience.

Let's add this feature to our app, starting by adding the models that are needed.

Creating the user model

First, we will define a simple user model that will hold the user information we will receive upon successful authentication:

```
data class User(
    val id: String,
    val name: String,
    val email: String,
    // Add other fields as necessary
)
```

In this code, we are defining the basic fields needed to hold the user information (depending on the requirements of your app, these fields will be different).

Then, to build the login request that we are going to send to the backend to obtain the authentication token, we will need another data class to hold the credentials:

```
data class LoginRequest(val email: String, val password:
String)
```

Here, we are including the email and password fields, which will be mandatory to be able to log users in.

Once this request reaches the backend, if the credentials are correct, the backend will return an authorization token, which our app will store in a secure place and will use to authenticate the following API calls to the backend. We will need another model to hold this token information:

```
data class AuthToken(val token: String)
```

Now, let's set Retrofit to get this authorization token.

Using Retrofit to get the authorization token

To obtain the authorization token, we need our app to request it when the user provides their credentials. In order to send this request to the backend, we are going to use Retrofit. We already used Retrofit in *Chapter 4*, so let's skip the introductions and start with the setup of an interface that Retrofit will use to make the HTTP requests:

```
interface AuthService {
    @POST("auth/login")
    suspend fun login(@Body loginRequest: LoginRequest):
        Response<AuthToken>
}
```

This code defines an interface called `AuthService` with a unique login function. We will pass a `LoginRequest` object with the data needed for the request and then will obtain an `AuthToken` response.

Let's build those models. First, we'll build the `LoginRequest` model:

```
data class LoginRequest(val email: String, val password:
String)
```

In this model, we will send the user's credentials – their email and password – to the backend.

Then, if the login has been successful, the backend should answer with a response including an authorization token. We will structure this response as follows:

```
data class AuthToken(val token: String)
```

This `AuthToken` model will include the aforementioned authorization token. Note that, usually, these tokens have a time window and so have to be renewed before they have expired. For simplicity, we are going to assume this token will not expire.

Now, let's create our remote data source to retrieve the authorization token:

```
class LoginRemoteDataSource(
    private val authService: AuthService
) {

    suspend fun login(email: String, password: String):
    Result<String> {
        return authService.login(
            LoginRequest(
                email = email,
                password = password
            )
        ).run {
            val token = this.body()?.token
            if (this.isSuccessful && token != null) {
                Result.success(token)
            } else {
                Result.failure(getError(this))
            }
        }
    }
}
```

Here, we define the `LoginRemoteDataSource` class, which will act as a data source layer for handling login functionality by interacting with the remote authentication service. This class will have a single dependency, `authService`, which is an interface (presumably Retrofit or a similar networking library) responsible for making network requests related to authentication. The primary function within this class, `login`, is a suspended function that takes two parameters, `email` and `password`, which are used to construct a `LoginRequest` object. This object is then passed to the `authService.login` method, initiating a network request to log the user in.

Upon receiving the response from `authService.login`, the `run` block is executed to handle the response. Inside this block, the response is checked to determine whether the request was successful (`isSuccessful`) and whether the response body contains a non-`null` token. If both conditions are met, `Result.success(token)` is returned, encapsulating the token in a successful result. This indicates that the login was successful and provides the caller with the token. Conversely, if either condition is not satisfied – meaning the request failed or the token was null – a failure result is returned by calling `Result.failure(getError(this))`. The `getError` function will analyze the `Response<AuthToken>` object to determine the nature of the failure and return an appropriate `Throwable` object that describes the error.

At this point, let's build the `getError()` function:

```
private fun getError(response: Response<AuthToken>):
Throwable {
    return when (response.code()) {
        401 -> LoginException.AuthenticationException(
            "Invalid email or password.")
        403 -> LoginException.AccessDeniedException(
            "Access denied.")
        404 -> LoginException.NotFoundException(
            "Login endpoint not found.")
        in 500..599 -> LoginException.ServerException(
            "Server error: ${response.message()}.")
        else -> LoginException.HttpException(
            response.code(),
            "HTTP error: ${response.code()}
                ${response.message()}."
        )
    }
}
```

In this `getError` function, we map the possible values of the status code from the response to different errors. If we wanted to, we could later process those errors and show messages to the user accordingly.

Let's also define those errors, in which we will map the server response. We will define them as part of a `LoginException` sealed class, which is a special type of class in Kotlin that restricts the inheritance hierarchy to a specific set of subclasses, providing exhaustive when expressions and ensuring that every possible type of error is handled:

```
sealed class LoginException(loginErrorMessage: String, val
code: Int? = null) : Exception(loginErrorMessage) {
    class AuthenticationException(message: String) :
        LoginException(message)
    class AccessDeniedException(message: String) :
        LoginException(message)
    class NotFoundException(message: String) :
        LoginException(message)
    class ServerException(message: String) :
        LoginException(message)
    class HttpException(code: Int, message: String) :
        LoginException(message, code)
}
```

Now that we have our `LoginRemoteDataSource` component, it is time to define how to store the token.

Using DataStore to store the token

Introduced by Google, **DataStore** is a data storage solution that provides an efficient, secure, and asynchronous way of persisting small pieces of data. It uses Kotlin coroutines and flow streams to store data asynchronously, ensuring UI thread safety and smoother performance.

DataStore comes with several features that make it a preferable data storage option in Android applications:

- **Asynchronous by default**: DataStore operations are performed asynchronously using Kotlin coroutines, preventing blocking the main thread and improving app performance.

- **Safe and consistent**: With built-in transactional data APIs, DataStore ensures data consistency and integrity, even if an app process is killed during a write operation.

- **Type safety**: DataStore offers two implementations: Preferences DataStore, which stores and retrieves key-value pairs, and Proto DataStore, which allows for storing type-safe objects using Protocol Buffers.

- **Security**: DataStore can be integrated with encryption mechanisms to securely store sensitive information. DataStore can be combined with encryption libraries such as Tink to encrypt the data before saving, making it a more secure option for handling user credentials, tokens, and other sensitive information.

Why will we use DataStore and not Room (which we used previously for our WhatsPackt messenger project)? While both are robust data persistence libraries, they serve different purposes and have distinct use cases:

- **Use case suitability**: DataStore is designed for storing small collections of data, such as settings, preferences, or application state. It excels in handling lightweight tasks where the data structure is simple. RoomDatabase is a SQLite abstraction that significantly reduces the amount of boilerplate code needed to use SQLite. It's intended for more complex data storage requirements, such as storing large datasets, relational data, or when we need to perform complex queries.

- **Performance and complexity**: DataStore provides a simpler API for data storage with minimal setup, making it ideal for straightforward tasks. Its performance is optimized for small datasets and simple data structures. RoomDatabase, being a database, is more suited for complex queries and large datasets. It involves more setup and is heavier than DataStore but offers more features and capabilities for comprehensive data management.

- **Data security**: DataStore, especially with Proto DataStore, can easily be integrated with encryption mechanisms to store data securely, making it a more secure option for sensitive information. RoomDatabase supports SQLite encryption, but integrating encryption requires additional setup and possibly third-party libraries.

As we just need to store a small value (the token) and given its security features, DataStore is the best option.

So, to start using it, first, we need to set up the DataStore dependency and its version in our version catalog:

```
[versions]
datastore = "1.0.0"

[libraries]
datastore = { module = "androidx.datastore:datastore-
preferences", version.ref = "datastore" }
```

Then, need to add it to our modules' gradle.build.kts files:

```
dependencies {
    ...
    implementation(libs.datastore)
}
```

With this code, we are only adding it to the modules where we would need to use the dependency – initially, this will just be in the :feature:login module.

Now, we can start using the DataStore library. We are going to build a `LoginLocalDataSource` component, which will be responsible for storing and retrieving the token in and from the DataStore:

```
val Context.dataStore by preferencesDataStore(name = "user_
preferences")

class LoginLocalDataSource(private val context: Context) {

    companion object {
        val TOKEN_KEY = stringPreferencesKey("auth_token")
    }

    suspend fun saveAuthToken(token: String) {
        context.dataStore.edit { preferences ->
            preferences[TOKEN_KEY] = token
        }
    }

    suspend fun getAuthToken(): Result<String> {
        val preferences = context.dataStore.data.first()
        val token = preferences[TOKEN_KEY]
        return if (token != null) {
            Result.success(token)
        } else {
            Result.failure(TokenNotFoundError())
        }
    }
}

class TokenNotFoundError : Throwable("Auth token not
found")
```

In `LoginLocalDataSource`, first, we leverage Kotlin's property delegation feature to initialize the DataStore. By defining `val Context.dataStore` with `preferencesDataStore(name: "user_preferences")`, we ensure a single instance of the DataStore is lazily initialized and tied to the application's context. This method optimizes resource use and simplifies subsequent data operations.

Within `LoginLocalDataSource`, we define a companion object to hold `TOKEN_KEY`, a key used to store and retrieve the authentication token from the DataStore. This key is defined using `stringPreferencesKey("auth_token")`, indicating the data type we intend to store – in this case, a `String` type.

In the `saveAuthToken` function, we perform a write operation on the DataStore by calling `edit` and passing a lambda that assigns the provided token to `TOKEN_KEY`. This operation is atomic and thread-safe, ensuring the integrity of our data.

To retrieve the authentication token, `getAuthToken` also employs suspending semantics to facilitate asynchronous execution. It accesses the DataStore's data as a flow, immediately fetching the first emitted value with `.data.first()`. This operation suspends the coroutine, effectively making the data retrieval feel synchronous while maintaining the benefits of asynchronous execution. The function then checks whether the token exists and returns it wrapped in `Result<String>`, providing a straightforward way to handle success and failure. In the absence of a token, it returns `Result.failure` with a custom `TokenNotFoundError`, offering precise error handling.

Now, it is time to implement `LoginRepository`, which is responsible for coordinating between the remote and local data sources. We will build it, as always, by creating an interface in the domain layer and the implementation in the data layer. This is because the domain shouldn't have any explicit dependency from the data layer, to respect the clean architecture. So, we define the interface like so:

```
interface LoginRepository {
    suspend fun getToken(): Result<String>
    suspend fun loginWithCredentials(email: String,
        password: String): Result<Unit>
}
```

Here, the interface will have two functions: one to obtain the token so it can be used elsewhere (for example, for the backend requests to authenticate the user once it has been obtained) and another to perform the login and store the newly obtained authentication token.

Now, let's implement the repository:

```
class LoginRepositoryImpl(
    private val localDataSource: LoginLocalDataSource,
    private val remoteDataSource: LoginRemoteDataSource
): LoginRepository {

    override suspend fun getToken(): Result<String> {
        return localDataSource.getAuthToken()
    }

    override suspend fun loginWithCredentials(email:
    String, password: String): Result<Unit> {
        return remoteDataSource.login(email, password)
            .fold(
                onSuccess = {
                    localDataSource.saveAuthToken(it)
                    Result.success(Unit)
```

```
            },
            onFailure = {
                Result.failure(it)
            }
        )
    }
}
```

The `LoginRepositoryImpl` class serves as an implementation of the `LoginRepository` interface, acting as a mediator between the application's data sources and its use cases or view models. This class abstracts the details of data retrieval and storage, providing a cohesive API for authentication processes. It relies on two primary data sources: `localDataSource` for local data storage and retrieval, and `remoteDataSource` for handling network requests related to user authentication.

In the `getToken` function, the repository directly delegates the call to `localDataSource.getAuthToken()`, which fetches the authentication token from local storage. This method returns a `Result<String>` object, encapsulating the outcome of the operation in a type-safe manner. The token retrieval is critical for checking the user's authentication status or for subsequent authenticated API calls that require a token.

The `loginWithCredentials` function implements the process of authenticating a user with their email and password. It first attempts to log in through the `remoteDataSource.login(email, password)` method. Upon a successful login, indicated by the `onSuccess` branch of the fold, it saves the received authorization token using `localDataSource.saveAuthToken(it)` and then signals the completion of the login process with `Result.success(Unit)`. Conversely, if the remote login attempt fails (`onFailure`), it propagates the failure as `Result.failure(it)`, allowing the calling code to handle the error appropriately. This design effectively separates concerns between local and remote data handling, ensuring that the repository remains the single source of truth for all authentication-related data flows within the application.

Now, we can build a use case to perform the login, consuming this `LoginRepository` component:

```
interface DoLoginUseCase {
    suspend fun doLogin(email: String, password: String):
        Result<Unit>
}

class DoLogin(
    private val loginRepository: LoginRepository
) : DoLoginUseCase {
    override suspend fun doLogin(email: String, password:
    String): Result<Unit> {
        return loginRepository.loginWithCredentials(email,
            password)
```

```
    }
  }
```

The DoLogin class implements the DoLoginUseCase interface, encapsulating the logic required to authenticate a user by their email and password. By delegating the authentication process to loginRepository, it invokes loginRepository.loginWithCredentials(email, password) to perform the actual login operation. The DoLogin use case simplifies the process of user authentication into a single method call, ensuring that the details of how the login is performed are encapsulated within the repository, thereby promoting the separation of concerns and making the code easier to maintain and test.

Now, we are all set to use the login functionality. Next, let's use those tokens to validate the app requests.

Sending the authorization token in requests

To finish the users authentication:authorization token, sending in requests" authentication tasks, there is still one thing we have to do. The reason we were obtaining this authentication token was to be used in the requests the app is going to send to the backend, so it will guarantee the authenticity of the user that has generated the request. To include the token in every request, we are going to take advantage of Retrofit interceptors.

A Retrofit **interceptor** is a powerful mechanism provided by OkHttp (the underlying HTTP client used by Retrofit) that allows you to intercept and manipulate the request and response chain. Interceptors can modify requests and responses or perform actions such as logging, adding headers, handling authentication, and much more, before the request is sent to the server or after the response is received by the client.

Interceptors can be broadly categorized into two types:

- **Application interceptors**: These interceptors are called once for any single call to the server. They don't need to worry about network specifics such as retries and redirects. Application interceptors are perfect for tasks such as adding a common header to all requests, logging the request and response body for debugging purposes, or managing application-level caching.

- **Network interceptors**: These interceptors can monitor the data at the network level. They can observe and manipulate requests and responses that come from and go to the server, including any retries and redirects that occur as part of the network call process.

To add an authentication token to all outgoing requests, we will choose an application interceptor. We will choose an application interceptor in this scenario because they are designed to operate at the application layer, directly modifying requests before they are sent out and processing responses once they are received. This makes them well suited for tasks such as adding headers that should be included in every request to the server, such as authentication tokens.

So, let's write our interceptor:

```
class AuthInterceptor(private val loginRepository:
LoginRepository) : Interceptor {
    override fun intercept(chain: Interceptor.Chain):
    Response {
        val originalRequest = chain.request()
        val token = runBlocking {
            loginRepository.getToken().getOrNull() }
        val requestWithToken = originalRequest.newBuilder()
            .apply {
                if (token != null) {
                    header("Authorization",
                        "Bearer $token")
                }
            }
            .build()
        return chain.proceed(requestWithToken)
    }
}
```

This class plays a critical role in enriching outgoing HTTP requests with authentication details. It achieves this by integrating with `LoginRepository`, from which it retrieves the current user's authorization token. Upon intercepting a request, the interceptor fetches theusers authentication:authorization token, sending in requests" token synchronously using `runBlocking` (a mechanism that allows for the seamless integration of coroutine-based asynchronous token retrieval into the synchronous flow expected by interceptors).

If a token is present, it's appended to the request as an `Authorization` header, adhering to the widely accepted bearer token format (the bearer token format is a security scheme where a client sends a token in the header of the requests to authenticate access, prefixed with the word `Bearer` followed by a space and the token itself), thereby ensuring that the request carries the necessary credentials for authentication by the server.

Using `runBlocking` within the interceptor is a pragmatic approach to accommodate the synchronous nature of the `intercept()` method, allowing for the immediate availability of the token. However, it's crucial to ensure that the token retrieval operation is efficient and non-blocking to avoid performance bottlenecks – ideally, by fetching the token from a local cache or storage.

Finally, at the end of the function, we return `chain.proceed(requestwithToken)`, which will allow Retrofit to continue processing the request, including the interceptor changes (in this case, adding the authentication header).

Now, we should include `AuthInterceptor` as an interceptor when we are building the Retrofit client:

```
@Provides
@Singleton
fun provideRetrofit(
    moshi: Moshi,
    authInterceptor: AuthInterceptor
): Retrofit {
    val okHttpClient = OkHttpClient.Builder()
        .addInterceptor(authInterceptor)
        .build()

    return Retrofit.Builder()
        .baseUrl("https://your.api.url/") // Replace
                                          with your
                                          actual
                                          base URL
        .addConverterFactory(
            MoshiConverterFactory.create(moshi))
        .client(okHttpClient)
        .build()
}
```

Here, we can see how we can integrate the interceptor we've created into our network layer setup, specifically within a Retrofit configuration.

Within the function, an `OkHttpClient` instance is created and configured to include the `authInterceptor` instance via the `addInterceptor` method. This setup ensures that every HTTP request made by this client will first pass through the `authInterceptor`, allowing it to modify the request as needed before it is sent out.

Following the configuration of the `OkHttpClient` instance, the Retrofit instance is built. The configured `OkHttpClient` instance is set as the client for Retrofit, linking the HTTP client, with its interceptor, to the Retrofit instance. Now, all the requests using this Retrofit instance will include the authentication token in the header, if it exists.

After that, weusers authentication:authorization token, sending in requests" handled the app authentication, from obtaining the token and storing it to providing this token in every request. Now, it's time to build the main screen: the list of movies and series.

Creating your movie list

One of the goals of our Packtflix app is for users to have the freedom to explore and enjoy an extensive range of movies (or TV series), ensuring they stay engaged with our app. To achieve this, we must present our movie catalog in the most appealing manner possible. For that reason, in this section, we will focus on building a movie (or series!) catalog screen.

To start building the classical main screen of our streaming app, we first need to create the models we will use to represent the information.

Building the models

Start by building the `Movie` model:

```
data class Movie(
    val id: Int,
    val title: String,
    val imageUrl: String,
)
```

This is the model that will represent a movie – it includes the movie identification (`id`), its title, and a URL to an image of the movie.

Generally, movies in a streaming app are arranged by genres, so let's create a `Genre` model too:

```
data class Genre(
    val name: String,
    val movies: List<Movie>
)
```

Here we defined the name of the genre (needed to render it on the screen) and a list of the movies included in that genre.

Finally, we need a `MoviesViewState` class to represent the movie list screen state:

```
data class MoviesViewState(
    val genres: List<Genre>
)
```

In this `MoviesViewState` class, we are including just one property, `genres`, which will store the list of genres we want to show in the list of our streaming app.

Now, we are ready to start creating the `MoviesScreen` composable.

Building the MoviesScreen composable

To build the `MoviesScreen` composable, enter the following code:

```
@Composable
fun MoviesScreen(moviesViewState: MoviesViewState =
sampleMoviesScreen()) {
    Scaffold(
        containerColor = Color.Black,
        topBar = { PacktflixTopBar() },
        bottomBar = { PacktflixBottomBar() }
    ) { innerPadding ->
        GenreList(
            genres = moviesViewState.genres,
            modifier = Modifier.padding(innerPadding)
        )
    }
}
```

As we can see, we have created our `MoviesScreen` composable and a `Scaffold` inside of it. As a `topBar` component of the `Scaffold`, we are including a new composable called `PacktflixTopBar`, then as a `bottomBar` component, we are including another new composable called `PacktflixBottomBar`. Finally, in the content of the Scaffold, we are showing a `GenreList` composable.

Now, let's build these three composables: `PacktflixTopBar`, `PacktflixBottomBar`, and `GenreList`.

PacktflixTopBar

Here is how we create the `PacktflixTopBar` composable:

```
@Composable
fun PacktflixTopBar() {
    TopAppBar(
        title = {
            Text(
                text = "PACKTFLIX",
                color = Color.Red,
                fontSize = 48.sp,
                modifier = Modifier.padding(bottom = 32.dp)
            )
        },
```

```
    actions = {
        IconButton(onClick =
        { /* Handle profile action */ }) {
            Icon(
                painter = painterResource(id =
                    R.drawable.ic_profile),
                contentDescription = "Profile"
            )
        }
        IconButton(onClick = { /* Handle more action */ }) {
            Icon(
                painter = painterResource(id =
                    R.drawable.ic_more),
                contentDescription = "More"
            )
        }
    },
    )
}
```

Inside `TopAppBar`, there's a title that displays the text **PACKTFLIX** on the screen – the text will be colored in red, with a large font size and some padding to create some space.

Additionally, `TopAppBar` includes two icons on the right side: the first icon is for a **Profile** button – when you tap on it, it's meant to handle a user profile-related task, although the actual function to do this hasn't been implemented yet. The second icon is for a **More** button – this is also set up to handle additional actions when clicked, but the specifics of these actions are not defined in this snippet. Each icon button has been created with an `IconButton` composable that contains an icon, and each icon gets its image from a resource file.

This is how `TopAppBar` will look:

Figure 7.4: Top bar in MoviesScreen

Let's continue with the bottom bar.

PacktflixBottomBar

Now, let's build the `PacktflixBottomBar` composable:

```
@Composable
fun PacktflixBottomBar() {
    NavigationBar (
        containerColor = Color.Black,
        contentColor = Color.White,
    ) {
        NavigationBarItem(
            icon = { Icon(Icons.Filled.Home,
                contentDescription = "Home") },
            selected = false,
            onClick = { /* Handle Home navigation */ }
        )
        NavigationBarItem(
            icon = { Icon(Icons.Filled.Search,
                contentDescription = "Search") },
            selected = false,
            onClick = { /* Handle Search navigation */ }
        )
        NavigationBarItem(
            icon = { Icon(Icons.Filled.ArrowDropDown,
                contentDescription = "Downloads") },
            selected = false,
            onClick = { /* Handle Downloads navigation */ }
        )
        NavigationBarItem(
            icon = { Icon(Icons.Filled.MoreVert,
                contentDescription = "More") },
            selected = false,
            onClick = { /* Handle More navigation */ }
        )
    }
}
```

This navigation bar sports a sleek black background with icons illuminated in white, offering a stark and stylish contrast. We're also introducing four navigation items, each symbolized by a distinct icon. We've opted for icons from the Material Icons collection, assigning specific and intuitive symbols to signify **Home**, **Search**, **Downloads**, and **More** functionalities.

For each navigation item within `NavigationBarItem`, we have set up an icon along with an `onClick` listener. Initially, all these items are not selected (`selected = false`) to indicate that their selection state will be managed dynamically through user interactions or specific logic to be implemented in the future. The implementation of these sections is beyond the scope of this book.

We are also pairing each icon with `contentDescription`. This approach enhances app accessibility by offering screen readers a concise explanation of each button's function.

Once it is finished, this is how `PacktflixBottomBar` will look:

Figure 7.5: Bottom bar in MoviesScreen

Now, let's continue with the next step and complete this screen by implementing the list of movies.

GenreList

Now, let's start building the `GenreList` composable. Generally, the content of a movie screen in a streaming app is composed of a list of genres, where each one contains a list of movies. Let's use the `Genre` model we defined previously and create this list of lists. We will start creating a vertical list composed of rows where every row will show the content of every `Genre` instance:

```
@Composable
fun GenreList(genres: List<Genre>, modifier: Modifier =
Modifier) {
    LazyColumn(modifier = modifier) {
        items(genres.size) { index ->
            GenreRow(genre = genres[index])
        }
    }
}
```

To efficiently display the `GenreList` composable, we employed `LazyColumn`, chosen for its ability to render items lazily – this means it only draws the items visible on the screen, enhancing performance, especially for long lists.

Inside `LazyColumn`, we iterate over the genre list. For each genre, we call items, specifying the size of our genre list to determine the number of items it should prepare to display.

Then, for every item (or genre, in our context), we invoke `GenreRow`, a custom composable function that we will define in a moment. This function is responsible for rendering a single row in our list, which represents a genre. We pass each genre to `GenreRow` by indexing it into our genres list with `genres[index]`.

Now, let's build the `GenreRow` composable that we just mentioned:

```
@Composable
fun GenreRow(genre: Genre) {
    Column(modifier = Modifier.fillMaxWidth()) {
        Text(text = genre.name, style =
            MaterialTheme.typography.headlineSmall)
        LazyRow {
            items(genre.movies.size) { index ->
                MovieCard(movie = genre.movies[index])
            }
        }
    }
}
```

We start with a vertical container, `Column`, that stretches across the full width of the screen. At the top of this container, we place the genre's name in large, readable text. This makes it clear to the user which genre they're looking at.

Right below the genre's name, we set up a horizontal scroll area, `LazyRow`, filled with movie cards. Each card represents a movie in the genre, and users can scroll through them horizontally.

For each movie in the genre, we will create a `MovieCard` composable that will show the movie thumbnail image and the name:

```
@Composable
fun MovieCard(movie: Movie) {
    Card(
        modifier = Modifier
            .padding(8.dp)
            .size(120.dp, 180.dp)
    ) {
        Image(
            painter = rememberAsyncImagePainter(model =
                movie.imageUrl),
            contentDescription = movie.title,
            contentScale = ContentScale.Crop
        )
    }
}
```

We start by using a `Card` composable that provides a Material Design card layout. This card is given specific dimensions and padding to ensure that it looks neat and uniform across the app. Specifically, we set each card to be `120dp` wide and `180dp` tall, with an 8dp padding around it. This size is ideal for displaying movie posters without taking up too much screen space or looking too cramped.

Inside the card, we place an `Image` composable to show the movie's poster. To load the image (the movie's poster in this case) from a URL, we use `rememberAsyncImagePainter`, a handy function that handles asynchronous image loading and caching. This means our app can fetch movie posters from the internet efficiently and display them as they become available, without blocking the UI thread.

The image is set to crop to fit the card's dimensions, ensuring that the most visually important part of the poster remains visible, even if the original image's aspect ratio doesn't exactly match the card's dimensions. This cropping also maintains a consistent appearance across all movie cards.

Finally, we include `contentDescription` for the image, using the movie's title, to make our list as accessible as possible.

With this component, we have finished our movie screen (or series screen – you just have to change the title and the content!). We can now test it using the `@Preview` annotation and providing a list of genres:

```
@Preview(showBackground = true)
@Composable
fun DefaultPreview() {
    MoviesScreenUI(moviesViewState = sampleMoviesScreen())
}
```

Here, we are using the preview feature of Jetpack Compose to see what our list will look like. We would need to create some sample content, and that's what the `sampleMoviesScreen()` function will do for us. For example, we could create this fake list of movies:

```
fun sampleMoviesScreen(): MoviesViewState {
    return MoviesViewState(
        genres = listOf(
            Genre(
                name = "Comedy",
                movies = listOf(
                    Movie(
                        id = 1,
                        title = "The Hangover",
                        imageUrl = "https://upload.wikimedia.org/
wikipedia/en/b/b9/Hangoverposter09.jpg"
                    ),
                    Movie(
                        id = 2,
```

```
                                    title = "Superbad",
                                    imageUrl = "https://upload.wikimedia.org/
wikipedia/en/8/8b/Superbad_Poster.png"
                                ),
                            Movie(
                                    id = 3,
                                    title = "Step Brothers",
                                    imageUrl = "https://upload.wikimedia.org/
wikipedia/en/d/d9/StepbrothersMP08.jpg"
                                ),
                            Movie(
                                    id = 4,
                                    title = "Anchorman",
                                    imageUrl = "https://upload.wikimedia.org/
wikipedia/en/6/64/Movie_poster_Anchorman_The_Legend_of_Ron_Burgundy.
jpg"
                                )
                        )
                ),
            Genre(
                    name = "Mystery",
                    movies = listOf(
                        Movie(
                                id = 1,
                                title = "Se7en",
                                imageUrl = "https://upload.wikimedia.org/
wikipedia/en/6/68/Seven_%28movie%29_poster.jpg"
                            ),
                        Movie(
                                id = 2,
                                title = "Zodiac",
                                imageUrl = "https://upload.wikimedia.org/
wikipedia/en/3/3a/Zodiac2007Poster.jpg"
                            ),
                        Movie(
                                id = 3,
                                title = "Gone Girl",
                                imageUrl = "https://upload.wikimedia.org/
wikipedia/en/0/05/Gone_Girl_Poster.jpg"
                            ),
                        Movie(
                                id = 4,
                                title = "Shutter Island",
```

```
                        imageUrl = "https://upload.wikimedia.org/
wikipedia/en/7/76/Shutterislandposter.jpg"
                        )
                    )
                ),
            Genre(
                name = "Documentary",
                movies = listOf(
                    Movie(
                        id = 1,
                        title = "March of the Penguins",
                        imageUrl = "https://upload.wikimedia.org/
wikipedia/en/1/19/March_of_the_penguins_poster.jpg"
                        ),
                    Movie(
                        id = 2,
                        title = "Bowling for Columbine",
                        imageUrl = "https://upload.wikimedia.org/
wikipedia/en/e/e7/Bowling_for_columbine.jpg"
                        ),
                    Movie(
                        id = 3,
                        title = "Blackfish",
                        imageUrl = "https://upload.wikimedia.org/
wikipedia/en/b/bd/BLACKFISH_Film_Poster.jpg"
                        ),
                    Movie(
                        id = 4,
                        title = "An Inconvenient Truth",
                        imageUrl = "https://upload.wikimedia.org/
wikipedia/en/1/19/An_Inconvenient_Truth_Film_Poster.jpg"
                        )
                    )
                )
            )
```

Here, we are creating fake data to make the testing of `MoviesScreen` easier. Note that the URLs provided are not the actual image URLs, so you would have to replace them for actual movie posters.

Once finished, our list screen should look like this:

Figure 7.6: Movies list screen

Now that we have our list of genres and movies, let's build the movie (or series) details page.

Making the movie and series detail screen

In this section, we will create the detail screen, which is the screen that will be shown when the user clicks a movie or series from the list. This screen will include information such as the plot summary, cast, year of release, and so on.

Before building the necessary composables, we need to think about the models we need. Let's start creating them.

Creating the detail models

To define the models, we need to take into account the data we want to show in the detail screen. As we would like to create the same model for both movies and series, we will build an `ItemDetail` model as follows:

```
data class ItemDetail(
    val type: Type,
    val title: String,
    val imageUrl: String,
    val rating: String,
    val year: String,
    val cast: List<String>,
    val description: String,
    val creators: List<String>,
    val episodes: List<Episode>,
    val movieUrl: String
) {
    enum class Type {
        MOVIE, SERIES
    }
}
```

In the case that `ItemDetail` represents a streaming series item, we also should define the `Episode` model:

```
data class Episode(
    val title: String,
    val imageUrl: String,
    val duration: String,
    val episodeUrl: String
)
```

Now that we have our models ready, we can start building the `DetailScreen` composable.

Building the DetailScreen

As we have done on other occasions, we will first build the structure we want the screen to have:

```
@Composable
fun ItemDetailScreen(item: ItemDetail =
createFakeItemDetail()) {
    val scrollState = rememberScrollState()
    Column(
        verticalArrangement = Arrangement.Top,
        modifier = Modifier
            .fillMaxSize()
            .background(Color.Black)
            .padding(all = 8.dp)
            .verticalScroll(scrollState)
    ) {
        ItemBannerImage(item.imageUrl)
        ItemTitleAndMetadata(item.title, item.isHD,
            item.year, item.duration)
        ItemActions(item.movieUrl)
        Text(text = item.description, color = Color.Gray)
        CastAndCreatorsList(item.cast, item.creators)
        AdditionalMovieDetails(item)
    }
}
```

In `ItemDetailScreen`, all the composables included are shown in a vertical `Column`, which allows us to build the UI progressively as we add new composables.

Now, let's start building all those composables, starting with `ItemBannerImage`:

```
@Composable
fun ItemBannerImage(imageUrl: String) {
    Box(modifier = Modifier.fillMaxWidth()) {
        Image(
            painter = rememberAsyncImagePainter(model =
                imageUrl),
            contentDescription = "Movie Banner",
            contentScale = ContentScale.Crop,
            modifier = Modifier
                .height(200.dp)
                .fillMaxWidth()
        )

        IconButton(
```

```
            onClick = {
                /* TODO: Handle back action */
            },
            modifier = Modifier
                .align(Alignment.TopStart)
                .padding(top = 32.dp, start = 16.dp)
        ) {
            Icon(
                imageVector = Icons.Default.ArrowBack,
                contentDescription = "Back",
                tint = Color.White
            )
        }
    }
}
```

This composable displays a banner image at the top of the screen, stretching it to fill the screen's width. It uses a `Box` composable with a `Modifier` parameter that will make sure it takes up the full width of the screen, and an `Image` composable that loads an image from a given URL with the `rememberAsyncImagePainter` function. The image is set to be 200 dp tall and automatically adjusts its width to fit the screen, ensuring that it's properly cropped to the allocated space.

On top of the image, there's an `IconButton` composable that's meant to act as a **Back** button. We place this button in the top-left corner with some padding. Inside this button, there's an icon shaped like an arrow pointing back, suggesting that pressing it should take you back to the previous screen. The icon is white to make sure it's visible on top of the banner image.

Now, let's build the `ItemTitleAndMetadata` composable:

```
@Composable
fun ItemTitleAndMetadata(
    title: String,
    isHD: Boolean,
    year: String,
    duration: String
) {
    Column {
        Text(
            text = title,
            style = MaterialTheme.typography.bodyMedium,
            fontWeight = FontWeight.Bold,
            color = Color.White
        )
        Row(verticalAlignment = Alignment.CenterVertically)
```

```
    {
        if (isHD) {
            Box(
                modifier = Modifier
                    .border(BorderStroke(1.dp,
                        Color.White), shape =
                            RoundedCornerShape(4.dp))
                    .padding(horizontal = 6.dp,
                        vertical = 2.dp)
            ) {
                Text(
                    text = "HD",
                    style =
                    MaterialTheme.typography.bodySmall,
                    color = Color.White
                )
            }
            Spacer(modifier = Modifier.width(8.dp))
        }
        Text(
            text = year,
            style =
                MaterialTheme.typography.bodyMedium,
            color = Color.Gray
        )
    }
    Text(
        text = duration,
        style = MaterialTheme.typography.bodyMedium,
        color = Color.Gray
    )
    }
}
```

We start by creating a `Column` layout because we want the details to stack vertically.

In this column, we will display the title of the item. The style we choose here is `bodyMedium` from the Material Theme, ensuring it fits nicely with the overall design of the app.

Next, we align our HD indicator and the year of release in a row, centering them vertically to ensure that they line up perfectly. We include a conditional check – only if `isHD` is `true` do we display an **HD** badge. We give this badge a white border and a bit of padding to make it pop against any background.

Following a small spacer, which adds some breathing room between our **HD** badge and the year, we place the text for the year. It's styled to be less prominent than the title, using a medium gray color.

Finally, below the row, we will show the duration of the item. It's also in medium gray, matching the year, and using the same bodyMedium style for consistency.

The next step is to create the ItemActions composable:

```
@Composable
fun ItemActions(
    itemUrl: String
) {
    Column(
        modifier = Modifier
            .fillMaxWidth()
            .padding(16.dp),
    ) {
        ActionButton(
            icon = Icons.Filled.PlayArrow,
            label = "Play",
            onClick = { /* TODO: Handle play action */ }
        )
        ActionButton(
            icon = Icons.Default.Add,
            label = "My List",
            onClick = {
                /* TODO: Handle add to list action */ }
        )
    }
}


@Composable
fun ActionButton(icon: ImageVector, label: String, onClick:
() -> Unit) {
    Column(
        horizontalAlignment = Alignment.CenterHorizontally,
        modifier = Modifier.clickable(onClick = onClick)
    ) {
        Icon(
            imageVector = icon,
            contentDescription = label
        )
        Text(text = label)
    }
}
```

We start by laying this function in a column format so that our action buttons stack vertically – this column will take up the full width available and will have padding all around for some space from the screen edges.

Inside this column, we're placing two action buttons: one for playing the item and another for adding the item to a user's personal list. To create these buttons, we are using the `ActionButton` composable function, which neatly bundles an icon and a label together into a clickable area. For the **Play** action, we are using a play arrow icon, and for adding to the list, we are using an **Add** icon.

> **Note**
>
> We have left placeholders in the code where the play and add-to-list actions can be written. In the next chapter, we will implement the **Play** button; however, I will leave you to add the add-to-list feature yourself. To do this, one solution could be to call an endpoint when the **Add To List** button is pressed, so the backend can store it in the user list (of course, imagining that we have a backend that handles this feature). You can refer to *Chapter 4* where we connected Packtagram with `NewsFeed` to understand how this can be done.

Now, let's continue with the next composable, `CastAndCreatorsList`:

```
@Composable
fun CastAndCreatorsList(cast: List<String>, creators:
List<String>) {
    Column(modifier = Modifier.fillMaxWidth()) {
        Text(
            text = "Cast",
            style = MaterialTheme.typography.titleSmall,
            color = Color.White,
            modifier = Modifier.padding(horizontal = 16.dp,
                vertical = 8.dp)
        )
        LazyRow(
            contentPadding = PaddingValues(horizontal =
                16.dp),
            horizontalArrangement =
                Arrangement.spacedBy(8.dp)
        ) {
            items(cast) { actorName ->
                Text(
                    text = actorName,
                    style =
                        MaterialTheme.typography.bodyMedium,
                    color = Color.White,
                    modifier = Modifier.background(
```

```
                color = Color.DarkGray,
                shape = RoundedCornerShape(4.dp)
            ).padding(horizontal = 8.dp,
                vertical = 4.dp)
        )
    }
}

Spacer(modifier = Modifier.height(16.dp))

Text(
    text = "Created by",
    style = MaterialTheme.typography.titleMedium,
    color = Color.White,
    modifier = Modifier.padding(horizontal = 16.dp,
        vertical = 8.dp)
)
LazyRow(
    contentPadding = PaddingValues(horizontal =
        16.dp),
    horizontalArrangement =
        Arrangement.spacedBy(8.dp)
) {
    items(creators) { creatorName ->
        Text(
            text = creatorName,
            style =
                MaterialTheme.typography.bodyMedium,
            color = Color.White,
            modifier = Modifier.background(
                color = Color.DarkGray,
                shape = RoundedCornerShape(4.dp)
            ).padding(horizontal = 8.dp,
                vertical = 4.dp)
        )
    }
}
        }
    }
}
```

We start with `Column`, which is going to stack our elements vertically. We want this to take up the full width available, so we use `Modifier.fillMaxWidth()`.

Then, we put a header labeled `Cast` at the top. We style this text to make it stand out using `MaterialTheme.typography.titleSmall` and set the color to white. To give it some breathing room, we add padding around it.

Next, we introduce a `LazyRow` composable to display each actor's name from the cast list using a `Text` composable. We style the names to stand out against the background by applying `MaterialTheme.typography.bodyMedium` and setting the text color to white. To further distinguish each name, we give them a tag-like appearance with a dark gray background and rounded corners using `RoundedCornerShape(4.dp)`. Additionally, we add padding around the text to ensure that it doesn't touch the edges of its gray backdrop, enhancing readability and visual appeal.

Then, we separate the cast from the creators with a `Spacer` composable. This just adds a bit of vertical space between the two sections, so they don't run into each other.

For the creators, the setup is pretty much the same. We have a header labeled `"Created by"`, styled similarly to the `Cast` header but a bit larger using `titleMedium`. Then, we list out the creators in another `LazyRow`, giving them the same styled text tags as the cast.

Now, it's time to work on the last composable of the screen, `AdditionalMovieDetails`:

```
@Composable
fun AdditionalMovieDetails(item: ItemDetail) {
    Column(modifier = Modifier.fillMaxWidth()) {
        // Assuming item.episodes is a list of episodes
            with their details
        item.episodes.forEach { episode ->
            EpisodeItem(episode = episode)
        }
    }
}


@Composable
fun EpisodeItem(episode: Episode) {
    Row(
        modifier = Modifier
            .fillMaxWidth()
            .clickable {
                /* TODO: Handle episode playback */ }
            .padding(16.dp),
        verticalAlignment = Alignment.CenterVertically
    ) {
        // Episode image
        Image(
            painter = rememberAsyncImagePainter(model =
                episode.imageUrl),
```

```
        contentDescription = "Episode Thumbnail",
        modifier = Modifier
            .size(width = 120.dp, height = 68.dp)
            .clip(RoundedCornerShape(4.dp)),
        contentScale = ContentScale.Crop
    )


    // Space between image and text details
    Spacer(modifier = Modifier.width(16.dp))

    // Episode title and duration
    Column {
        Text(
            text = episode.title,
            style =
                MaterialTheme.typography.bodyMedium,
            color = Color.White
        )
        Text(
            text = "Duration: ${episode.duration}",
            style = MaterialTheme.typography.bodySmall,
            color = Color.Gray
        )
    }
}
    Divider(color = Color.Gray, thickness = 0.5.dp)
}
```

In AdditionalMovieDetails, we're setting up a column that expands to the maximum width of its parent container. Inside this column, we're going through each episode in the item.episodes list and, for each one, we're calling the EpisodeItem composable to render the details of that episode.

Now, moving on to the EpisodeItem composable function, this is where we lay out each episode's information. We create a row that stretches across the full width, which can be tapped – this is where we will want to add the code for what happens when someone clicks to play the episode. We are also adding some padding for spacing.

Within this row, the first thing is the episode image. We use rememberAsyncImagePainter to load the image from the episode URL, and we make sure it's nicely rounded and cropped to fit a specific size. This image will act as a thumbnail for the episode.

Next to the image, we add a spacer to give some breathing room before the text details of the episode. This is followed by a column that holds two pieces of text: the episode's title, which stands out more, and below it, the duration of the episode in a smaller and less prominent color.

Lastly, after each episode item, we draw a thin gray line, a divider, to visually separate the episodes from one another. It's a common design pattern that helps users distinguish between different pieces of content.

And with this composable, we have finished the detail screen and this chapter. Our detail screen should look like this:

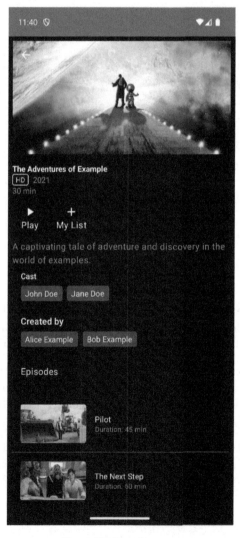

Figure 7.7: Detail screen

In the next chapter, we will bring those movies and series to life by implementing the playback.

Summary

As we close this chapter, we have laid a solid foundation for Packtflix, our video streaming app. We began by conceptualizing the project's structure and modules, setting the stage for an organized and scalable app. This structure is pivotal for our journey ahead, where complexity will grow as we add more features.

We then created the login screen, before venturing into the world of user authentication. Through the integration of OAuth2, we've equipped Packtflix with a secure authentication system that respects user privacy and guards against unauthorized access, ensuring a trustworthy environment for our users to enjoy their favorite content.

Our progress continued as we crafted a UI to display a curated list of movies, leveraging the power of Jetpack Compose to create a dynamic and engaging experience. This attention to detail in presenting content is what will turn first-time users into loyal fans of Packtflix.

In the next chapter, we will learn more about how to implement the playback, so our users can not only see the movies and series information but also play their videos.

8

Adding Media Playback to Packtflix with ExoPlayer

In the journey of Android development, the ability to create rich, engaging multimedia applications is a crucial skill that sets apart great apps from the good ones. As we venture further into the creation of our Netflix-like app, we'll transition from the foundational structures and user interfaces for browsing movie lists and details to the core of multimedia experiences: video playback. This chapter is dedicated to unlocking the potential of video content within our application, a feature that will significantly enhance user engagement and satisfaction. Here, we will travel into the world of media playback on Android, focusing on the powerful and versatile library known as ExoPlayer.

ExoPlayer stands out in the Android ecosystem as a robust, open-source library that provides an alternative to the standard Android MediaPlayer API. It offers extensive customization options and supports a wide range of media formats, including those not natively supported by Android. Our exploration will begin with an overview of media options in Android, setting the stage for why ExoPlayer is the library of choice for modern Android applications seeking to offer a superior media playback experience.

Following the introduction to media options, we will learn the basics of ExoPlayer, covering its architecture, key components, and how it integrates within an Android application. This foundational knowledge will prepare us to tackle the practical aspects of implementing video playback. This chapter will guide you through creating a responsive, intuitive video playback UI that meets the expectations of today's users.

The journey will continue with hands-on examples and detailed guidance on playing videos using ExoPlayer. This includes managing playback controls, adjusting video quality, and handling various media sources. Additionally, while recognizing the importance of accessibility and global reach, you'll learn how to add subtitles to your videos, ensuring your content is accessible to a wider audience.

By the end of this chapter, you will have mastered the essentials of video playback in Android, equipped with the skills to enrich your applications with high-quality video content, creating immersive experiences for your users.

In this chapter, we will cover the following topics:

- Reviewing media options in Android

- Reviewing Android's media options

- Creating the video playback user interface

- Playing video using ExoPlayer

- Adding subtitles to the video player

Technical requirements

As in the previous chapter, you will need to have Android Studio (or another editor of your preference) installed.

We will continue working on the same project we started in *Chapter 7*. You can find the complete code that we are going to build throughout this chapter in this book's GitHub repository: `https://github.com/PacktPublishing/Thriving-in-Android-Development-using-Kotlin/tree/main/Chapter-8`.

Reviewing Android's media options

Android, as a versatile mobile operating system, offers comprehensive support for various types of media, including but not limited to audio files (such as MP3, WAV, and OGG) and video content (such as MP4, WebM, and MKV). This broad support empowers developers to incorporate a wide range of media types into their applications that can be used for diverse user preferences and use cases. From educational apps that leverage video tutorials for learning to entertainment platforms streaming movies and music, media playback is at the heart of modern mobile applications, driving user engagement and satisfaction.

To start our journey, let's look at which options we have in the Android ecosystem so that we can choose the most appropriate option to build the playback functionality of our app. We will start with MediaPlayer API and VideoView before considering ExoPlayer.

Learning about the MediaPlayer API

The **MediaPlayer** API is a powerful and flexible class that allows Android developers to handle audio and video playback with a high degree of control. The API is designed to be easy to use yet capable of catering to complex media playback requirements.

Its main features are as follows:

- **Versatile media source support**: MediaPlayer can play media from various sources, including local files (such as device storage or SD cards), raw resources (which are bundled within the app), and network streams (HTTP/HTTPS).

- **Playback control**: It offers comprehensive control over media playback, including play, pause, stop, rewind, and fast-forward options, as well as the ability to seek specific timestamps.

- **Volume control**: The MediaPlayer API in Android allows developers to programmatically adjust the volume of audio playback. This is achieved through methods such as `setVolume(float leftVolume, float rightVolume)`, which controls the volume level of the left and right speakers independently. This feature is essential for creating applications that can dynamically adjust the playback volume based on specific user settings, environmental conditions, or application scenarios. For instance, an app might automatically lower the volume during nighttime hours or increase it in a noisy environment to enhance user experience.

- **Event handling**: MediaPlayer provides listeners that can be used to respond to media life cycle events, such as completion, preparation, error handling, and buffering updates.

- **Audio focus management**: Essential for apps that play audio, MediaPlayer can handle audio focus to ensure a smooth user experience when multiple apps potentially play sounds simultaneously.

As we can see, MediaPlayer provides the basic functionality we need for simple audio and video handling, so it could be a good solution for the following cases:

- **Music players**: MediaPlayer is well-suited for apps that play music or podcast files, whether it's stored locally or streamed over the internet

- **Video players**: Although MediaPlayer requires more setup for video playback compared to VideoView, it's ideal for custom video player applications where developers need control over rendering and playback

- **Game sound effects**: For games that need to play short sound effects, MediaPlayer can be used for its simplicity and ability to handle various audio formats

Here's an example of how to reproduce an audio file using MediaPlayer:

```
@Composable
fun AudioPlayerComposable() {
    val context = LocalContext.current
    val mediaPlayer = remember { MediaPlayer.create(
        context, R.raw.my_audio_file) }

    // Observe lifecycle to release MediaPlayer
    ObserveLifecycle(owner = ProcessLifecycleOwner.get()) {
        onExit = {
```

```
                    mediaPlayer.release()
            }
    }

    Column(modifier = Modifier.padding(16.dp)) {
        Button(onClick = {
            if (!mediaPlayer.isPlaying) {
                mediaPlayer.start()
            }
        }) {
            Text("Play")
        }
        Button(onClick = {
            if (mediaPlayer.isPlaying) {
                mediaPlayer.pause() // Use pause or stop
                                    based on your need
            }
        }) {
            Text("Stop")
        }
    }
}

@Composable
fun ObserveLifecycle(owner: LifecycleOwner, onExit: () ->
Unit) {
    // Use DisposableEffect to manage lifecycle
    DisposableEffect(owner) {
        val observer = LifecycleEventObserver { _, event ->
            if (event == Lifecycle.Event.ON_DESTROY) {
                onExit()
            }
        }
        owner.lifecycle.addObserver(observer)

        onDispose {
            owner.lifecycle.removeObserver(observer)
        }
    }
}
```

In this example, `MediaPlayer.create()` is used within the `remember` block to ensure that the media player is only instantiated once, maintaining this instance across recompositions of the composable. Then, the `ObserveLifecycle` composable function is used to observe the life cycle of the entire application (using `ProcessLifecycleOwner` here for simplicity). This function ensures that `mediaPlayer.release()` is called to free up resources when the app is destroyed, although you might adapt this to more specific life cycle events as needed.

The UI consists of two buttons for play and stop functionalities. The play button's `onClick` logic checks if the media is not currently playing before starting playback. This is done to avoid restarting the audio and video if the button is pressed during playback. Similarly, the stop button pauses the playback.

This example demonstrates how to integrate MediaPlayer with Jetpack Compose while managing the media player life cycle and providing a simple UI for controlling playback. You can find more examples in the official documentation: `https://developer.android.com/media/platform/mediaplayer`.

Although our example illustrates how to provide the playback control UI, we still need to show the video so that our users can watch it. This is where VideoView comes in.

Learning about VideoView

VideoView is a higher-level UI component in Android that encapsulates the functionality of MediaPlayer and SurfaceView to provide a convenient way to play video files. It simplifies the process of video playback by managing the underlying media playback mechanics, making it ideal for use cases that require straightforward video playback without the need for fine-grained control over the media pipeline.

> **Note**
>
> SurfaceView is a specialized component in the Android framework that provides a dedicated drawing surface within the app's view hierarchy. Unlike standard views, which are drawn onto a single canvas managed by the UI thread, SurfaceView can be rendered independently in a separate thread. This allows for more efficient redrawing, especially for demanding content such as video playback or dynamic graphics. SurfaceView is particularly useful when you need to update your views frequently or when the rendering process is computationally intensive as it does not block user interaction while drawing.

Let's explore some of VideoView's features so that we can appreciate the practical benefits it offers:

- **Simplicity**: VideoView simplifies the implementation of video playback. You can start playing a video with just a few lines of code, handling preparation and playback of the video file automatically.

- **Control integration**: It can be easily integrated with media controls (using MediaController), allowing users to play, pause, and seek through the video.

- **Format support**: VideoView supports various video formats that Android's MediaPlayer supports, including MP4, 3GP, and more, depending on the device and platform version.

- **Layout flexibility**: Being a view, VideoView can be placed anywhere in your application's layout and can be resized and styled as needed, just like any other UI component.

Understanding VideoView's features sets the stage for its practical applications. Now, let's pinpoint exactly where VideoView shines. Here are the best scenarios for using VideoView in your app:

- **Simple video playback**: When you need to play videos without requiring advanced playback features such as adaptive streaming, VideoView is a straightforward and effective choice. Adaptive streaming, such as **HTTP Live Streaming (HLS)** and **Dynamic Adaptive Streaming over HTTP (DASH)**, allows videos to be delivered in varying qualities, depending on network conditions. HLS is widely used for live and on-demand streaming on the web, as well as dynamically adjusting video quality based on the viewer's internet speed. Similarly, DASH is a flexible standard that enables high-quality streaming of media content over the internet.

- **Local and network videos**: It's suitable for playing videos stored locally on the device or streamed over the network.

- **Embedded video content**: VideoView is great for applications that need to embed video content directly within their UI, such as tutorial apps, video players, or social media apps with video feeds.

Now that we know its features and recommended use cases, let's look at an example so that we understand how it works. In this example, we're using the 1.7.0 version of the androidx.media:media library:

```
@Composable
fun VideoPlayer(modifier: Modifier = Modifier, videoUrl:
String) {
    val context = LocalContext.current

    AndroidView(
        modifier = modifier,
        factory = { ctx ->
            VideoView(ctx).apply {
                val mediaController = MediaController(ctx)
                setMediaController(mediaController)
                mediaController.setAnchorView(this)
                setVideoURI(Uri.parse(videoUrl))
                start() // Auto-start playback
            }
        }
    )
}
```

Here, we start by declaring a composable called `VideoPlayer`. This composable accepts a `videoUrl` string as a parameter. This specifies the location of the video to be played.

Within the function, `LocalContext.current` is used to obtain the current context from the Compose environment. The `AndroidView` composable is then employed to bridge the gap between traditional Android UI components and the Compose world. It takes a factory Lambda expression where `VideoView` is instantiated by using the context.

Next, `MediaController` is created and associated with `VideoView` through `setMediaController()`, providing standard media controls such as play, pause, and seek to enhance user interaction with the video playback.

The media controller is anchored to `VideoView` using `setAnchorView(this)`, ensuring that the control interface is displayed correctly concerning the video view. The video URL that's passed to the function is parsed into a `Uri` component and set on `VideoView` with `setVideoURI()`, pointing the player to the video content.

Finally, `start()` is called on `VideoView` to initiate video playback automatically as soon as the setup is complete and the video is ready to be shown.

In this section, we took a sneak peek at how the MediaPlayer API and VideoView work and their features. Now, it's time for the crown jewel: ExoPlayer.

Understanding the basics of ExoPlayer

ExoPlayer stands as a significant advancement over Android's basic MediaPlayer, offering a level of flexibility, customization, and support for advanced streaming formats that MediaPlayer simply cannot match. This superiority makes ExoPlayer the go-to choice for developers needing robust, feature-rich media playback capabilities in their applications.

One of ExoPlayer's most compelling advantages is its adaptability. Unlike the relatively static MediaPlayer, ExoPlayer can be easily adapted and extended to suit specific application needs. Its modular architecture allows developers to include only the components they need, reducing the app's overall size. Furthermore, ExoPlayer's customization options extend to its user interface, with the ability to create custom controls and layouts that seamlessly integrate with the rest of the application's design. This adaptability ensures that developers can craft a unique media playback experience that aligns perfectly with their app's branding and user interface guidelines.

In the realm of streaming, ExoPlayer's strengths become even more apparent. It offers out-of-the-box support for modern streaming protocols such as HLS and DASH. These adaptive streaming protocols are essential for delivering content efficiently over the internet, adjusting the quality of the stream in real time based on the user's current network conditions. This ensures an optimal viewing experience that minimizes buffering and playback interruptions even under fluctuating network speeds.

MediaPlayer, by contrast, offers limited support for such streaming protocols, often requiring developers to implement additional solutions or workarounds to achieve similar functionality. With ExoPlayer, developers gain direct access to these advanced features, simplifying the development process and enhancing the end user experience.

As we can see, ExoPlayer's functionality is widely superior due to its flexibility and wide format support and those are the reasons we will use it in this project. On the other hand, as it is more complex, we will have to learn more about it before we start to implement our video player using it.

Well, let's do exactly that and break down ExoPlayer's architecture.

Exploring ExoPlayer's architecture

ExoPlayer's architecture is designed to be both flexible and extensible, making it capable of handling a wide range of media playback scenarios. ExoPlayer has several core components that work together to provide a robust and efficient media playback experience. Understanding these components is key to leveraging ExoPlayer's full capabilities in our applications. Let's take a look at them here.

The ExoPlayer instance – the central media playback engine

The ExoPlayer instance itself acts as the central hub for media playback, orchestrating the interaction between the various components involved in the playback process, managing the playback state, and coordinating the fetching, decoding, and rendering of media. Unlike Android's MediaPlayer, which operates as a black box, ExoPlayer provides developers with detailed control over playback and access to the playback pipeline, enabling fine-tuned adjustments to fit the application's specific needs.

Here's a simple example of how to initialize ExoPlayer and prepare it to play a media item:

```
val context = ... // Your context here
val player = ExoPlayer.Builder(context).build().apply {
    // Media item to be played
    val mediaItem =
        MediaItem.fromUri("http://example.com/media.mp3")
    // Set the media item to be played
    setMediaItem(mediaItem)
    // Prepare the player
    prepare()
    // Start playback
    playWhenReady = true
}
```

The process begins with creating an `ExoPlayer` instance, utilizing a context-aware builder pattern that ensures the player is configured for the environment where it operates. Following its instantiation, a media item is specified through a URI, which could either point to a local resource or a remote media file. This media item is then associated with the `ExoPlayer` instance, indicating what content it should be prepared to play.

Once the media item has been set, the player enters a preparation phase by invoking the `prepare()` method. During this phase, ExoPlayer analyzes the media, setting up necessary buffers and decoding resources to ensure smooth playback.

The final step in the process involves setting the player's `playWhenReady` property to `true`, a command that triggers playback as soon as the player is fully prepared. This property provides flexibility, allowing developers to control when playback should start. This can be immediately after preparation or delayed based on additional conditions or user interactions.

MediaItem – sourcing the media resource

In ExoPlayer, **MediaItem** encapsulates details about a media source, such as its URI, metadata, and any configuration related to playback. It is a versatile and essential component that tells ExoPlayer what content to load and play. These are the key functions of MediaItem:

- **Media source specification**: The primary function of MediaItem is to specify the location of the media to be played. This can be a file path, a URL, or a content URI, among other formats.

- **Media configuration**: Beyond just specifying a media source, MediaItem allows for detailed configuration of the playback. This includes setting DRM configurations, specifying subtitles, and defining custom attributes through metadata.

- **Adaptive streaming**: For adaptive streaming content (such as DASH and HLS), MediaItem can include the necessary information for ExoPlayer to adapt the stream's quality dynamically based on network conditions. This information includes metadata such as the URLs of the various stream segments, available quality levels, and codecs.

- **Playback options**: Developers can use MediaItem to configure specific playback options, such as start and end positions, looping, and more. These options provide fine-grained control over how the media is played.

In practice, once a MediaItem is created and configured, it is passed to the ExoPlayer instance so that it can be prepared for playback. You can load a single MediaItem for simple playback scenarios or manage a playlist by loading multiple MediaItems. Let's see a brief example:

```
val mediaItem =
    MediaItem.fromUri("https://example.com/video.mp4")
player.setMediaItem(mediaItem)
player.prepare() // Prepares the player with the provided
                 MediaItem
```

```
player.playWhenReady = true // Starts playback as soon as
                              preparation is complete
```

In this example, we are creating `mediaItem` from a URL and preparing it to be reproduced by the ExoPlayer instance.

TrackSelector – managing media tracks

The `TrackSelector` instance is a critical component of ExoPlayer that's responsible for selecting the specific tracks to be played. A video might contain multiple audio tracks in different languages, several video qualities, or various subtitle tracks, and `TrackSelector` decides which of these tracks are best suited for the current playback context based on the device's capabilities, user preferences, and network conditions. This selection process is crucial for adaptive streaming scenarios as a single video is encoded at multiple quality levels and stored on the server.

Here's an example of its use:

```
val trackSelector =
    DefaultTrackSelector(context).apply {
        setParameters(buildUponParameters()
            .setPreferredAudioLanguage("en")
}
val player = ExoPlayer.Builder(context)
    .setTrackSelector(trackSelector)
    .build()
```

The process starts with the creation of a `DefaultTrackSelector` instance. The `Default-TrackSelector` instance is a component of `ExoPlayer` that decides which tracks (audio, video, or text) are played from the media based on various criteria, such as the user's device capabilities and the tracks' properties. In this example, the track selector is configured to prefer audio tracks in English. This preference is set by modifying the track selector's parameters, indicating that if the media contains multiple audio tracks in different languages, the English one should be chosen, if available.

After configuring the track selector, it's used in the construction of the `ExoPlayer` instance. Here, `ExoPlayer.Builder` is provided with the application context and the customized track selector when building the player. This ensures that when the `ExoPlayer` instance prepares and plays media, it uses the logic defined in `DefaultTrackSelector` for track selection. Essentially, this setup allows for more control over which audio track is selected during playback, based on the predefined criteria (in this case, the language preference).

This approach to configuring ExoPlayer is particularly beneficial in applications that deal with media containing multiple tracks for different audience demographics or in scenarios where the application needs to adhere to user preferences or settings, such as a language selection option. By customizing the track selector, developers can ensure that the media playback experience is optimized for the specific needs and preferences of their users, enhancing overall usability and satisfaction.

LoadControl – handling buffering and loading

The LoadControl component oversees the strategy for buffering and loading media resources. Efficient buffering is essential for smooth playback, especially in streaming scenarios where network conditions can vary widely. The LoadControl component determines how much media data to buffer at any given time, striking a balance between reducing initial loading times and minimizing the likelihood of playback interruptions. We can customize the buffering policy to cater to specific requirements, such as prioritizing quick start times or ensuring uninterrupted playback.

The following is an example of creating a custom LoadControl component to modify the buffer policy:

```
val loadControl = DefaultLoadControl.Builder().apply {
    // Set minimum buffer duration to 2 minutes
    setBufferDurationsMs(
        minBufferMs = 2 * 60 * 1000,
        maxBufferMs =
            DefaultLoadControl.DEFAULT_MAX_BUFFER_MS,
        bufferForPlaybackMs =
            DefaultLoadControl
            .DEFAULT_BUFFER_FOR_PLAYBACK_MS,
        bufferForPlaybackAfterRebufferMs =
            DefaultLoadControl
            .DEFAULT_BUFFER_FOR_PLAYBACK_AFTER_REBUFFER_MS
    )
}.build()

val player = ExoPlayer.Builder(context)
    .setLoadControl(loadControl)
    .build()
// Continue setting up the player as before
```

The example begins by creating an instance of DefaultLoadControl using Builder. Here, DefaultLoadControl is an implementation of the LoadControl interface provided by ExoPlayer and is designed to manage media buffering based on various parameters that I will explain now.

The setBufferDurationsMs method is called on the builder to specify custom buffer durations. Specifically, it sets the minimum buffer duration (minBufferMs) to 2 minutes (120,000 milliseconds). This means that ExoPlayer will attempt to buffer at least 2 minutes of media before starting playback, which can help ensure smooth playback under varying network conditions.

The other parameters (maxBufferMs, bufferForPlaybackMs, and bufferForPlayback-AfterRebufferMs) are set to their default values, which are predefined in DefaultLoadControl. These parameters control the maximum buffer size, the minimum amount of media that must be buffered for playback to start, and the minimum amount of media that must be buffered to resume playback after a rebuffer, respectively.

> **Note**
>
> If you want to learn more about the aforementioned options, you can find all the details in the documentation for DefaultLoadControl.Builder: https://developer.android. com/reference/androidx/media3/exoplayer/DefaultLoadControl. Builder.

After configuring the buffer durations, the build() method is called to create the DefaultLoadControl instance with the specified settings.

This custom LoadControl component is then set on a new ExoPlayer instance through the setLoadControl method of ExoPlayer.Builder. This step integrates the custom buffering strategy with the player, meaning that the player will use the specified buffer durations during playback.

Finally, the build method is called on ExoPlayer.Builder to create the ExoPlayer instance that was configured with the custom LoadControl component.

Renderers – rendering media to outputs

Renderers are the components that output the media to the appropriate destination, such as rendering video frames to the screen or audio samples to speakers. ExoPlayer uses separate renderers for different types of tracks, allowing for parallel processing and rendering of audio, video, and text tracks. This separation enables ExoPlayer to support a wide range of media types and formats efficiently. Moreover, developers can implement custom renderers to handle non-standard media types or apply special processing to media before playback.

To illustrate this, consider the following example, where a custom renderer is being used to apply a grayscale filter to video content:

```
class GrayscaleVideoRenderer(
    eventHandler: Handler,
    videoListener: VideoRendererEventListener,
    maxDroppedFrameCountToNotify: Int
) : SimpleDecoderVideoRenderer(eventHandler, videoListener,
maxDroppedFrameCountToNotify) {

    override fun onOutputFormatChanged(format: Format,
    outputMediaFormat: MediaFormat?) {
        super.onOutputFormatChanged(format,
            outputMediaFormat)
        // Setup to modify the color format to grayscale
    }

    override fun renderOutputBufferToSurface(buffer:
    OutputBuffer, surface: Surface,
```

```
        presentationTimeUs: Long) {
            // Apply grayscale effect to the buffer before
            rendering to the surface
        }
    }
}
```

The `GrayscaleVideoRenderer` class extends ExoPlayer's `SimpleDecoderVideoRenderer` to apply a grayscale effect to video frames during playback. This customization allows it to not just decode and display the video but also transform each frame to grayscale in real time, enhancing the visual presentation for stylistic choices or accessibility.

When initializing, this renderer takes a `Handler` component for thread-safe event dispatching, a `VideoRendererEventListener` component for managing video events, and an integer that sets the threshold for notifying about dropped frames. This setup helps keep the playback smooth and responsive.

It overrides the `onOutputFormatChanged` method, where it prepares for video format changes. This is where adjustments for grayscale processing would be set up. The `renderOutputBufferToSurface` method is where the grayscale effect is applied to each video frame before they are rendered to the screen.

Now that we are familiar with the most important components of ExoPlayer, let's integrate it into our project.

Integrating ExoPlayer into our project

To integrate ExoPlayer, we have to include the necessary library dependencies in our version catalog:

```
[versions]
...
exoPlayer = "1.2.1"

[libraries]
...
exoPlayer-core = { module = "androidx.media3:media3-exoplayer",
version.ref = "exoPlayer" }
exoPlayer-ui = { module = " androidx.media3:media3-ui", version.ref =
"exoPlayer" }
```

As with every dependency that we have included, we must add them to the `build.gradle` file of the module where we are going to use them. In this case, we'll add it them the `build.gradle` file for `:feature:playback`:

```
dependencies {
    implementation(libs.exoPlayer.core)
    implementation(libs.exoPlayer.ui)
}
```

With these two dependencies, we have all the components we need to use ExoPlayer:

- `androidx.media3:media3-exoplayer`: This is the core module of ExoPlayer in the Media3 library. It includes the essential classes and interfaces needed for media playback functionality. This module provides the fundamental components for media playback, including the ExoPlayer interface, media source handling, and playback control logic. It is the backbone of media playback in Media3, offering high-performance, low-level media playback capabilities.

- `androidx.media3:media3-ui`: This module provides user interface components for media playback in the Media3 library. It includes pre-built UI components such as `PlayerView` (a view that displays video content and playback controls) and other UI elements for controlling media playback. These components can be customized or replaced with custom implementations if needed. This module helps developers quickly integrate ExoPlayer with a functional UI for media playback.

Now, we're all set. In the next section, we will build our playback UI and connect it with ExoPlayer.

Creating the video playback user interface

In this section, we're going to build the video playback UI and focus on the essentials: a title bar, close, play/pause, forward and rewind buttons, a progress bar, and a time indicator. We will start by creating the `PlaybackScreen` composable, the main composable for this new screen, after which we will add the additional components required to make it function.

Building PlaybackScreen and its composables

Let's start building the `PlaybackScreen` composable:

```
@Composable
fun PlaybackScreen() {
    Box(
        modifier = Modifier
            .fillMaxSize()
            .background(Color.Black)
    ) {
        TopMediaRow(Modifier.align(Alignment.TopCenter))
        PlayPauseButton(Modifier.align(Alignment.Center))
        ProgressBarWithTime(Modifier
            .align(Alignment.BottomCenter))
    }
}
```

We start by declaring a Box container that fills the entire screen and sets its background to black, mimicking the dark mode typically preferred in video playback interfaces. Within this Box, we place three key components that constitute our playback UI: a top media row, a play/pause button, and a progress bar with a time indicator.

Here, TopMediaRow is positioned at the top center of the screen, likely containing the title bar and close button. Then, PlayPauseButton is placed right in the center of the screen, making it easy for users to start or pause playback with a simple tap. Finally, ProgressBarWithTime is aligned at the bottom center, allowing users to see how much of the video has played and how much is left. Each of these components is aligned within the Box container using the Modifier.align method, ensuring they are positioned exactly where we want them in the UI.

Now that we have built the base of the screen, including every composable needed, it's time to build them. We will start with the TopMediaRow composable:

```
@Composable
fun TopMediaRow(modifier: Modifier = Modifier) {
    Row(
        modifier = modifier.fillMaxWidth().padding(20.dp),
        horizontalArrangement = Arrangement.SpaceBetween,
        verticalAlignment = Alignment.CenterVertically
    ) {
        Text(text = "S1:E1 - Pilot", color = Color.White)
        Icon(imageVector = Icons.Default.Close,
            contentDescription = "Close",
                tint = Color.White)
    }
}
```

In this TopMediaRow composable function, we're designing the top part of our video playback UI, which is specifically tailored for displaying the episode information and a close button. This function uses a Row layout to arrange its elements horizontally across the screen. The modifier that's applied to this Row layout ensures it stretches to fill the maximum width of its parent container and applies a padding of 20 **density-independent pixels (dp)** around its edges for a neat, uncluttered look.

Within the Row layout, we use two main components: Text and Icon:

- The Text component displays the episode information, such as **S1:E1 'Pilot'**, in white color, making it easily visible against the dark background typical of video playback screens.

- The Icon component uses the default "close" symbol with its tint also set to white to maintain consistency and visibility. The horizontalArrangement property is set to Arrangement. SpaceBetween to ensure the text and icon are placed on opposite ends of the row, while verticalAlignment keeps them centered vertically within the row.

Now, let's move to the next row, which contains the `PlayPauseButton` composable:

```
@Composable
fun PlayPauseButton(modifier: Modifier = Modifier) {
    Row(
        horizontalArrangement = Arrangement.Center,
        verticalAlignment = Alignment.CenterVertically,
        modifier = modifier
    ) {
        IconButton(
            modifier = Modifier.padding(20.dp),
            onClick = { /* Rewind action */ })
        {
            Icon(
                modifier = Modifier
                    .height(80.dp)
                    .width(80.dp),
                imageVector = Icons.Default.ArrowBack,
                contentDescription = "Rewind 10s",
                tint = Color.White)
        }
        IconButton(
            modifier = Modifier
                .padding(20.dp),
            onClick = { /* Play/Pause action */ }
        ) {
            Icon(
            modifier = Modifier
                .height(80.dp)
                .width(80.dp),
            imageVector = Icons.Default.PlayArrow,
            contentDescription = "Play/Pause",
            tint = Color.White)
        }
        IconButton(
            modifier = Modifier
                .padding(20.dp),
            onClick = { /* Fast-forward action */ }) {
            Icon(
                modifier = Modifier
                    .height(80.dp)
                    .width(80.dp),
                imageVector = Icons.Default.ArrowForward,
                contentDescription = "Fast-forward 10s",
```

```
                    tint = Color.White)
            }
        }
    }
```

The `PlayPauseButton` composable function will provide the central control mechanism for video playback and incorporate rewind, play/pause, and fast-forward actions within a single, intuitive interface. This function employs a `Row` layout to horizontally align its child elements – the buttons for each control action – so that they're centered both horizontally and vertically.

Each button is created using the `IconButton` component. These buttons are spaced out with a padding of 20 dp to ensure they're comfortably tappable without the risk of accidental presses. The icons for rewind, play/pause, and fast-forward are sized uniformly at 80 dp by 80 dp, making them large enough to be easily tapped and visually recognized.

The `Icon` components within each `IconButton` are specifically chosen to visually represent their respective actions: an arrow pointing backward for rewind, a play arrow for play/pause, and an arrow pointing forward for fast-forward, each accompanied by a content description for accessibility purposes. The placeholder comments within the `onClick` parameters indicate where the functionality for each button – rewinding the video by 10 seconds, toggling between playing and pausing, and fast-forwarding by 10 seconds – would be implemented.

Finally, we have one last composable to build, the `ProgressBarWithTime` composable:

```
@Composable
fun ProgressBarWithTime(modifier: Modifier = Modifier) {
    Row(
        modifier = modifier
            .fillMaxWidth()
            .wrapContentHeight()
            .padding(horizontal = 16.dp, vertical = 8.dp),
        horizontalArrangement = Arrangement.SpaceBetween,
        verticalAlignment = Alignment.CenterVertically
    ) {
            val progress = remember { mutableStateOf(0.3f)
                } // Dummy progress
            val formattedTime = "22:49" // Dummy time

            Row(
                modifier = Modifier.fillMaxWidth(),
                verticalAlignment =
                    Alignment.CenterVertically
```

```
        ) {
            Slider(
                value = progress.value,
                onValueChange =
                    { progress.value = it },
                modifier = Modifier.weight(1f)
            )

            Spacer(modifier = Modifier.width(8.dp))

            Text(text = formattedTime,
                color = Color.White)
        }

    }
}
```

This composable is wrapped in a Row layout, which spans the maximum width available (to accommodate the length of the video) and adjusts its height to wrap the content closely, ensuring a tidy appearance with ample padding around its edges for a balanced layout.

The core functionality centers around two elements:

- The Slider component represents the video's progress. It uses a mutable state initialized at 0.3 (30% progress) to simulate the current position of the video playback. This state is interactively adjustable, allowing users to seek through the video. The onValueChange event updates the progress state, reflecting the user's input. To visually separate the progress bar from the time indicator and to ensure the layout remains intuitive, a spacer is inserted between these elements, maintaining a clear distinction.

- Adjacent to the Slider component, the Text component displays the current playback time (set to **22:49** for now, until we integrate the playback functionality) in white color. The time is displayed to provide users with exact information about how much of the video has been played or how much is left, enhancing the user experience by offering precise control over video playback.

Although it may seem that our playback UI is complete, there is still one thing that we should take care of before integrating the playback feature itself. When we are watching a video, we don't want all those controls to be occupying the screen, making it difficult to watch the content. The controls usually disappear automatically after the user hasn't been interacting with the screen. So, let's implement this change.

Making the controls disappear when playing the content

We know our playback controls should disappear if they haven't been used for a while. The easiest way to do this is to have a value that will indicate if the controls should be visible or not, and we will modify its value to `false` when the screen has been idle for a time. Let's make these modifications in the `PlaybackScreen` composable, as follows:

```
@Composable
fun PlaybackScreen() {
    val isControlsVisible = remember { mutableStateOf(true) }
    val coroutineScope = rememberCoroutineScope()

    Box(
        modifier = Modifier
            .fillMaxSize()
            .background(Color.Black)
            .pointerInput(Unit) {
                detectTapGestures(
                    onPress = {
                        // Reset the visibility timer on
                            user interaction
                        isControlsVisible.value = true
                        coroutineScope.launch {
                            delay(15000) // 15 seconds
                                         delay
                            isControlsVisible.value = false
                        }
                    }
                )
            }
    ) {
        if (isControlsVisible.value) {
            TopMediaRow(Modifier.align(Alignment.TopCenter))
            PlayPauseButton(Modifier.align(
                Alignment.Center))
            ProgressBarWithTime(Modifier.align(
                Alignment.BottomCenter))
        }
    }
}
```

The core idea of these modifications is to track user interaction and use a timer to determine when to hide the controls. Initially, as mentioned previously, we'll introduce a state to manage the visibility of the controls. This state will likely be a Boolean that toggles between visible and invisible (`true` and `false`) based on user interaction and the passage of time without interaction.

For detecting user interactions, we could wrap the `Box` layout that contains our playback UI components in a `Modifier.pointerInput` Lambda. Inside this Lambda, we can listen for touch input events, and each time a touch is detected, we can reset the timer – a coroutine launched with `LaunchedEffect` keyed to the visibility state might handle this. This coroutine will wait for 15 seconds of inactivity (no touch events detected) before setting the controls' visibility state to `false`, effectively hiding them. To ensure the controls reappear when the user interacts with the screen again, the same touch input detection mechanism will set the visibility state back to `true`, and the coroutine will restart its countdown.

Incorporating this functionality requires making modifications to the `PlaybackScreen` composable function so that it includes state handling for visibility and can modify the `TopMediaRow`, `PlayPauseButton`, and `ProgressBarWithTime` functions so that they accept and react to the visibility state. This means each of these components will only be rendered when the state indicates they should be visible.

Once we've finished, our playback UI should look like this:

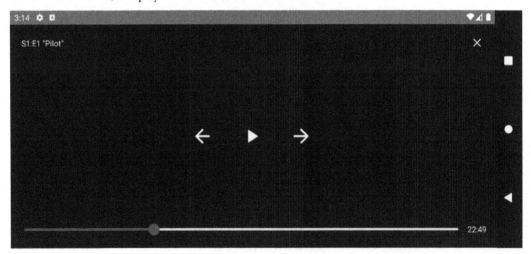

Figure 8.1: Finished playback UI (with controls shown)

When the controls are hidden, it should just show the video content (this isn't visible yet as it hasn't been implemented):

Figure 8.2: Finished playback UI (with controls hidden)

In this section, we created a UI to display the videos. In the next section, we will integrate ExoPlayer so that our app can start playing videos.

Playing video using ExoPlayer

In this section, we'll harness the full power of ExoPlayer so that we can integrate it into our newly created video playback UI. Let's learn how we can do this.

Creating PlaybackActivity

We'll start by creating a new `Activity` for this functionality called `PlaybackActivity`:

```
class PlaybackActivity: ComponentActivity() {
    override fun onCreate(savedInstanceState: Bundle?) {
        super.onCreate(savedInstanceState)
        setContent {
            PlaybackScreen()
        }
    }
}
```

This `PlaybackActivity` activity will show our already created `PlaybackScreen()` in its content.

We also want our playback UI to be always displayed in landscape mode. To do so, we'll configure this activity in the `AndroidManifest.xml` file, as follows:

```xml
<?xml version="1.0" encoding="utf-8"?>
<manifest xmlns:android =
"http://schemas.android.com/apk/res/android">
    <application>
        <activity android:name =
        "com.packt.playback.presentation.PlaybackActivity"
        android:screenOrientation="landscape"/>
    </application>
</manifest>
```

Here, we are declaring `PlaybackActivity` so that it has landscape as a forced screen orientation. This will ensure it will only be rendered in landscape mode, despite what orientation the user is holding their phone.

Creating PlaybackViewModel

Now, we need to create the player, which is the component that's responsible for managing the media playback. We will create `PlaybackViewModel` to handle the ExoPlayer instance and all the logic needed for the view to interact with the video player and watch the media.

To start, we are going to build the basic setup logic for our player in `PlaybackViewModel`:

```kotlin
@HiltViewModel
class PlaybackViewModel @Inject constructor(): ViewModel()
{

    lateinit var player: ExoPlayer

    @OptIn(UnstableApi::class)
    private fun preparePlayerWithMediaSource(exoPlayer:
    ExoPlayer) {
        val mediaUrl = "https://example.com/media.mp4"

        val mediaSource = ProgressiveMediaSource.Factory(
            DefaultHttpDataSource.Factory())
            .createMediaSource(MediaItem.fromUri(mediaUrl))

        exoPlayer.setMediaSource(mediaSource)
        exoPlayer.prepare()
    }
```

```
fun setupPlayer(context: Context) {
    player = ExoPlayer.Builder(context).build().also {
    exoPlayer ->
        preparePlayerWithMediaSource(exoPlayer)
    }
}

override fun onCleared() {
    super.onCleared()
    player.release()
    progressUpdateJob?.cancel()
}
}
```

This is the start of our `PlaybackViewModel` composable, which is designed to manage the media playback functionality of an Android app.

The core component of this `ViewModel` is the ExoPlayer instance, which is stored in a property named `player`. This `player` property is responsible for all media playback operations. However, when `ViewModel` is first created, the player is not initialized; it's declared with `lateinit`, meaning it will be initialized later but before any other component needs to access it.

The `setupPlayer` function is publicly exposed and intended to be called with a `Context` object, which provides access to application-specific resources and classes. Inside this function, `ExoPlayer.Builder` is used to create an instance of `ExoPlayer`. This setup process involves calling the `build()` method on the builder, which returns a fully configured `ExoPlayer` instance. Immediately after creating this instance, the `also` block executes, calling the `preparePlayerWithMediaSource` method with the newly created player.

The `preparePlayerWithMediaSource` method is where the actual media source is set up. It takes an `ExoPlayer` instance as an argument and configures it to play a specific media file. The URL of the media file is defined as `https://example.com/media.mp4`. To play this media, `ProgressiveMediaSource` is created, which is suitable for playing regular media files such as MP4s over HTTP. This media source is then attached to the `ExoPlayer` instance using the `setMediaSource` method, and `prepare()` is called to prepare the player for playback. It's worth noting that this method is marked as private, meaning it's intended to be used only within the `PlaybackViewModel` class. The `@OptIn(UnstableApi::class)` annotation indicates that this method uses APIs that are not yet stable and may change in the future.

Lastly, the `onCleared` method overrides a `ViewModel` life cycle callback that gets called when `ViewModel` is about to be destroyed. This method releases the `ExoPlayer` instance by calling `player.release()`, ensuring that resources are freed and preventing memory leaks.

Now, we'll add the view that will render the media content in `PlaybackScreen` and connect it to the player:

```
@Composable
fun PlaybackScreen() {
    val viewModel: PlaybackViewModel = hiltViewModel()
    val isControlsVisible = remember { mutableStateOf(true) }
    val coroutineScope = rememberCoroutineScope()

    viewModel.setupPlayer(LocalContext.current)

    Box(
        modifier = Modifier
            .fillMaxSize()
            .background(Color.Black)
            .pointerInput(Unit) {
                detectTapGestures(
                    onPress = {
                        isControlsVisible.value = true
                        coroutineScope.launch {
                            delay(15000) // 15 seconds
                                            delay
                            isControlsVisible.value = false
                        }
                    }
                )
            }
    ) {
        VideoPlayerComposable(
            modifier = Modifier.matchParentSize(),
            player = viewModel.player
        )

        if (isControlsVisible.value) {
            ...
        }
    }
}
```

In the `PlaybackScreen` composable, we obtain an instance of `PlaybackViewModel` using `hiltViewModel()`. This `ViewModel` is central to managing the media playback life cycle and interactions within the app.

Once `ViewModel` is ready, we call `viewModel.setupPlayer(LocalContext.current)` to initialize `ExoPlayer`. This setup is crucial because it prepares the player with the appropriate Android context, allowing it to load and play media files effectively. Ensuring that ExoPlayer is initialized with the current context helps manage resources efficiently, which is essential for smooth playback.

The UI component responsible for displaying the video is `VideoPlayerComposable`. We pass the initialized player from `ViewModel` to this composable, which is placed inside a `Box` layout. This layout is configured to fill the maximum size of its parent and sets a black background to emphasize the video content. The `Box` layout also handles user interactions, listening for tap gestures to toggle the visibility of playback controls. When a tap is detected, it makes the controls visible and starts a coroutine that hides these controls again after 15 seconds if no further interaction occurs.

Inside the `Box` layout, conditional logic checks the value of `isControlsVisible`. If `true`, playback controls are rendered on top of the video. This allows users to interact with the video, such as pausing, skipping, or adjusting the volume, but only when they choose to display the controls.

Finally, we will explore how to implement `VideoPlayerComposable` so that we can effectively utilize the player to render the video while responding dynamically to user interactions with playback controls.

Let's see how we can implement this new composable. Unfortunately, at the time of writing, the library doesn't provide a Jetpack Compose option to show the player, so we need to create one inside an `AndroidView` composable, as follows:

```
@Composable
fun VideoPlayerComposable(
    modifier: Modifier = Modifier,
    player: ExoPlayer
) {
    AndroidView(
        factory = { ctx ->
            PlayerView(ctx).apply {
                layoutParams = ViewGroup.LayoutParams(
                    MATCH_PARENT, MATCH_PARENT)
                setPlayer(player)
                useController = false
            }
        },
        modifier = modifier,
        update = { view ->
            view.player = player
        }
    )
}
```

The `VideoPlayerComposable` function takes two parameters:

- The `Modifier` instance allows you to customize the layout or appearance of this composable when it's used elsewhere in your UI

- The `ExoPlayer` instance is the media player that will handle the actual playback of the video content

Inside the `AndroidView` composable, the factory Lambda is where the traditional Android view is created – in this case, `PlayerView`. Here, `PlayerView` is a view provided by the `ExoPlayer` library to display video content and playback controls. Here, it's initialized with the application context (`ctx`).

After creating `PlayerView`, some properties are set on it:

- Here, `layoutParams` is set to `MATCH_PARENT` for both width and height, making `PlayerView` fill the entire space allocated to it. This ensures that the video will take up as much space as possible, typically the entire screen or the parent container.

- Then, `setPlayer(player)` attaches the passed `ExoPlayer` instance to `PlayerView`. This connection is what allows the video loaded in `ExoPlayer` to be displayed in this view.

- Finally, `useController` is set to `false`, indicating that the default playback controls provided by `PlayerView` (such as play, pause, and seek bar) will not be used. We will implement our own controls next.

Finally, the update Lambda of `AndroidView` is where you can update the properties of `PlayerView` based on changes to the composable's state or properties.

With these changes, our player is ready to start rendering the media via `ViewPlayer`. But we still have work to do. We need to bind the already developed controls to the player controls and keep the time and the progress bar of the video updated.

Connecting the controls with ExoPlayer

Let's start modifying the `PlayPauseButton` composable. In this case, we will need to bind the control functions with the ViewModel:

```
@Composable
fun PlayPauseButton(
    isPlaying: Boolean,
    onRewind: () -> Unit,
    onPlayPause: () -> Unit,
    onFastForward: () -> Unit,
    modifier: Modifier = Modifier,
    ) {
```

```
Row(
    horizontalArrangement = Arrangement.Center,
    verticalAlignment = Alignment.CenterVertically,
    modifier = modifier
) {
    IconButton(
        onClick = onRewind,
        modifier = Modifier.padding(20.dp)
    ) {
        Icon(
            modifier = Modifier
                .height(80.dp)
                .width(80.dp),
            imageVector = Icons.Default.ArrowBack,
            contentDescription = "Rewind 10s",
            tint = Color.White
        )
    }

    IconButton(
        onClick = onPlayPause,
        modifier = Modifier.padding(20.dp)
    ) {
        Icon(
            modifier = Modifier
                .height(80.dp)
                .width(80.dp),
            imageVector = if (isPlaying)
                Icons.Default.Close else
                Icons.Default.PlayArrow,
            contentDescription = if (isPlaying) "Pause"
                else "Play",
            tint = Color.White
        )
    }

    IconButton(
        onClick = onFastForward,
        modifier = Modifier.padding(20.dp)
    ) {
        Icon(
            modifier = Modifier
                .height(80.dp)
```

```
                              .width(80.dp),
                        imageVector = Icons.Default.ArrowForward,
                        contentDescription = "Fast-forward 10s",
                        tint = Color.White
                )
            }
        }
    }
```

Now, the `PlayPauseButton` composable takes several parameters, each serving a specific purpose within the UI component:

- `isPlaying` (Boolean): This parameter indicates the current playback state of the video. It is used to determine which icon to display on the play/pause button – either a play icon when the video is paused or a pause icon when the video is actively playing. This allows for intuitive control interactions from the user's perspective.

- `onRewind` (Lambda function): This is a callback function that's triggered when the user presses the rewind button. It should contain the logic for what happens when the video is rewound, such as moving the playback position backward by a fixed amount.

- `onPlayPause` (Lambda function): This function is executed when the play/pause button is pressed. It handles toggling between playing and pausing the video based on the current state, facilitating seamless user control over video playback.

- `onFastForward` (Lambda function): Similar to `onRewind`, this callback is activated when the fast-forward button is pressed. It controls the logic for fast-forwarding the video, advancing the playback position forward by a predetermined interval.

- `modifier` (modifier): This parameter allows the appearance and layout of the button row within the composable to be customized. As we've seen previously, wt can be used to apply padding, define alignment, and set dimensions.

Now that we've added these new parameters, we need to pass them from the parent composable. Here's how you can include and invoke this composable with the required parameters:

```
val isPlaying = viewModel.isPlaying.collectAsState()
PlayPauseButton(
    isPlaying = isPlaying.value,
    onRewind = { viewModel.rewind() },
    onFastForward = {viewModel.fastForward() },
    onPlayPause = {viewModel.togglePlayPause() },
    modifier = Modifier.align(Alignment.Center)
)
```

As we can see, we have bound every Lambda parameter to `ViewModel` functions (that are yet to be implemented) and we are providing an `isPlaying` state to reflect the current playing status of the player.

Now, let's implement those functions in `ViewModel`:

```
private val _isPlaying = MutableStateFlow<Boolean>(false)
val isPlaying: MutableStateFlow<Boolean> = _isPlaying

fun setupPlayer(context: Context) {
    player = ExoPlayer.Builder(context).build().also {
    exoPlayer ->
        preparePlayerWithMediaSource(exoPlayer)

        exoPlayer.addListener(object : Player.Listener {
            override fun onIsPlayingChanged(isPlaying:
            Boolean) {
                _isPlaying.value = isPlaying
            }

            override fun onPlaybackStateChanged(
            playbackState: Int) {
                super.onPlaybackStateChanged(playbackState)
            }

            override fun onPositionDiscontinuity(
            oldPosition: Player.PositionInfo, newPosition:
            Player.PositionInfo, reason: Int) {
                super.onPositionDiscontinuity(oldPosition,
                    newPosition, reason)
            }

            override fun onTimelineChanged(timeline:
            Timeline, reason: Int) {
                super.onTimelineChanged(timeline, reason)
            }
        })
    }
}

fun togglePlayPause() {
    if (player.isPlaying) {
        player.pause()
    } else {
```

```
        player.play()
    }
}

fun rewind() {
    val newPosition =
        (player.currentPosition - 10000).coerceAtLeast(0)
    player.seekTo(newPosition)
}

fun fastForward() {
    val newPosition =
        (player.currentPosition + 10000)
            .coerceAtMost(player.duration)
    player.seekTo(newPosition)
}
```

First, we have defined a private mutable state flow, _isPlaying, to track whether the video is currently playing. This same state flow is exposed as a public MutableStateFlow component named isPlaying. In this case, isPlaying acts as a single source of truth for the playback state, allowing our UI components to update reactively based on whether the video is playing or paused.

The setupPlayer function, which we've already implemented, initializes the ExoPlayer instance. Now, it also attaches a listener to respond to playback events. The listener added overrides several methods, but most importantly, onIsPlayingChanged is used to update _isPlaying.value based on the player's state.

We've also included the functions to manipulate playback that we were already being called from the composable:

- togglePlayPause: This checks if the player is currently playing and toggles between play and pause. This method directly controls the player's state, making it the primary way the user interacts with the playback.

- rewind and fastForward: These options calculate a new position based on the current playback position and seek to that position. The rewind function moves the playback position backward by 10 seconds, while fastForward moves it forward by 10 seconds. These methods enhance user control over the video, allowing for quick navigation within the content.

Now, let's connect the next (and last) composable, ProgressBarWithTime:

```
@Composable
fun ProgressBarWithTime(
    currentPosition: Long,
    duration: Long,
```

```
    onSeek: (Long) -> Unit,
    modifier: Modifier = Modifier,
) {
    val progress =
        if (duration > 0) currentPosition.toFloat() /
            duration else 0f
    val formattedTime =
        "${formatTime(currentPosition)} /
            ${formatTime(duration)}"

    Row(
        modifier = modifier
            .fillMaxWidth()
            .wrapContentHeight()
            .padding(horizontal = 16.dp, vertical = 8.dp),
        horizontalArrangement = Arrangement.SpaceBetween,
        verticalAlignment = Alignment.CenterVertically
    ) {
        Slider(
            value = progress,
            onValueChange = { newValue ->
                val newPosition =
                    (newValue * duration).toLong()
                onSeek(newPosition)
            },
            modifier = Modifier.weight(1f),
            valueRange = 0f..1f
        )

        Spacer(modifier = Modifier.width(8.dp))

        Text(text = formattedTime, color = Color.White)
    }
}
```

The function now accepts three new parameters: currentPosition and duration to represent the current playback position and the total length of the video in milliseconds, respectively, and an onSeek Lambda function that defines what to do when the user seeks to a new position.

The progress variable calculates how far along the video is, represented as a float between 0 and 1. This is achieved by dividing currentPosition by duration, which specifies a proportion of the video that has been played. If the duration is 0 (to avoid division by zero), progress is set to 0f, indicating no progress.

The `formattedTime` string provides a user-friendly display of the current position and total duration of the video by using a custom formatting function, `formatTime()` (as we'll see next), to convert milliseconds into a more readable format (HH:MM:SS).

Finally, slider progress is now bound to the progress value, and its `onValueChange` event is wired to call `onSeek` with the new position when the user interacts with it. This allows the user to seek through the video by moving the slider, with the `onSeek` function updating the video playback position accordingly.

Regarding the aforementioned `formatTime` function, it will work as follows:

```
fun formatTime(millis: Long): String {
    val totalSeconds = millis / 1000
    val hours = totalSeconds / 3600
    val minutes = (totalSeconds % 3600) / 60
    val seconds = totalSeconds % 60

    return if (hours > 0) {
        String.format("%02d:%02d:%02d", hours, minutes,
            seconds)
    } else {
        String.format("%02d:%02d", minutes, seconds)
    }
}
```

The input to the function is `millis`, which represents the time duration in milliseconds. This is a common way to represent time in programming because it's precise. However, milliseconds aren't very human-friendly, so the first step inside the function is to convert milliseconds into total seconds by dividing by `1000`. We're doing this because there are 1,000 milliseconds in a second.

Once you have the total seconds, the function calculates hours, minutes, and seconds. It divides the total seconds by `3600` (the number of seconds in an hour) to get hours. The remainder from that division (using the modulo operator, `%`) is then used to calculate minutes by dividing by `60` (since there are 60 seconds in a minute). Finally, the remainder from the minutes calculation gives you the seconds.

The last part is where the function formats the time string. If the duration includes hours (that is, if the duration is longer than 60 minutes), it formats the time as HH:MM:SS using `String.format()`. This method is used to create a formatted string with placeholders (`%02d`) for hours, minutes, and seconds. Here's a breakdown of the format:

- The `%` symbol indicates the start of a format specifier.
- The `0` specifies that the number should be padded with leading zeros if it has fewer digits than specified.
- The `2` indicates that the number should be at least two digits long.
- The `d` stands for 'decimal' and specifies that the placeholder is for an integer number.

So, %02d ensures that the number is at least two digits long and padded with zeros if necessary.

Going back to the composable, we also need to modify where ProgressBarWithTime is called in PlaybackScreen:

```
val currentPosition =
    viewModel.currentPosition.collectAsState()
val duration = viewModel.duration.collectAsState()

ProgressBarWithTime(
    currentPosition = currentPosition.value,
    duration = duration.value,
    onSeek = { newPosition ->
        viewModel.seekTo(newPosition)
    },
    modifier = Modifier.align(Alignment.BottomCenter)
)
```

As we can see, we have bound the seekTo Lambda parameter to a ViewModel function (that is yet to be implemented) and we are also providing duration and currentPosition states.

Now, let's modify PlaybackViewModel so that we can implement the pending functions related to the progress bar.

Implementing the video controls in PlaybackViewModel

The last step to make the progress bar work is to modify PlaybackViewModel. We can add the necessary functionality to control the progress bar like so:

```
private val _currentPosition = MutableStateFlow<Long>(0L)
val currentPosition: StateFlow<Long> = _currentPosition

private val _duration = MutableStateFlow<Long>(0L)
val duration: MutableStateFlow<Long> = _duration

private var progressUpdateJob: Job? = null

fun setupPlayer(context: Context) {
    player = ExoPlayer.Builder(context).build().also {
    exoPlayer ->
        preparePlayerWithMediaSource(exoPlayer)

        exoPlayer.addListener(object : Player.Listener {
            override fun onIsPlayingChanged(isPlaying:
            Boolean) {
```

```
                _isPlaying.value = isPlaying
                if (isPlaying) {
                    startPeriodicProgressUpdate()
                } else {
                    progressUpdateJob?.cancel()
                }
            }
            override fun onPlaybackStateChanged
            (playbackState: Int) {
                super.onPlaybackStateChanged(playbackState)
                if (playbackState == Player.STATE_READY ||
                playbackState == Player.STATE_BUFFERING) {
                    _duration.value = exoPlayer.duration
                }
            }

            override fun onPositionDiscontinuity(
            oldPosition: Player.PositionInfo, newPosition:
            Player.PositionInfo, reason: Int) {
                super.onPositionDiscontinuity(oldPosition,
                    newPosition, reason)
                _currentPosition.value =
                    newPosition.positionMs
            }

            override fun onTimelineChanged(timeline:
            Timeline, reason: Int) {
                super.onTimelineChanged(timeline, reason)
                if (!timeline.isEmpty) {
                    _duration.value = exoPlayer.duration
                }
            }
        }
    })
    }
}

private fun startPeriodicProgressUpdate() {
    progressUpdateJob?.cancel()
    progressUpdateJob = viewModelScope.launch {
        while (coroutineContext.isActive) {
            val currentPosition = player.currentPosition
            _currentPosition.value = currentPosition
            delay(1000)
```

```
                }
            }
        }

    fun seekTo(position: Long) {
        if (::player.isInitialized && position >= 0 &&
        position <= player.duration) {
            player.seekTo(position)
        }
    }

    override fun onCleared() {
        super.onCleared()
        player.release()
        progressUpdateJob?.cancel()
    }
```

With that, we've declared private mutable state flows called _currentPosition and _duration for tracking the current playback position and the total video duration, respectively. These are exposed as read-only StateFlows to the rest of the app, ensuring that the UI components can observe these values and react to changes, but cannot modify them directly.

The listener in the setupPlayer function has also been modified to include functionality to keep the two states, _currentPosition and _duration. The following modifications have been made to the listener callbacks:

- onIsPlayingChanged: This updates the _isPlaying state and controls the start and stop of a job, which periodically updates the current playback position. This is essential for keeping the UI in sync with the actual playback.

- onPlaybackStateChanged: This checks if the player is ready or buffering and updates the _duration state with the total duration of the video. This is necessary for setting up the progress bar.

- onPositionDiscontinuity and onTimelineChanged: These ensure that changes in the video playback position or timeline (such as seeking or switching to another video) update _currentPosition and _duration correctly.

Then, the new function, startPeriodicProgressUpdate, launches a coroutine that periodically updates the _currentPosition state with the player's current position. This loop runs every second, providing a near-real-time update of the playback position to the UI. It's crucial for making the progress bar move smoothly as the video plays.

Building on this functionality, the `seekTo` function allows the video to be seeked to a new position. It checks that the position is within the bounds of the video before calling `seekTo` on the ExoPlayer instance, effectively letting the user jump to different parts of the video through the progress bar.

Finally, the `onCleared` method has been modified to cancel the new `progressUpdateJob` composable in case we have to release the resources.

With these changes, our video player is ready. We just have to modify the hardcoded media URL in `PlaybackViewModel(val mediaUrl = "https://example.com/media.mp4")` so that we can provide a URL to an actual video and let the magic happen! At this point, we should see the playback of the provided video.

In the last section of this chapter, we are going to enhance the functionality of our video player a little bit further by learning how to add subtitles.

Adding subtitles to the video player

In this section, we'll be adding subtitles to our video player. Subtitles are crucial for making videos accessible to everyone, but they can also be great for watching videos in noisy environments or when you need to keep the volume down. In this section, we'll learn how to load and display subtitles alongside our video while handling various formats and ensuring they sync up perfectly with our content.

To add subtitles, follow these steps:

1. Create a MediaSource for your video file, just as you would for any video playback in ExoPlayer. We did this in the previous section.

2. Create a MediaSource for your subtitle file. This often involves using `SingleSampleMediaSource` for single subtitle files or similar approaches for different formats.

3. Use `MergingMediaSource` to combine the video and subtitle sources. This merged source is then passed to the ExoPlayer instance for playback.

4. Initialize ExoPlayer with the merged source; it will handle the playback of both video and subtitles.

ExoPlayer supports a wide range of subtitle formats so that it can cater to various use cases and standards. Some of the most popular formats are as follows:

-   **WebVTT** (`.vtt`): A widely used format for HTML5 video subtitles that's supported by many web browsers and platforms:

    -   **Advantages**: WebVTT is extensively supported across most modern web browsers, making it ideal for online streaming services. It offers options for styling, positioning, and cue settings, allowing for a customizable viewing experience.

    -   **Disadvantages**: Compared to simpler formats such as SRT, WebVTT's additional features can make it more complex to create and edit. Also, different platforms and browsers may interpret styling and formatting cues differently, leading to inconsistent presentations.

- **SubRip** (`.srt`): One of the most common subtitle formats that's simple in structure and supported by a wide range of media players:

  - **Advantages**: The structure of SRT files is straightforward, making them easy to create, edit, and debug. It is also supported by almost all media players, making it universally applicable for offline and online video playback.

  - **Disadvantages**: It provides basic text formatting, which limits its ability to customize the appearance of subtitles.

To give you an idea of what one of these formats looks like, here's an example of the content of a SubRip (`.srt`) file:

```
1
00:00:01,000 --> 00:00:03,000
Hello, welcome to our video!

2
00:00:05,000 --> 00:00:08,000
Today, we'll be discussing how to create a simple SRT file.

3
00:00:10,000 --> 00:00:12,000
Let's get started.

4
00:00:15,000 --> 00:00:20,000
Subtitles primarily enhance accessibility and also can be very helpful
for understanding dialogue, especially in noisy environments.

5
00:00:22,500 --> 00:00:25,000
And that's all there is to it!
```

Each block starts with a sequence number (for example, 1, 2, 3, and so on), followed by the time range on the next line (start time --> end time), and then the text of the subtitle. This text can be one or more lines and is followed by a blank line to indicate the end of the subtitle entry. This format can be edited with any text editor and saved with the `.srt` extension.

Now that we know a bit more about how to add subtitles to a video in ExoPlayer, let's add them by default to our already-implemented playback functionality. We just need to change the logic for the player setup in `PlaybackViewModel`:

```
@OptIn(UnstableApi::class)
private fun preparePlayerWithMediaSource(exoPlayer:
```

```
ExoPlayer) {
        val mediaUrl = "https://example.com/media.mp4"
        val subtitleUrl =
            "https://example.com/subtitles.srt"

        val videoMediaSource =
            ProgressiveMediaSource.Factory(
                DefaultHttpDataSource.Factory()
        ).createMediaSource(MediaItem.fromUri(mediaUrl))
        val subtitleSource =
            MediaItem.SubtitleConfiguration.Builder(
                Uri.parse(subtitleUrl)).build()
        val subtitleMediaSource =
            SingleSampleMediaSource.Factory(
                DefaultHttpDataSource.Factory()
        ).createMediaSource(subtitleSource, C.TIME_UNSET)

        val mergedSource =
            MergingMediaSource(videoMediaSource,
                subtitleMediaSource)
        exoPlayer.setMediaSource(mergedSource)
        exoPlayer.prepare()
    }
```

In the preceding code, we modified the already existing preparePlayerWithMediaSource function. We started by adding a new media with the subtitles URL.

Then we created MediaSource for the subtitles, and we created a MediaItem. SubtitleConfiguration object from the subtitle URL (subtitleUrl). This configuration specifies how the subtitle should be loaded and displayed.

Then, SingleSampleMediaSource is created for the subtitle configuration. Here, SingleSampleMediaSource is used because subtitle files are typically a single piece of content rather than streamed content. The createMediaSource method here is slightly different from the video one; it takes the subtitle configuration and a duration parameter, which is set to C.TIME_UNSET to indicate that the duration is unknown or should be determined from the content itself.

Once both the video and subtitle sources have been created, they're combined into a single source using MergingMediaSource. This merged source tells ExoPlayer to play the video with the subtitles overlaying it.

Finally, the merged source is set on the ExoPlayer instance with setMediaSource, and prepare() is called. This action causes ExoPlayer to load the media and get ready for playback. When the video plays, the subtitles from the specified SRT file will be displayed at the correct times, as defined in the file.

The following figure shows the subtitles added:

Figure 8.3: Playback with subtitles

With that, our player is ready to play back videos. By including subtitles, it offers a more accessible experience for our users.

Summary

In this chapter, we tackled the essentials of adding video playback in our Android app while focusing on the powerful ExoPlayer library. We started by comparing media options in Android before quickly realizing ExoPlayer's superiority due to its flexibility and wide format support. This set the stage for us to learn how ExoPlayer fits into an app and how to use it for playing videos smoothly.

We then walked through building a user-friendly video playback interface, covering everything from setting up ExoPlayer to managing playback controls. Finally, we explored adding subtitles to make your videos accessible to a wider audience, highlighting ExoPlayer's capability to enhance inclusivity.

Now that you have a solid grasp of video playback using ExoPlayer, you're ready to elevate your app with picture-in-picture mode and media casting.

9

Extending Video Playback in Your Packtflix App

Have you ever wanted your users to continue enjoying their favorite videos even when they switch apps or turn off the screen? This chapter dives deep into the world of extended video playback on Android, bringing you the skills to create a more engaging and versatile user experience.

We'll be exploring two key functionalities: **picture-in-picture** (**PiP**) mode and media casting. With PiP, you'll learn how to create a miniature video player that overlays other apps, allowing users to keep an eye on the video while multitasking. With media casting, we'll use `MediaRouter` and the Cast SDK, which enable users to transfer the video playback to a larger screen, such as a TV with Google Chromecast.

By the end of this chapter, you'll have gained a solid understanding of the PiP functionalities and unlocked the potential of extended video playback in our Android app.

So, in this chapter, we will cover the following topics:

- Getting to know the PiP API
- Using PiP to continue playback in the background
- Getting to know `MediaRouter`
- Connecting to Google Chromecast devices

Technical requirements

As in the previous chapter, you will need to have installed Android Studio (or another editor of your preference).

We will follow the project started in *Chapter 7* with the changes we have made in *Chapter 8*.

You can find the complete code that we are going to build through this chapter available in this repository: `https://github.com/PacktPublishing/Thriving-in-Android-Development-using-Kotlin/tree/main/Chapter-9`.

Getting to know the PiP API

The first step on our extended video playback journey is to understand the PiP API, which lets us use PiP mode. **PiP mode** allows users to minimize your app and continue watching a video in a resizable and movable miniature player. This functionality enhances user experience by providing flexibility and convenience.

This section will provide you with the knowledge to leverage PiP effectively in your app. We'll cover the most important aspects such as understanding the PiP requirements and learning how to enter and exit PiP mode programmatically, and review some different listener events. So, let's get started.

PiP requirements

Not every device is created equal when it comes to PiP. Before we go deep into the exciting functionalities, let's ensure a smooth user experience by understanding the requirements and compatibility aspects of PiP mode.

Regarding the requirements, there are two variables to take into account:

- **Minimum Android version**: PiP mode relies on specific APIs introduced in Android 8.0 (Oreo). Targeting devices running older versions of Android will not only prevent PiP functionality but could also lead to crashes or unexpected behavior.

  To check if the user's device is compatible with PiP, we could implement the following code:

  ```
  val minApiLevel = Build.VERSION_CODES.O
  if (android.os.Build.VERSION.SDK_INT < minApiLevel) {
    // PiP not supported on this device
    return false
  }
  ```

  This code ensures our app gracefully handles devices that can't use PiP mode. First, we define the minimum Android version required for PiP (typically Android 8.0 or Oreo). Then, we check the device's current version. If it's older than the minimum, the code recognizes that PiP functionality isn't available and signals this back (potentially by returning `false`) to prevent the app from attempting to use PiP features that would cause issues on incompatible devices.

  This allows you to gracefully handle situations where PiP isn't available and potentially offer alternative functionalities for users on older devices (for example, we could offer them to send the playback to a different device).

- **Screen size requirements**: While PiP mode can be technically implemented on various screen sizes, smaller displays might not provide an optimal user experience. Imagine trying to watch a movie in a tiny PiP window on a phone with a 4-inch screen! Therefore, it's essential to consider screen size limitations.

Now that we've established the requirements, let's explore the exciting part: initiating PiP mode within our app.

Entering and exiting PiP mode programmatically

As we already know, PiP mode offers users the convenience of continuing video playback in a miniature window even when they switch apps or turn off the screen. To do this, we'll use the `enterPictureInPictureMode()` method available in the `Activity` class:

```
activity.enterPictureInPictureMode()
```

Calling this method allows you to programmatically trigger PiP mode from within your activity, and the system will handle resizing the video player window and placing it on top of other apps. It's important to note that you should typically only call this method when the user explicitly requests it, such as upon tapping a dedicated PiP button within your app's UI.

While entering PiP mode is initiated programmatically, exiting is primarily user-driven. The user can exit PiP mode by swiping the miniature player away or tapping a designated **Close** button provided by the system. However, as developers, we can still play a role in ensuring a smooth transition back to the fullscreen experience. The system triggers specific callbacks within your activity when PiP mode is exited. Here's how we can utilize these callbacks:

```
override fun onPictureInPictureExited() {
  super.onPictureInPictureExited()
  // Any logic that we want to add when the user comes back
    to the full screen experience in our app
}
```

This function will be called every time the user closes the PiP miniature screen. This is not the only function that we can use to handle PiP status changes, though; the listener provides various events to keep our app informed about changes in the PiP window. These events allow us to react and update our app's behavior accordingly, ensuring a seamless user experience:

- `OnPictureInPictureEntered()`: This event gets triggered when the user successfully enters PiP mode. You can use this opportunity to potentially update UI elements to reflect the PiP state (for example, hide unnecessary controls) or perform any necessary optimizations for PiP playback (for example, adjust video quality).

- `OnPictureInPictureExited()`: As discussed previously, this event signifies the user exiting PiP mode. Here, you can clean up resources associated with the PiP window or update the UI to reflect the return to fullscreen playback.

- `OnPictureInPictureUiStateChanged()`: This event gets fired whenever any change occurs to the PiP window, such as resizing or moving it. You might use this to adjust your UI layout based on the new PiP window dimensions or update video playback based on potential performance changes due to resizing.

By effectively handling PiP events and listener callbacks, you can keep your app in sync with the changing PiP window state. Now, let's see how we can integrate it into our existing project.

Using PiP to continue playback in the background

The first step before we can use PiP in our project is that we must declare support for it in our `AndroidManifest.xml` file. This step is crucial for informing the Android system that our `PlaybackActivity` class is capable of running in PiP mode. We do this like so:

```xml
<?xml version="1.0" encoding="utf-8"?>
<manifest
    xmlns:android =
        "http://schemas.android.com/apk/res/android">
    <application>
        <activity
            android:name = "com.packt.playback.presentation
                .PlaybackActivity"
            android:supportsPictureInPicture="true"
            android:resizeableActivity="true"
            android:screenOrientation="landscape"/>
    </application>
</manifest>
```

For PiP specifically, the key attribute in our manifest is `android:supportsPicture InPicture="true"`, which explicitly declares that your activity supports PiP mode.

The `resizeableActivity` attribute, while related to the ability of an activity to be resized, is implicitly set to `true` for all activities when targeting API level 24 or higher. This means if your app targets API level 24+, you don't need to explicitly set `resizeableActivity="true"` for PiP mode to work because the system already considers all activities to be resizable to support multi-window mode.

However, explicitly setting `resizeableActivity="true"` can be a good practice for clarity, especially if your app is designed to take advantage of multi-window features beyond just PiP, or if you want to ensure compatibility across different Android versions and devices. It's also useful for documentation purposes, making it clear to anyone reading your `AndroidManifest.xml` file that your activity is intended to support resizable behaviors, including PiP.

Implementing PiP

Now that we have explicitly opted in our `Activity` class to use the PiP feature, let's implement it. We will override the `onUserLeaveHint()` callback, which is triggered when the user presses the **Home** button or switches to another app:

```
override fun onUserLeaveHint() {
    super.onUserLeaveHint()
    val aspectRatio = Rational(16, 9)
    val params = PictureInPictureParams.Builder()
        .setAspectRatio(aspectRatio)
        .build()
    enterPictureInPictureMode(params)
}
```

As we said, we are overriding the `onUserLeaveHint()` existing function. Here, we still have to include the call to `super.onUserLeaveHint()` as it ensures that the `Activity` class properly handles any additional underlying operations defined by Android's framework before executing custom behavior.

Within this method, the aspect ratio for the PiP window is defined as $16:9$, a common choice for video content, by using the `Rational` class. This aspect ratio is crucial as it dictates the proportional relationship between the width and height of the PiP window, ensuring the video maintains its intended appearance without distortion.

To apply this aspect ratio, the `PictureInPictureParams.Builder` class is utilized to construct a configuration object. By invoking `setAspectRatio(aspectRatio)` on the builder, the previously defined aspect ratio is applied to this configuration.

While `setAspectRatio(Rational)` sets the preferred aspect ratio of the PiP window, meaning that the system will try to maintain this aspect ratio when displaying the PiP window, it may not always be possible depending on the device and screen size constraints. Android 11 (API level 30) introduced `setMaxAspectRatio(Rational)` and `setMinAspectRatio(Rational)` for defining the maximum and minimum aspect ratios. Additionally, `setMaxSize(int, int)` allows setting the maximum size of the PiP window, providing greater control over how the PiP window appears on different devices.

> **Note**
>
> There are also other `PictureInPictureParams.Builder` options that could be applied. For more information about these options, refer to the documentation: `https://developer.` `android.com/reference/android/app/PictureInPictureParams.Builder`.

The `build()` method then compiles these configurations into a `PictureInPictureParams` object, which encapsulates all the necessary settings for entering PiP mode.

Finally, the `enterPictureInPictureMode(params)` method is invoked, signaling the system to transition the current `Activity` class into PiP mode using the specified parameters.

Now that we have integrated this feature, when we are on the playback screen and we leave the application, we should still see the video on the PiP screen:

Figure 9.1: Playback using the PiP feature

The `PictureInPictureParams.Builder` class in Android provides a customizable way to configure the behavior and appearance of an app when it enters PiP mode. Apart from setting the aspect ratio with `setAspectRatio()`, as we did in the previous instruction, there are several other options available to tailor the PiP experience:

- **Actions**: Using `setActions(List<RemoteAction>)`, developers can specify a list of actions that the user can perform while in PiP mode. These actions are represented as `RemoteAction` objects and can include things such as play, pause, or skip. These actions appear as buttons in the PiP window, providing interactive elements for the user without needing to return to the full app interface.

- **Auto enter/exit**: Through `setAutoEnterEnabled(boolean)` and `setAutoExitEnabled(boolean)` (introduced in later Android versions), developers can control whether the app should automatically enter or exit PiP mode based on certain conditions, such as media playback state.

- **Seamless resize**: By invoking `setSeamlessResizeEnabled(boolean)`, it's possible to enable or disable seamless resizing for the PiP window. This option, available in later Android versions, helps make the transition into and out of PiP mode smoother visually.

- **Source rect hint**: `setSourceRectHint(Rect)` allows developers to suggest a preferred area of the screen that the PiP mode should try to align with when entering PiP mode. This can be useful for guiding the system on where the PiP window should ideally be placed based on the app's UI layout.

Let's use these options to add actions so that the user can toggle between play and pause in the PiP view. But first, a little theory.

Understanding how to add actions to the PiP mode

Integrating actions into PiP mode enhances user interaction by allowing direct control over app functionality without leaving the PiP window. By using the `setActions(List<RemoteAction>)` method, you can create a more immersive and user-friendly experience, offering controls such as play, pause, or skip directly within the PiP overlay. This capability is especially valuable in media applications, where users often need to manage playback without disrupting their current onscreen activities.

In a moment, we will learn how to effectively create and manage these `RemoteAction` objects, ensuring our app's PiP mode is both functional and engaging, complementing the existing array of PiP features. But let's dig into the concepts further.

Each `RemoteAction` object represents an actionable element in the PiP window, such as a button for play, pause, or skip functionality. To create these actions, we would have to specify an icon, a title, a `PendingIntent` object that defines the action to take when the user interacts with the button, and a description for accessibility purposes.

The utilization of a `PendingIntent` object is crucial here, as it allows the action to trigger specific behaviors in your app when invoked. An `Intent` object in Android is like a message that can signify a wide range of events, including system boot completion, network changes, or custom events defined by the application. Typically, these intents are directed toward a `BroadcastReceiver` instance within your application.

A `BroadcastReceiver` instance in Android is a fundamental component that enables applications to listen for and respond to broadcast messages from other applications or from the system itself. When an intent that matches a `BroadcastReceiver` instance's filter is broadcasted, the `BroadcastReceiver` instance's `onReceive()` method is invoked, allowing the app to execute logic in response to the event. This mechanism provides a powerful way for applications to react to global system events or inter-app communication without needing to be running in the foreground, making `BroadcastReceiver` instances a key tool for event-driven programming in Android.

In our case, this `BroadcastReceiver` instance is responsible for listening to and processing the broadcasted intents sent by PiP actions. For instance, when a user presses the **Play** button in the PiP window, the `PendingIntent` object associated with the play action is broadcasted, and the corresponding receiver in your app catches this intent and triggers the media to play.

The need for a `BroadcastReceiver` instance arises from the decoupled nature of PiP action intents from direct method calls within your app. Since these actions occur outside the regular UI flow, using a broadcast mechanism allows your app to respond to these actions asynchronously and perform the necessary operations, such as updating the media playback state. This setup ensures that your app can handle PiP controls effectively, providing a seamless experience for users even when interacting with the app from the PiP window.

Now that we know how to create `RemoteAction` objects, let's apply our learnings in our project.

Adding actions to the PiP mode

Let's start by creating our `BroadcastReceiver` subclass. This class will extend `BroadcastReceiver` and override the `onReceive()` method, where you'll define how your app should react to PiP action `Intent` objects:

```
class PiPActionReceiver(private val togglePlayPause: () -> Unit) :
BroadcastReceiver() {
    override fun onReceive(context: Context?, intent:
    Intent?) {
        when (intent?.action) {
            ACTION_TOGGLE_PLAY -> {
                togglePlayPause()
            }
        }
    }
}
```

```
    companion object {
        const val ACTION_TOGGLE_PLAY =
            "com.packflix.action.TOGGLE_PLAY"
    }
}
```

In the onReceive method, a check is performed on the Intent action to determine if it matches the ACTION_TOGGLE_PLAY action. If it does, the play/pause toggle logic will be executed. In this case, we will execute a callback, as the logic to play or pause the playback will likely be outside this receiver.

Next, we need to register the BroadcastReceiver instance so that it can receive the Intent object. This can be done in two ways:

- **Manifest declaration**: Registering in the AndroidManifest.xml file is suitable for actions that should be received even if your app is not running. However, for PiP actions, dynamic registration in the activity or service that handles PiP mode is often more appropriate.

- **Dynamic registration**: Since PiP actions are specifically related to when our app is in PiP mode, registering the BroadcastReceiver instance dynamically in our PlaybackActivity class allows for more control and is contextually relevant.

We will register the BroadcastReceiver instance using dynamic registration. In our PlaybackActivity class, the implementation will look like this:

```
private lateinit var pipActionReceiver: PiPActionReceiver

override fun onCreate(savedInstanceState: Bundle?) {
    super.onCreate(savedInstanceState)

    pipActionReceiver = PiPActionReceiver {
        //TODO handle there the play/pause logic
    }

    val filter =
        IntentFilter(PiPActionReceiver.ACTION_TOGGLE_PLAY)

    if (Build.VERSION.SDK_INT >=
    Build.VERSION_CODES.TIRAMISU) {
        registerReceiver(pipActionReceiver, filter,
            RECEIVER_NOT_EXPORTED)
    } else {
        registerReceiver(pipActionReceiver, filter)
    }

    setContent {
```

```
        PlaybackScreen()
    }
}
```

First, we will declare a `BroadcastReceiver` variable named `pipActionReceiver`. This receiver is not initialized immediately (it is declared as `lateinit var`) because it will be set up in the `onCreate` method of our activity.

In the `onCreate` method, we will initialize the `BroadcastReceiver` variable. The `pipActionReceiver` variable is instantiated and assigned a lambda function as its argument. This function is intended to contain the logic that handles the play/pause action.

Then, we will register the `BroadcastReceiver` variable, indicating the `Intent` filter signal it will listen to. The registration method differs depending on the SDK version:

- For SDK versions Tiramisu (Android 13, API level 33) and above, you use the `register-Receiver` method with an additional flag, `RECEIVER_NOT_EXPORTED`, for enhanced security, ensuring that your receiver does not inadvertently become accessible to other apps.

- For earlier versions, you register the receiver without this flag. This ensures backward compatibility while adhering to best practices for app security on newer devices.

Now, let's create the action that will trigger the `Intent` action needed to launch the `BroadcastReceiver` instance:

```
private fun getIntentForTogglePlayPauseAction():
RemoteAction {
    val icon: Icon = Icon.createWithResource(this,
        R.drawable.baseline_play_arrow_24)
    val intent =
    Intent(PiPActionReceiver.ACTION_TOGGLE_PLAY).let {
    intent ->
        PendingIntent.getBroadcast(this, 0, intent,
            PendingIntent.FLAG_UPDATE_CURRENT or
                PendingIntent.FLAG_IMMUTABLE)
    }
    return RemoteAction(icon, "Toggle Play", "Play or pause
        the video", intent)
}
```

In this code, we are creating a `RemoteAction` method. The first line inside the method creates an `Icon` object from a drawable resource (`R.drawable.baseline_play_arrow_24`). This icon visually represents the toggle play/pause action to the user.

Then, a new `Intent` object is instantiated with the `PiPActionReceiver.ACTION_TOGGLE_PLAY` action. This `Intent` object is designed to be broadcasted when the `RemoteAction` method is invoked by the user. The `let` block is utilized to directly chain the creation of a `PendingIntent` object that wraps this `Intent` object, making it executable from outside the application context.

The `PendingIntent.getBroadcast` method is called to create a `PendingIntent` object that broadcasts the `Intent` object. This `PendingIntent` object is configured with `PendingIntent.FLAG_UPDATE_CURRENT` to ensure that if the pending `Intent` object already exists, it will be reused but with its extra data updated. `PendingIntent.FLAG_IMMUTABLE` is used for security purposes, marking the `Intent` object as immutable to prevent alterations after creation.

Finally, a `RemoteAction` object is instantiated and returned. This object takes the previously created icon, a title (**Toggle Play**), a content description (**Play or pause the video**), and the `PendingIntent` object as its parameters. The title and content description should be concise yet descriptive enough to inform the user of the action's purpose, adhering to accessibility standards.

Now, we need to configure this action as a parameter for our PiP configuration. We will modify the existing configuration as follows:

```
override fun onUserLeaveHint() {
    super.onUserLeaveHint()
    val aspectRatio = Rational(16, 9)
    val params = PictureInPictureParams.Builder()
        .setAspectRatio(aspectRatio)
        .setActions(listOf(
            getIntentForTogglePlayPauseAction()))
        .build()
    enterPictureInPictureMode(params)
}
```

Here, we are using the `setActions()` function to add a list including the new action.

The last step is to handle the logic to effectively toggle between play and pause. We already have this functionality implemented in the `ViewModel` component, so we just have to inject the `PlaybackViewModel` component in the `Activity` class and call the `togglePlayPause()` function:

```
@AndroidEntryPoint
class PlaybackActivity: ComponentActivity() {

    private val viewModel: PlaybackViewModel by
    viewModels()

    override fun onCreate(savedInstanceState: Bundle?) {
        super.onCreate(savedInstanceState)
```

```
        pipActionReceiver = PiPActionReceiver {
            viewModel.togglePlayPause()
        }

        ...
    }
}
```

As we can see, we are injecting `PlaybackViewModel` and then, the `viewModel.toggle PlayPause()` function will be invoked when the receiver detects that the user has sent a broadcast with the play/pause action.

If we execute the code with these changes, we should see the **Play** button in our PiP UI:

Figure 9.2: PiP view with some actions

Having implemented PiP mode, let's move on to connecting with other devices for media playback using the `MediaRouter` API, which allows your app to cast or stream content to devices such as smart TVs or Chromecast. We'll cover how to use `MediaRouter` to identify compatible devices and manage media streaming to them, enhancing our app's functionality.

Getting to know MediaRouter

`MediaRouter` is a pivotal component in Android development, especially for applications that deal with multimedia content. It acts as a bridge between devices running your app and external devices such as Google Chromecast, smart TVs, and various speakers that support media routing capabilities.

The core function of `MediaRouter` is to facilitate the streaming of multimedia content—be it audio, video, or images—from the user's current device to another device that provides a better or more suitable playback experience. It intelligently discovers available media routes and allows the application to connect to them, thereby extending the multimedia capabilities beyond the confines of the user's primary device.

Android's `MediaRouter` API provides a framework that developers can utilize to search for and interact with media route providers registered on the local network. These providers represent devices or services capable of media playback. With `MediaRouter`, applications can not only discover these routes dynamically but also present the user with a streamlined interface for choosing their preferred playback devices, all while managing the connections and playback state seamlessly across devices.

The use of `MediaRouter` in Android apps opens up a myriad of possibilities for enhancing the user's media consumption experience. Here are some typical use cases:

- **Casting videos to larger screens**: One of the most common uses of `MediaRouter` is casting videos from a mobile device to a larger display, such as a smart TV or a monitor with Chromecast. This is particularly appealing for watching movies, TV shows, or user-generated content on a bigger screen that offers a more immersive viewing experience.

- **Streaming music to external speakers**: `MediaRouter` allows apps to stream music to external speakers, amplifying the audio experience. This is ideal for parties, workouts, or simply enhancing the quality of music playback beyond what the phone's or tablet's built-in speakers can provide.

- **Displaying images on a shared screen**: Apps can use `MediaRouter` to send images to a smart TV or a connected display, making it perfect for sharing photos with a group, conducting presentations, or viewing artwork in higher resolution.

- **Gaming**: With the capability to cast screen content to a larger display, gaming apps can leverage `MediaRouter` to provide a console-like gaming experience on the TV while using the mobile device as a controller.

- **Fitness and education**: For apps focused on fitness or education, casting instructional videos or workout routines to a TV allows users to follow along more comfortably and effectively.

In each of these use cases, `MediaRouter` significantly enhances the functionality of apps by leveraging the power of connected devices, thus offering users a more flexible and enriched media playback experience. Through its comprehensive API, developers can create applications that are not just confined to the small screens of mobile devices but are instead capable of bringing content to life on any compatible device within the home network.

Setting up MediaRouter

Integrating `MediaRouter` into our Android app involves a few key setup steps, including adding the necessary dependencies to your project and ensuring you have the correct permissions in place.

First, we'll need to include the `MediaRouter` library dependencies in our `libs.versions.toml` file. This library provides the classes and interfaces needed to discover and interact with media route providers:

```
[versions]
...
mediarouter = "1.7.0"
google-cast = "21.4.0"

[libraries]
...
media-router = { group = "androidx.mediarouter", name="mediarouter",
version.ref="mediarouter"}
google-cast = { group = "com.google.android.gms", name="play-services-
cast-framework", version.ref="google-cast"}
```

As we plan to support casting to Chromecast devices or other Google Cast-enabled devices, we need the `play-services-cast-framework` library. This library facilitates the integration with Google Cast devices and extends the capabilities of `MediaRouter`.

The next step will be to add it to our `build.gradle` module:

```
        implementation(libs.media.router)
        implementation(libs.google.cast)
```

Now, to enable `MediaRouter` to discover and interact with devices on the local network, we must declare the necessary permissions in our app's `AndroidManifest.xml` file:

```
<uses-permission android:name="android.permission.ACCESS_NETWORK_
STATE"/>
<uses-permission android:name="android.permission.ACCESS_WIFI_STATE"/>
<uses-permission android:name="android.permission.INTERNET"/>
<uses-permission android:name="android.permission.BLUETOOTH_CONNECT"
/>
```

```
<uses-permission android:name="android.permission.BLUETOOTH_SCAN" />
<uses-permission android:name="android.permission.POST_NOTIFICATIONS"
/>
```

We are including permissions here for the following:

- **Internet permission**: Since `MediaRouter` may use the network to communicate with media route providers, your app needs permission to access the internet. We have already needed to declare this permission for the previous chapters, so it shouldn't be new.

- **Network state permissions**: These permissions are required for the app to monitor changes in network connectivity, which is essential for discovering devices on the network.

- **Local network permissions (Android 12 and above)**: Starting with Android 12 (API level 31), if your app targets API level 31 or higher and needs to discover devices on the local network, you must also declare the permission.

- **Post notifications**: For Android 12+, to access the local network for device discovery, it is mandatory to have this permission.

After adding the necessary dependencies and permissions, our project is ready to use `MediaRouter` for discovering media route providers and enabling media streaming to external devices.

Discovering media routes

Once your app is set up with the necessary `MediaRouter` dependencies and permissions, the next step is discovering available media routes. This involves identifying external devices or services your app can stream media to. Android's `MediaRouter` framework simplifies this by providing tools to both discover media routes and present them to users.

Learning about MediaRouteProvider

`MediaRouteProvider` is a component that publishes media routes to `MediaRouter`. It acts as a bridge between your app and external devices or services, such as speakers, TVs, or other Cast-enabled devices. There are two options to use `MediaRouteProvider`:

- The default `MediaRouteProvider` implementation: For most use cases, especially when integrating with Google Cast devices, Android provides a default `MediaRouteProvider` implementation, so you don't need to implement your own. The Google Cast framework automatically discovers compatible devices and makes them available as media routes.

- A custom `MediaRouteProvider` implementation: If you need to discover devices for a custom protocol or a specific type of media routing not covered by Google Cast, you can implement your own `MediaRouteProvider` instance by extending the `MediaRouteProvider` class. This involves defining the discovery logic and publishing routes to `MediaRouter`.

However, creating a custom `MediaRouteProvider` implementation is beyond the scope of basic media routing and requires in-depth knowledge of the specific hardware or protocol you're targeting. If you want to know more, here is the official documentation to create a customized `MediaRouteProvider` implementation: `https://developer.android.com/media/routing/mediarouteprovider`.

We will use the default `MediaRouteProvider` implementation instead.

Using the MediaRouter class

The `MediaRouter` class is your primary tool for interacting with media routes. Here's how you can use it to discover and monitor available media routes.

We will begin by defining a `MediaRouteSelector` instance and allow it to start discovering other devices to send the media to. We will use `LaunchedEffect` to tie the discovery process to the composable's lifecycle:

```
@Composable
fun MediaRouteDiscoveryOptions(mediaRouter: MediaRouter) {

    val context = LocalContext.current
    val routeSelector = remember {
        MediaRouteSelector.Builder()
            .addControlCategory(
                MediaControlIntent.CATEGORY_REMOTE_PLAYBACK
            )
            .build()
    }
    val mediaRoutes = remember {
    mutableStateListOf<MediaRouter.RouteInfo>() }

    DisposableEffect(mediaRouter) {
        mediaRouter.addCallback(routeSelector, callback,
            MediaRouter.CALLBACK_FLAG_PERFORM_ACTIVE_SCAN)
        onDispose {
            mediaRouter.removeCallback(callback)
        }
    }
}
```

This composable function accepts a `MediaRouter` instance as a parameter, highlighting its dependency on this framework for discovering media routes.

The function begins by obtaining the current `Context` value using `LocalContext.current`, then it creates a `MediaRouterSelector` instance. This selector is specifically configured to filter for routes supporting live video content. The use of `remember` ensures that the `MediaRouteSelector` instance is preserved across recompositions of the composable, optimizing performance by preventing unnecessary reinitializations.

Then, we are adding a `DisposableEffect` composable, which encapsulates the logic for starting and stopping media route discovery in alignment with the composable's lifecycle. By passing `MediaRouter` as a key to `DisposableEffect`, the enclosed block of code is executed in a coroutine when the composable is first composed into the UI, and the coroutine is canceled when the composable is removed, effectively managing the lifecycle of the discovery process. Within this block, the `addCallback` method of `MediaRouter` is called to register a callback with the active scan flag, initiating the active scanning for media routes that match the criteria set by `routeSelector`. The `onDispose` block within `DisposableEffect` serves as a cleanup mechanism, where the callback is unregistered from `MediaRouter` when the composable is disposed of, ensuring resources are freed and background processing is minimized.

Now, we will create a callback that we have included in the `addCallback` function described previously:

```
val callback = remember {
    object : MediaRouter.Callback() {
        override fun onRouteAdded(router: MediaRouter,
        route: MediaRouter.RouteInfo) {
            mediaRoutes.add(route)
        }

        override fun onRouteRemoved(router: MediaRouter,
        route: MediaRouter.RouteInfo) {
            mediaRoutes.remove(route)
        }
    }
}
```

We are instantiating a `MediaRouter.Callback` listener, using `remember` to avoid needing to recreate it every time the app's UI updates.

This listener, `MediaRouter.Callback`, has two main jobs through its `onRouteAdded` and `onRouteRemoved` methods. When a new device becomes available for casting media, `onRouteAdded` gets called, and the app adds this new route to a list called `mediaRoutes`. This list is crucial for the app to know what devices are available at any moment. On the flip side, when a device goes offline or disconnects, `onRouteRemoved` is called, and the app removes that route from the list, ensuring the list stays current.

Effectively, this setup allows the app to dynamically adjust to changes in the available devices for media casting.

To provide users with an easy way to select from these available devices, we need to integrate a button designed for this purpose. The MediaRouter API offers a ready-made button that displays the available devices for casting. Although this button is an Android view and not a composable, we can still use it in Jetpack Compose by wrapping it with the AndroidView composable. Here's how we can do it:

```
AndroidView(
    factory = { ctx ->
        MediaRouteButton(ctx).apply {
            setRouteSelector(routeSelector)
        }
    },
    modifier = Modifier
        .wrapContentWidth()
        .wrapContentHeight()
)
```

Now, we just have to use the MediaRouteDiscoveryOptions composable from our playback screen:

```
@Composable
fun TopMediaRow(mediaRouter: MediaRouter, modifier:
Modifier = Modifier) {
    Row(
        modifier = modifier
            .fillMaxWidth()
            .padding(20.dp),
        horizontalArrangement = Arrangement.SpaceBetween,
        verticalAlignment = Alignment.CenterVertically
    ) {
        Text(text = "S1:E1 \"Pilot\"", color = Color.White)
        MediaRouteDiscoveryOptions(mediaRouter =
            mediaRouter)
    }
}
```

Here, we have added the MediaRouteDiscoveryOptions composable to our already existing TopMediaRow function.

When calling the TopMediaRow function we will pass it an instance of mediaRouter that we had obtained before, using LocalContext:

```
TopMediaRow(
    mediaRouter =
        MediaRouter.getInstance(LocalContext.current),
    modifier = Modifier.align(Alignment.TopCenter))
```

Now, we will see the **Cast** button in the right corner of our existing `PlaybackScreen` composable. If we click it, `MediaRouter` will automatically search for devices:

Figure 9.3: MediaRouter searching for devices

If it cannot find any device, it will show a message encouraging the user to check the connection:

Figure 9.4: MediaRouter functionality, prompting the user to check the device connections

After discovering available media routes using the `MediaRouter` API, the next step is connecting to a selected device for media playback. This involves two main actions: selecting a media route and then establishing a connection to that route. Here's how you can approach this process.

When utilizing the built-in media route selector with `MediaRouteButton`, the process of connecting to a device is streamlined. `MediaRouteButton` automatically handles the display of available media routes based on the criteria defined in a `MediaRouteSelector` instance. Users can then select their preferred device directly from the UI that `MediaRouteButton` presents.

Once a user selects a route from the dialog, the connection to that device is automatically managed by the `MediaRouter` framework based on the route's capabilities and the types of media specified in your `MediaRouteSelector` instance. There's no need for additional manual connection management in your application code.

With the route selected and a connection established, you can control media playback through the selected route. This typically involves using media control APIs that are appropriate for your application's media content and the capabilities of the selected route. We will learn how can we cast media playback for Google Cast devices in the next section.

Connecting to Google Chromecast devices

Google Cast is a powerful technology developed by Google that allows users to wirelessly stream audio and video content from their smartphones, tablets, or computers directly to Cast-enabled devices. This technology is embedded in a wide array of devices, including Chromecast dongles, smart TVs, and speakers, making it accessible to a vast user base. At its core, Google Cast works by establishing a connection between a Cast-enabled app on a mobile device or computer and a Cast-enabled receiver device. Once a connection is made, media can be played back on the receiver device, effectively turning it into a remote screen or speaker for the content being cast.

The functionality of Google Cast is not limited to streaming media from the internet. It also enables the mirroring of content from the sender device's screen, extending its utility to presentations, educational content, and more. Google Cast operates over Wi-Fi, ensuring high-quality streaming performance without the need for physical cables or adapters.

We have already done some steps: we have already included the library and we are already detecting the devices that allow casting. Now, we need to establish a cast session. This session facilitates a connection between your app and the selected Cast device, enabling media control and playback on the larger screen. This process hinges on effectively using `CastContext` and adeptly managing Cast session events.

`CastContext` is central to initiating and managing Cast sessions in your application, providing the necessary APIs to connect to the selected Cast device. Here's how to initiate a connection.

First, we need to ensure that you have initialized `CastContext` in your application. This is typically done in the `Application` subclass or your main activity. We will initialize it in our `PlaybackActivity` class:

```
val castContext = CastContext.getSharedInstance(context)
```

Then, we need to select a device. We have already implemented `MediaRouterbutton`, which will automatically handle the selection. Once a device is selected, the Cast SDK automatically initiates a connection to the device. This process is abstracted away from the developer, but it's crucial to listen for session events to manage the connection effectively.

The Cast SDK provides callbacks for session events such as starting, ending, resuming, and suspending. Handling these events allows your app to respond to changes in the session state, such as updating the UI or pausing media playback when the session ends.

To listen to these session events, we must implement `SessionManagerListener`:

```
private val sessionManagerListener = object :
SessionManagerListener<CastSession> {
    override fun onSessionStarted(session: CastSession,
    sessionId: String) {
        castSession = session
        updateUIForCastSession(true)
    }

    override fun onSessionEnded(p0: CastSession, p1: Int) {
        castSession = null
        updateUIForCastSession(false)
    }

    override fun onSessionResumed(session: CastSession, p1:
    Boolean) {
        castSession = session
        updateUIForCastSession(true)
    }

    override fun onSessionStarting(p0: CastSession) {}

    override fun onSessionStartFailed(
        p0: CastSession, p1: Int) {}

    override fun onSessionResuming(session: CastSession,
        p1: String) {}

    override fun onSessionResumeFailed(session:
        CastSession, p1: Int) { }

    override fun onSessionEnding(session: CastSession) {}
```

```
        override fun onSessionSuspended(p0: CastSession,
            p1: Int) {}
}
```

Here, we are implementing our `SessionManagerListener<CastSession>` interface, crucial for managing Google Cast sessions. This listener is designed to react to various events related to the lifecycle of a Cast session, including its start, end, resumption, and failure cases. Let's look deeper into this implementation:

- `onSessionStarted`: This callback is invoked when a new Cast session has successfully started. Here, the `session` parameter, which is an instance of `CastSession`, represents the newly established session. The method sets the global `castSession` variable to this instance, effectively marking the beginning of a session. Subsequently, it calls `updateUIForCastSession(true)`, a method that will be implemented to update the application's UI to reflect that casting has started.

- `onSessionEnded`: Triggered when an existing Cast session ends, this method clears the `castSession` variable by setting it to `null`, indicating that there is no longer an active Cast session. It also invokes `updateUIForCastSession(false)` to adjust the UI, signaling to the user that casting has stopped.

- `onSessionResumed`: Similar to `onSessionStarted`, this callback is called when a previously suspended Cast session is resumed. It updates `castSession` with the current session and calls `updateUIForCastSession(true)` to reflect the resumption of casting in the UI.

- `onSessionStarting` and `onSessionResuming`: Indicate that a session is in the process of starting or resuming but has not yet completed. No action is taken in these callbacks in our case.

- `onSessionStartFailed` and `onSessionResumeFailed`: Called when attempts to start or resume a session fail. Again, no action is specified in our case, but these would be appropriate places to handle errors, such as by notifying the user or attempting to restart the session.

- `onSessionEnding` and `onSessionSuspended`: These callbacks are triggered when a session is in the process of ending or being suspended. As with the start and resume events, no specific actions are taken in these cases.

Once we have implemented our listener, we need to register it using `castContext.sessionManager`:

```
override fun onStart() {
    super.onStart()
    castContext.sessionManager.addSessionManagerListener(
        sessionManagerListener, CastSession::class.java)
}
```

```
override fun onStop() {
    super.onStop()
    castContext.sessionManager.removeSessionManagerListener
        (sessionManagerListener, CastSession::class.java)
}
```

Here, we are registering the listener when the `Activity` class is started and removing it when it is stopped. That way, we ensure that the listener is only retained when the `Activity` class is in a started state.

Now, let's implement the `updateUIForCastSession` function:

```
private fun updateUIForCastSession(isCasting: Boolean) {
    viewModel.setCastingState(isCasting)
}
```

Here, we are calling a new function that we will include next in the `ViewModel` component, called `setCastingState`. We are passing a Boolean as the argument, indicating whether the app is casting or not.

In our `PlaybackViewModel` component, we will introduce the following changes. We will start adding a new property, `isCasting`:

```
private val _isCasting = MutableStateFlow<Boolean>(false)
val isCasting: MutableStateFlow<Boolean> = _isCasting
```

Then, we will change its value when the `setCastingState` function is called:

```
fun setCastingState(isCasting: Boolean) {
    _isCasting.value = isCasting
}
```

Then, we will use it in our `PlaybackScreen` composable:

```
@Composable
fun PlaybackScreen() {
    ...
    val isCasting = viewModel.isCasting.collectAsState()

    Box(
        ...
    ) {
        if (isCasting.value) {
            NowCastingView()
        } else {
            //VideoPlayerComposable and the rest of the UI...
```

```
        }
    }
}
```

In our already existing `PlaybackScreen` composable, we have added a new property, `isCasting`. This property is used to choose if the screen will show a **Now Casting** message or the complete playback UI.

Next, we will build a new `NowCastingView` composable:

```
@Composable
fun NowCastingView() {
    Card(
        modifier = Modifier
            .fillMaxWidth()
            .padding(16.dp),
    ) {
        Column(
            modifier = Modifier.padding(16.dp)
        ) {
            Text(
                text = "Now Casting",
                style =
                    MaterialTheme.typography.headlineMedium
            )
        }
    }
}
```

This composable is just placing and showing a text with the **Now Casting** content, just to make the user aware that the media content is currently being cast to another device.

There's just one thing that we must do: load the media in the remote device. We will modify the `onSessionStarted` callback in the `SessionManagerListener` interface, including a call to a new function to load the media:

```
override fun onSessionStarted(session: CastSession,
sessionId: String) {
    castSession = session
    updateUIForCastSession(true)
    loadMedia(session)
}
```

Finally, we will implement this function as follows:

```kotlin
private fun loadMedia(castSession: CastSession) {
    val mediaInfo = MediaInfo.Builder(viewModel.mediaUrl)
        .setStreamType(MediaInfo.STREAM_TYPE_BUFFERED)
        .setContentType("video/mp4")
        .build()
    val mediaLoadOptions = MediaLoadOptions
        .Builder()
        .setAutoplay(true)
        .setPlayPosition(0)
        .build()
    castSession.remoteMediaClient?.load(mediaInfo,
        mediaLoadOptions)
}
```

The function begins by constructing a `MediaInfo` object, which encapsulates all necessary details about the media file intended for playback. Utilizing the `MediaInfo.Builder` pattern, it starts with specifying the media's URL, sourced from `viewModel.mediaUrl`. This URL is the location of the media file, which the Cast-enabled device will stream. The builder then sets the stream type to `MediaInfo.STREAM_TYPE_BUFFERED`, indicating that the content is pre-recorded and can be buffered before playback, which is ideal for video content that isn't being streamed live. Furthermore, the content type is set to `"video/mp4"`, defining the **MIME** type (**Multipurpose Internet Mail Extensions**, used not only by email but also by web browsers and apps to interpret and display content correctly.) of the file as an MP4 video.

Following the creation of the `MediaInfo` object, the function proceeds to configure additional playback options through a `MediaLoadOptions` object. The options set include `setAutoplay(true)`, which commands the Cast device to automatically start playing the media as soon as it's loaded, and `setPlayPosition(0)`, ensuring that playback commences from the very beginning of the media file, for simplicity. One improvement to this could be to obtain the current play position from the `ViewModel` component so that the video can continue at the same point in time if the playback has already started.

The final step in the `loadMedia` function involves invoking the `load` method on the `castSession` variable's `remoteMediaClient` instance. This method call is where the media loading and playback command is actually sent to the Cast-enabled device. `remoteMediaClient` acts as the intermediary, transmitting commands from the app to the receiver. By passing the `MediaInfo` object and `MediaLoadOptions` to this method, the app specifies what to play and how it should be played, effectively initiating the streaming of video content to the Cast device.

Now, our app is ready to start casting to Google Cast devices. With that, we have finished this chapter and learned the vast possibilities of playback in Android and other connected devices.

Summary

In this chapter, we tackled the essentials of extended video playback on Android, focusing on making our app more engaging by allowing videos to play in other contexts. We covered two main areas: PiP mode and media casting, both aimed at keeping our users connected to their content, whether they're multitasking on their device or looking to enjoy videos on a larger screen.

Starting with PiP, we walked through how to enable a video to continue playing in a small window while users navigate away from the app. This section detailed everything from modifying your app's manifest to implementing PiP mode, ensuring users won't have to pause their viewing experience when they need to use another app.

Next, we shifted focus to media casting, particularly with `MediaRouter` and the Cast SDK for devices such as Google Chromecast. Here, you learned how to let users send video from their mobile device to a TV. We discussed using `MediaRouteButton` for easy device discovery and connection, as well as how to create a custom UI for users who want more control over the casting process.

By the end of this chapter, you should have understood how to implement PiP for in-app multitasking and set up casting to external devices. These skills are key to creating Android apps that offer flexible and user-friendly video playback experiences. Whether it's keeping a video running in a corner of the screen or sharing a favorite movie on a big TV, your app can now cater to various user needs, enhancing overall engagement with your video content.

And with that, we've reached the end of our journey, where we built key features for three types of apps: a messaging app, a social platform, and a video app. Each project aimed to deepen your Android and Kotlin development skills and inspire you to think about how you can apply these ideas to your own work.

Thank you for reading this book. I hope it has not only broadened your knowledge but also sparked new ideas for your projects. With the tools and techniques you've learned, you're well prepared to advance your career and start building your own innovative apps. Here's to your success in the field of mobile development – go out there and make great things!

Index

‹packt›

www.packtpub.com

Subscribe to our online digital library for full access to over 7,000 books and videos, as well as industry leading tools to help you plan your personal development and advance your career. For more information, please visit our website.

Why subscribe?

- Spend less time learning and more time coding with practical eBooks and Videos from over 4,000 industry professionals
- Improve your learning with Skill Plans built especially for you
- Get a free eBook or video every month
- Fully searchable for easy access to vital information
- Copy and paste, print, and bookmark content

Did you know that Packt offers eBook versions of every book published, with PDF and ePub files available? You can upgrade to the eBook version at packtpub.com and as a print book customer, you are entitled to a discount on the eBook copy. Get in touch with us at customercare@packtpub.com for more details.

At www.packtpub.com, you can also read a collection of free technical articles, sign up for a range of free newsletters, and receive exclusive discounts and offers on Packt books and eBooks.

Other Books You May Enjoy

If you enjoyed this book, you may be interested in these other books by Packt:

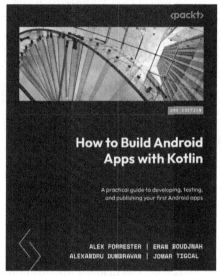

How to Build Android Apps with Kotlin - Second Edition

Alex Forrester, Eran Boudjnah, Alexandru Dumbravan, Jomar Tigcal

ISBN: 978-1-83763-493-4

- Create maintainable and scalable apps using Kotlin
- Understand the Android app development lifecycle
- Simplify app development with Google architecture components
- Use standard libraries for dependency injection and data parsing
- Apply the repository pattern to retrieve data from outside sources
- Build user interfaces using Jetpack Compose
- Explore Android asynchronous programming with Coroutines and the Flow API
- Publish your app on the Google Play store

Kickstart Modern Android Development with Jetpack and Kotlin

Catalin Ghita

ISBN: 978-1-80181-107-1

- Integrate popular Jetpack libraries such as Compose, ViewModel, Hilt, and Navigation into real Android apps with Kotlin

- Apply modern app architecture concepts such as MVVM, dependency injection, and clean architecture

- Explore Android libraries such as Retrofit, Coroutines, and Flow

- Integrate Compose with the rest of the Jetpack libraries or other popular Android libraries

- Work with other Jetpack libraries such as Paging and Room while integrating a real REST API that supports pagination

- Test Compose UI and the application logic through unit tests

Packt is searching for authors like you

If you're interested in becoming an author for Packt, please visit `authors.packtpub.com` and apply today. We have worked with thousands of developers and tech professionals, just like you, to help them share their insight with the global tech community. You can make a general application, apply for a specific hot topic that we are recruiting an author for, or submit your own idea.

Share Your Thoughts

Now you've finished *Thriving in Android Development Using Kotlin*, we'd love to hear your thoughts! Scan the QR code below to go straight to the Amazon review page for this book and share your feedback or leave a review on the site that you purchased it from.

`https://packt.link/r/1-837-63129-8`

Your review is important to us and the tech community and will help us make sure we're delivering excellent quality content.

Download a free PDF copy of this book

Thanks for purchasing this book!

Do you like to read on the go but are unable to carry your print books everywhere?

Is your eBook purchase not compatible with the device of your choice?

Don't worry, now with every Packt book you get a DRM-free PDF version of that book at no cost.

Read anywhere, any place, on any device. Search, copy, and paste code from your favorite technical books directly into your application.

The perks don't stop there, you can get exclusive access to discounts, newsletters, and great free content in your inbox daily

Follow these simple steps to get the benefits:

1. Scan the QR code or visit the link below

https://packt.link/free-ebook/9781837631292

2. Submit your proof of purchase
3. That's it! We'll send your free PDF and other benefits to your email directly

Made in the USA
Las Vegas, NV
09 December 2024